Contract L

Contract Law

Themes for the Twenty-First Century

Roger Brownsword   LLB, Barrister
Professor of Law and Head of Department, University of Sheffield

Butterworths
London, Edinburgh, Dublin
2000

United Kingdom	Butterworths, a Division of Reed Elsevier (UK) Ltd, Halsbury House, 35 Chancery Lane, LONDON WC2A 1EL and 4 Hill Street, EDINBURGH EH2 3JZ
Australia	Butterworths, a Division of Reed International Books Australia Pty Ltd, CHATSWOOD, New South Wales
Canada	Butterworths Canada Ltd, MARKHAM, Ontario
Hong Kong	Butterworths Asia (Hong Kong), HONG KONG
India	Butterworths India, NEW DELHI
Ireland	Butterworth (Ireland) Ltd, DUBLIN
Malaysia	Malayan Law Journal Sdn Bhd, KUALA LUMPUR
New Zealand	Butterworths of New Zealand Ltd, WELLINGTON
Singapore	Butterworths Asia, SINGAPORE
South Africa	Butterworths Publishers (Pty) Ltd, DURBAN
USA	Lexis Law Publishing, CHARLOTTESVILLE, Virginia

© Reed Elsevier (UK) Ltd 2000

A CIP Catalogue record for this book is available from the British Library.

ISBN 0 406 93413 4

Printed by Hobbs the Printers, Totton, Hampshire

Visit ButterworthsLEXIS *direct* at: http://www.butterworths.com

Preface

This book reproduces the text of the chapter (entitled 'General Considerations') which I contributed to the first volume in Butterworths' Common Law Series, *The Law of Contract* (1999). Prompted by the positive reception given to that chapter, the publishers have taken the unusual step of making the text available in a free-standing paperback form. The intention is that the material should reach a broader readership and, in particular, I hope that students who are seeking an overview of the principal themes of the law of contract will be assisted by this commentary.

As the law of contract prepares to enter the twenty-first century, it does so with a mixture of influences. The principles of freedom of contract and sanctity of contract, the classical inheritance, continue to be important. However, the modern pre-occupation with reasonableness, especially with standards crafted for consumer contracting, casts a long shadow over the classical principles. Further, as English law opens itself to ideas drawn from both the common law world and civilian Europe, contract doctrine evolves—the principle of good faith, for example, might be one such idea whose time has come. If there is a common denominator underlying these themes, perhaps it is the idea that the law of contract should protect and promote the parties' reasonable expectations.

Doctrinal themes, of course, develop in particular contexts. For contract law today, the most proximate domestic context is the (private) law of obligations; but contract law must cohere not only with the private law of obligations but also with the principles of public law. Given the sometimes complex overlapping of doctrinal domains (contract, tort, restitution, and so on), as well as the shifting boundary between public and private law, and given the increasing absorption into English law of the jurisprudence of European Community law, the enterprise of keeping contract law in line with reasonable expectations represents a considerable challenge.

In order to expedite the production of this book, the original text has been reproduced without alteration. Had there been some revision, I would have wanted to say rather more about electronic commerce as well as flagging up the potential impact of the Human Rights Act 1998 on contract law. With regard to the former, despite the rapid growth of on-line consumer contracting, I doubt that e-commerce (or m-commerce) will generate major new doctrinal themes—although the principle of 'functional equivalence' will serve as an important mediating standard between traditional and new contracting environments. Rather, it is the ease with which consumers will be able to contract with suppliers from other jurisdictions that will be significant. Initially, this will make conflicts of law questions much more urgent; but, at the same time, the pressure for harmonisation of contract law will increase. With regard to human rights, it remains unclear whether English law will accept that the newly incorporated rights will have a horizontal application in private law disputes. Potentially, though, there are significant implications here for freedom of contract—for example, as to whether one can contract out of human rights, and whether freedom of (and to) contract is restricted by human rights.

In a revised version of the text, a conclusion would also be added. Readers will find that in this original version of the text, the commentary comes to an end with some reflections on rationality in the law. Much more could be said about the quest for rational law in an age of pluralism and scepticism. However, I hope that readers who are interested in following up on rationality in relation to contract doctrine will be assisted by my earlier discussion (with John Adams) in *Key Issues in Contract* (Butterworths, 1995).

Finally, there are a number of acknowledgements that I am only too happy to make. First the ideas in this book, like the themes of contract law itself, have not arisen out of context. They are rooted in long-standing co-authorship with my colleagues John Adams and Deryck Beyleveld and in conversations with Robert Bradgate with whom I share the Contract teaching at Sheffield. Secondly, Michael Furmston read and commented on the entire draft of this text and I am grateful for the many helpful suggestions that he made. Thirdly, it was David Campbell who pressed me hardest to have the material published in its present form and I owe a considerable debt to him, and to Andrew Grubb, for supporting the idea. As always the final responsibility is mine; but, without the help and encouragement of others, the book would not have been published with this substance nor in this form.

Roger Brownsword
July 2000

Contents

Table of statutes

Table of statutory instruments

Table of cases

References in the right-hand column are to paragraph numbers

PARA

PARA

CHAPTER 1

The Nature of Contract

Definition

1.1 A contract, it seems, is one of those phenomena that is relatively easy to recognise but difficult to define. On the one hand, to state some truisms, one of the functions of the law of contract is to discriminate between those transactions that are enforceable as contracts and those that are not. Doctrine lays down the constituents of a contract (agreement, consideration, certainty, intention and, in exceptional cases, written formality) as well as stipulating the conditions of enforceability (the absence of fraud, coercion, illegal purpose and so on). There will be cases where, for one reason or another, doctrine is uncertain in its application. However, for the most part, lawyers will expect to recognise a 'contract', as specified by the law of contract, when they see one. On the other hand, whilst we might hope to construct a definition of a 'contract' around the shared idea of an enforceable transaction, there is little agreement about how this is best articulated. Some definitions might centre on the idea of an enforceable agreement; others might be anchored to the concept of an enforceable promise (or set of promises); and others might emphasise that contracts are essentially exchanges, or perhaps bargained-for exchanges[1]. Which definition, if any, is correct?

As with any question of definition, it is important to be clear about what kind of defining statement is at issue. Broadly speaking, definitions are either stipulative, prescriptive, or reportive. Whereas a stipulative definition specifies (in the definer's own lexicon) a particular meaning for a word (or a concept), and a prescriptive definition purports to lay down for others such a meaning, a reportive definition (as we might expect to find in a dictionary) purports to describe usage (in a particular place at a particular time by a particular group) of a particular word (or concept). When we ask for a general definition of a 'contract', we are not asking for a stipulation; we are not interested in a particular definer's idiosyncratic usage of the term. Nor are we asking for a prescription as to the usage of this term; in a sense, the law of contract already so prescribes. Rather, we are asking for an account that captures the employment of the idea within the law of contract and, thus, the exercise is akin to that of reportive definition. It follows that any proffered general definition will be deficient if it does not fit the various transactions that the law of contract picks out as 'contracts'.

A report that aspires to capture usage of a particular term (such as the term 'contract' as used in the law) might attempt to do so in the form of an essential definition (in which one or more elements are identified as the necessary and sufficient conditions for correct usage) or in the form of a cluster concept (in which several elements are identified with the usage, but where no single set of these elements can be combined to represent the necessary and sufficient conditions for correct usage). Insofar as the puzzle about defining a contract is approached as an exercise in essential (reportive) definition, a proffered definition will fail if the given condition, or conditions, (agreement, exchange, promise, or whatever) is or are not strictly necessary (ie, if a contract can exist without meeting such conditions); and, equally, it will fail if the given condition, or conditions, is/are not sufficient (ie, if, despite meeting such conditions, a transaction fails to be recognised as a contract). Insofar as the puzzle is approached as an exercise in non-essential cluster concept definition, the challenge is less demanding. Before we fall back on such an approach, however, we must consider where the difficulties lie in relation to the standard accounts interpreted as would-be essential definitions of a contract.

1   Cf *Chitty on Contracts: Volume 1, General Principles* (27th edn, 1994) para 1–001, where promise-based and agreement-based definitions of contract are presented as the principal options.

Agreement, exchange, and promise as essential definitions of contract

1.2   Any reportive definition must fit at least the most salient features of the usage in question. For present purposes, this means that any proposed definition of a 'contract' must fit with the three species of contract that are recognised in English law. These three species (expressed in the language of promises) are:

(i) 'unilateral' contracts (in which a promise is met, not with a reciprocal promise, but with a requested act of performance);
(ii) 'bilateral' (or 'synallagmatic'[1]) contracts (in which a promise is met with a reciprocal promise); and
(iii) 'formal' contracts (made in a deed, and in which a promise is not necessarily reciprocated by either a promise or a requested act of performance).

If we were content to describe rather than to define a 'contract', we might simply say that contracts are transactions that the law will enforce; and that English law currently recognises three such types of transaction, namely, unilateral, bilateral, and formal contracts. However, such a description does not purport to isolate the necessary and sufficient conditions for a contract. If, then, we try to capture all three species of 'contract' in a reportive essential definition (running in the language of agreement, exchange, or promise), where are we likely to encounter problems?

1   In *United Dominions Trust (Commercial) Ltd v Eagle Aircraft Services Ltd* [1968] 1 All ER 104, Diplock LJ, borrowing from the terminology of Articles 1102 and 1103 of the French Civil Code, defined a synallagmatic contract as one in which 'each party undertakes to the other party to do or to refrain from doing something, and, in the event of his failure to perform his undertaking, the law provides the other party with a remedy' (at 108). By contrast, in a unilateral (or 'if') contract, 'one party [the promisor] undertakes to do or to refrain from doing something on his part if another party [the promisee] does or refrains from doing something, but the promisee does not himself undertake to do or to refrain from doing that thing' (at 109). The standard example of a unilateral contract is that between the manufacturer (who promised £100) and Mrs Carlill (who did not promise anything, but who satisfied various conditions stipulated by the manufacturer) in *Carlill v Carbolic Smoke Ball Co* [1893] 1QB 256. See further paras 1.13 and 1.17.

1.3   First, can we present each species of contract as an agreement? The initial difficulty with this definitional strategy is that the concept of 'agreement' itself needs to be clarified. If 'agreement' is understood as connoting mutual assent to the terms of a transaction (as interpreted under an objective theory of offer and acceptance)[1], the definition apparently misses the category of formal contracts, where a promise in a deed can take effect even though the beneficiary of the promise has no knowledge of it[2]. That is to say, 'agreement' in this sense is not a necessary condition for a (formal) 'contract'. Similarly, if 'agreement' is understood in terms of reciprocity—either (bilaterally) as one party undertaking to do X in return for the other party undertaking to do Y, or (unilaterally) as one party undertaking to do X if the other party actually does Y—then the category of formal contracts again seems to be the problem. Alternatively, if 'agreement' is understood as meaning that a formal undertaking has been given, this fits with formal contracts but misses both bilateral and unilateral contracts (where formality is not generally required). Finally, if 'agreement' is taken to indicate that the beneficiary of an undertaking understands that an obligation has been assumed, then this seems too strong in relation to formal contracts and too weak in relation to bilateral or unilateral contracts. In other words, 'agreement' in this sense is neither a necessary nor a sufficient condition for a 'contract'.

1   See BCLS: CL (1999) ch 2, paras 2.106–2.108; and see, too, para 1.22 note 3.
2   *Hall v Palmer* (1844) 3 Hare 532; *Macedo v Stroud* [1922] 2AC 330.

1.4   Secondly, will a definition running in terms of exchange, or bargained-for exchange, fare any better? To identify contract with bargained-for exchange might make some sense in a context of *prescriptive* definition; for we might wish to avoid dignifying a transaction with the label 'contract' unless it is the outcome of genuine negotiation and bargaining. In the context of reportive definition, however, such a strategy must be rejected. Quite apart from the absence of bargained-for exchange in relation to formal contracts, it is clear that ordinary consumer dealing (whether in bilateral or unilateral contract form) simply does not fit such a description. Exchange *simpliciter* is less vulnerable. However, here, too, the category of formal contracts undermines the claim that exchange is a necessary condition for a contract; and, moreover, significant elements of commercial practice as well as much of the modern case-law invite the view that, even with informal contracts, exchange is not strictly speaking necessary[1].

1   The standard example of a commercial arrangement, treated as contractual, but lacking exchange in a real sense, is a banker's letter of credit. For the view that the technical requirement of consideration (exchange) will not defeat a serious commercial agreement, see eg *New Zealand Shipping Co Ltd v AM Satterthwaite and Co Ltd, The Eurymedon* [1975] AC 154, 167; *Thoresen Car Ferries v Weymouth Portland Borough Council* [1977] 2 Lloyd's Rep 614, 619; and *Williams v Roffey Bros & Nicholls (Contractors) Ltd* [1991] 1QB 1, see para 1.14.

1.5   Thirdly, what do we make of promise-based definitions of contract? On the face of it, a definition of this kind looks plausible. For each species of contract (unilateral, bilateral, and formal) is apparently grounded in a promise. In a unilateral contract, there is a promise in return for an act; in a bilateral contract there is a promise in return for a promise; and, in a formal contract, there is simply a promise. We should not conclude from this, however, that the making of a promise is the necessary and sufficient condition for every transaction recognised by English law as a contract. We can deal with reservations about a promise-based definition in two stages: first, by considering promise as a necessary condition; and then by considering it as a sufficient condition.

Promise as a necessary condition

1.6   What is the problem with viewing the giving of a promise as a necessary condition for the existence of a contract? Surely, there cannot be a contract without the giving of a promise. Is it not precisely non-performance or defective performance of a promise that the innocent party will cite in an action for breach?

1.7   To see how one kind of reservation unfolds, we can consider any typical marketplace transaction, any contract for the sale or supply of goods or services. Without doubt, many transactions of this kind exemplify not only contract as promise but also agreement and exchange. In a large-scale construction contract, for example, there is an agreement (however understood) that certain building work will be carried out for a certain price; there is an exchange (no one is making a gift); and the client's promise to pay is reciprocated by the contractor's promise to carry out the work. Alongside such tailored transactions, however, there is a myriad of routine transactions where commerce is conducted on a taken-for-granted basis. Suppose, for example, that the aforementioned construction contract is for a garage and self-service petrol station. When the garage has been built and is functioning, agreements to carry out repair work for customers may well resemble the tailored transacting of the construction project itself. However, motorists who call in at the garage simply to fill up their petrol tanks may well participate in a transaction that is so routine that nothing is actually said between the parties. Similarly, customers who purchase items from the garage self-service shop may complete the transaction by tendering the appropriate money—and, again, neither party to the transaction will necessarily give an express promise, the exchange will simply be made. In other words, in routine everyday transactions, an exchange will often take place in a setting where promising is implicit rather than explicit[1].

1   Cf Atiyah *Essays on Contract* (1986) pp 19–20.

1.8   If the only reservation about the necessity of a promise (in a promise-based definition) were that promises are sometimes implicit rather than explicit—that, for example, in routine consumer transactions the purchaser implicitly promises to pay for the goods and services at the advertised prices—this would give rise to no real difficulty. However, the legal backcloth presupposed by routine consumer transactions gives such a reservation a fresh twist. To a large extent, the law supplies the content for standard everyday transactions by writing in various types of implied terms, some of which are strictly non-negotiable. Although these implied terms do take the form of a promise, it would be a distortion to treat them as implicit promises in the sense that we have been using that term thus far. Rather, given widespread ignorance amongst contractors about the details of these implied term regimes, it would be more accurate to say that promises of this kind are attributed (or imputed) to the parties[1]. Nevertheless, so long as a promise-based definition allows for attributed (or imputed) promises, it can cover this difficulty.

1   Cf *National Carriers Ltd v Panalpina (Northern) Ltd* [1981] AC 675, 696, where Lord Wilberforce, albeit in the context of the frustration of commercial contracts, remarked: 'I think that the movement of the law of contract is away from a rigid theory of autonomy towards the discovery—or I do not hesitate to say imposition—by the courts of just solutions, which can be ascribed to reasonable men in the position of the parties.'

1.9   A further obstacle to treating promise as a necessary condition for contract might be thought to arise where the law shifts into a remedial gear, constructing contracts *ex post facto* in order to facilitate some form of relief or redress. For example, in cases such as *The Eurymedon*[1] where, in the context of the carriage of goods by sea, a contract was constructed between the owners of the goods (who contracted with the carriers) and the stevedores (who were sub-contracted by the carriers), the parties did not realise that they were entering into a transaction with one another, let alone that they were issuing promises to one another. To be sure, we might defend a promise-based definition by insisting that even such *ex post facto* rationalisation eventually returns to the idea of a promise. In other words, whether we reason forwards from promise to contract to remedy, or backwards from remedy to contract to promise, contract is essentially, and necessarily, about enforceable promises. Such a robust defence, however, might be thought to miss an opportunity to draw out the sophisticated way in which contract law is used to protect the expectations of those who are involved in transactions.

1   *New Zealand Shipping Co Ltd v AM Satterthwaite and Co Ltd, The Eurymedon* [1975] AC 154.

1.10   For instance, in *Blackpool and Fylde Aero Club Ltd v Blackpool Borough Council*[1], the defendants, who owned and managed Blackpool airport, raised revenue by granting concessions to operators to use it.

The plaintiff club was granted the concession in 1975, 1978 and 1980. Shortly before the plaintiff's last (1980) concession was due to expire, the council sent an invitation to the plaintiff to tender for the new concession to the club. The council also sent invitations to six other parties. The invitations stated *inter alia* that tenders received after 12 noon on 17 March 1983 would not be considered. The plaintiff's tender was put in the Town Hall letter box at 11 am on 17 March, but the box was not emptied as it was supposed to be. As a result, the plaintiff's letter was incorrectly recorded as having been received late, and it was not considered when the relevant committee met to award the concession. The plaintiff sued alleging a breach of warranty on the part of the defendants to the effect that, if the tender were received by the deadline, it would be considered along with the others. The Court of Appeal unanimously upheld the decision of the court at first instance that the defendants were liable for a breach of contract.

Amongst the arguments presented on behalf of the defendants, it was contended that a contract should not be implied merely because it was reasonable to do so[2]; and that there was a distinction between reasonable expectation and contractual obligation. Responding to these arguments, Bingham LJ observed:

> [W]hat if, in a situation such as the present, the council had opened and thereupon accepted the first tender received, even though the deadline had not expired and other invitees had not responded? Or if the council had considered and accepted a tender admittedly received well after the deadline? Counsel answered that although by so acting the council might breach its own standing orders, and might fairly be accused of discreditable conduct, it would not be in breach of any legal obligation because at that stage there would be none to breach. This is a conclusion I cannot accept, and if it were accepted there would in my view be an unacceptable discrepancy between the law of contract and the confident assumptions of commercial parties ... [W]here, as here, tenders are solicited from selected parties all of them known to the invitor, and where a local authority's invitation prescribes a clear, orderly and familiar procedure ... the invitee is in my judgment protected at least to this extent: if he submits a conforming tender before the deadline he is entitled, *not as a matter of mere expectation but of contractual right*, to be sure that his tender will after the deadline be opened and considered in conjunction with all other conforming tenders or at least that his tender will be considered if others are.[3]

These remarks might seem to gloss over a number of potentially important distinctions, in particular between intentional and unintentional violation of the principles of good tendering practice, and between holding the council contractually bound to consider all conforming tenders, as opposed to holding the council so bound *only if any tenders were considered.* However, for Bingham LJ's purposes, such nice points were largely immaterial: the critical question was simply whether tenderers reasonably assumed that the council would observe certain ground rules in dealing with the tenders; if they did, then an appropriate contractual relationship would be implied in line with their expectations[4].

1   [1990] 3 All ER 25.
2   Relying on cases such as *Liverpool City Council v Irwin* [1977] AC 239, and *Heilbut Symons and Co v Buckleton* [1913] AC 30.
3   Ibid, emphasis supplied. Cf the analysis in Craig 'Legitimate Expectations: A Conceptual Analysis' (1992) 108 LQR 79.
4   Cf *Harvela Investments Ltd v Royal Trust of Canada (CI) Ltd* [1986] AC 207, which, somewhat curiously was not cited in the *Blackpool* case. In *Harvela*, a reasonable expectation on the part of the tenderers was that referential bids would be excluded. Thus, the offer (inviting bids) was subject to an appropriate implied qualification. In the *Blackpool* case, essentially the same reasoning was applied except that, in a sense, it was carried one step further—not merely to read an implied qualification into an express offer, but actually to imply the offer itself.

1.11   Taking stock of these remarks, we cannot define a contract in a way that presupposes the giving of an express promise. If contract is to be defined in terms of promises, we must allow for express, implicit, and imputed promises. We must also allow, however, for promises constructed *ex post facto*; and the thought prompted by cases such as *Blackpool* and *The Eurymedon* is that, if a promise is necessary to give form to a contract, reasonable expectation is perhaps the key to contractual substance.

Promise as a sufficient condition

1.12   Suppose that an express promise is made: is this sufficient for a contract to come into existence? Given that it is axiomatic in English law that a gratuitous promise (a gift promise) is unenforceable unless it is in a deed, the making of a promise cannot be regarded as sufficient for a contract. In practice, however, the willingness of English judges to construct contracts for remedial purposes means that apparently gratuitous promises can sometimes be transformed into binding contractual obligations.

1.13   Consider, for example, that most famous of English contract cases, *Carlill v Carbolic Smoke Ball Co*[1]. The Carbolic Smoke Ball Co made a promise to pay £100 to anyone who, having used the smoke ball in the prescribed fashion, nevertheless caught influenza. On one reading of the facts, this promise was gratuitous, because Mrs Carlill's contract was with the chemist from whom she purchased the smoke ball. As the Court of Appeal construed the facts, however, the company's promise was not gratuitous, because Mrs Carlill reciprocated in some way by buying and using the smoke ball. A century on from the case, commentators would probably say that Mrs Carlill either relied on the company's promise (meaning that she would not otherwise have purchased and used the smoke ball) or that she formed the reasonable expectation that, if she contracted influenza, the company would compensate her to the tune of £100[2]. Either way, a collateral contract with the company would be put in place to protect Mrs Carlill's reasonable expectation.

1   [1893] 1QB 256.
2   Cf *Bowerman v ABTA* [1995] NJLR 1815, CA; NLJ Law Reports, December 8, 1995.

1.14   In line with the thinking in *Carlill*, the thrust of the modern case-law is that a promisor will be held to an apparently gratuitous promise where that promise engenders reasonable reliance or reasonable expectation. To some extent, the binding effect of such a promise can be achieved by invoking the doctrine of promissory estoppel[1]; but, in the landmark case of *Williams v Roffey Bros & Nicholls (Contractors) Ltd*[2], the Court of Appeal went one step further by weakening the orthodox requirement of consideration and easing the way to finding a contract[3].

In *Williams v Roffey*, the defendants were main contractors employed by Shepherds Bush Housing Association Ltd to refurbish 27 flats in a block of flats in London. The defendants engaged the plaintiff to carry out the carpentry work on the roof of the block and the first and second fix carpentry work in the flats themselves. The contract price for the work was £20,000. Before the subcontract work was completed, however, the plaintiff ran into financial difficulties, partly, so the judge found, because the work had been underpriced and partly because of the plaintiff's inadequate supervision of his men. At the material time, the plaintiff had completed the roofing work, the first fix to all 27 flats, and he had substantially completed the second fix to 9 of the flats. The defendants, fearing that the carpentry work would not be completed on time, and facing an agreed damages clause[4] in the main contract should it overrun, promised to pay the plaintiff an additional sum of £10,300. This extra money was to be paid at the rate of £575 for each flat on which the carpentry work was completed. In the light of this agreement, the plaintiff proceeded with the work. However, with the carpentry work on 17 flats substantially completed, he ceased working. On these facts, the trial judge held *inter alia* that the plaintiff was entitled to £2,800 in respect of the additional sums promised (calculated as 8 flats at £575 each (£4,600) less deductions for minor defects and incomplete items).

The Court of Appeal unanimously rejected the defendants' contention, grounded in the long-standing authority of *Stilk v Myrick*[5], that the promise to pay additional sums was not supported by consideration. Building on a number of analogous cases[6], Glidewell LJ summarised the evolving legal position as follows[7]:

(i)   if A has entered into a contract with B to do work for, or to supply goods or services to, B in return for payment by B; and,

(ii) at some stage before A has completely performed his obligations under the contract B has reason to doubt whether A will, or will be able to, complete his side of the bargain; and

(iii) B thereupon promises A an additional payment in return for A's promise to perform his contractual obligations on time; and

(iv) as a result of giving his promise, B obtains in practice a benefit, or obviates a disbenefit; and

(v)   B's promise is not given as the result of economic duress or fraud on the part of A; then

(vi) the benefit to B is capable of being consideration for B's promise, so that the promise will be legally binding.

But, in the light of (iv), what practical benefit did accrue to the defendants? Counsel for the defendants conceded that the promise to pay additional sums improved the chances of the plaintiff continuing to work which, in turn, meant that the defendants might avoid not only having to pay liquidated damages to the Housing Association for late completion, but also the inconvenience and expense involved in engaging another carpenter to complete the sub-contract work[8].

1   See BCLS: CL (1999) ch 2.
2   [1990] 1 All ER 512.
3   For discussion concerning the relative merits of (i) a promissory estoppel or (ii) a relaxed consideration approach, see Chen-Wishart 'Consideration: Practical Benefit and the Emperor's New Clothes' in Beatson and Friedmann (eds) *Good Faith and Fault in Contract Law* (1995) 123. See, too, Carter, Phang and Poole, 'Reactions to *Williams v Roffey*' (1995) 8 JCL 248.
4   The judgments refer to the relevant clause as a 'penalty' clause. Although it is commonplace in the construction industry to talk about the contractor being liable to 'penalties' for late completion, presumably the clause in question was simply a liquidated damages clause.
5   (1809) 2 Camp 317.
6   Namely, *Ward v Byham* [1956] 1 WLR 496; *William v Williams* [1957] 1 WLR 148; and *Pao On v Lau Yiu Long* [1980] AC 614. In *The Alev* [1989] 1 Lloyd's Rep 138, 147, Hobhouse J rejected the contention that cases like *Ward v Byham* showed that performance of an existing duty constituted good consideration. Yet, in the light of the developing doctrine of economic duress,

he indicated that there was no warrant to refuse to recognise an item as consideration 'even though it may be insignificant and even though there may be no mutual bargain in any realistic use of that phrase'.

7   [1990] 1 All ER 512, 521–522.
8   For the risks involved in a main contractor having to find a new sub-contractor, see *Percy Bilton Ltd v Greater London Council* [1982] 2 All ER 623.

1.15   Whilst there is room for argument about the precise scope and significance of the decision in *Williams v Roffey*[1], there is little doubt that it exemplifies the view that a commercial contractor's word (albeit expressed without the formalities of a deed) is his bond. It follows that, in practice, notwithstanding the formal doctrinal position, at least some gratuitous promises that are intended to[2] (and do) induce reasonable reliance or expectation on the part of the promisee are enforced as contracts. In other words, in practice, contracts are on occasion sufficiently constituted by what are effectively informal gratuitous promises.

1   See Adams and Brownsword 'Contract, Consideration, and the Critical Path' (1990) 53 MLR 536; and see discussion in *Musumeci v Winadall Pty Ltd* (1994) 34 NSWLR 723.
2   In business contexts, the presumption made by English law is that promises are intended to be contractually binding. However, in social and domestic settings, the opposite presumption is made: see eg *Balfour v Balfour* [1919] 2KB 571. It follows that a gratuitous promise given in the latter settings will generally fail to qualify as contractual on the ground not only that there is a want of consideration but also that the promisor did not intend to create legal relations.

Synthesis

1.16   If we start with the idea that a contract is an enforceable transaction, and given that English law recognises three species of contracts (unilateral, bilateral, and formal), how well does the notion of a promise (or a set of promises) capture the essence of a contractual transaction?

First, the form of each of the recognised species of contracts presupposes that one party at least has given a promise. Secondly, however, the practice of recognising contracts is such that the giving of a promise can only be regarded as a necessary condition if, over and above express undertakings, we allow for promises to be implied, imputed, and constructed *ex post facto*. Thirdly, the giving of a promise is not sufficient for a contract. Formally, a gratuitous promise will constitute a contract only if it is in a deed; and, although some non-deed gratuitous promises are enforced in practice, this will arise only where the promise is intended to, and does, induce reasonable reliance or expectation.

Even though a promise-based definition runs into difficulties when offered as an essential report, it works rather better perhaps if we treat a 'contract' as a cluster concept. Cast in this form, we can say that a contract is an enforceable transaction; that contractual transactions are formally rooted in a promise (express, implied, imputed, or constructed); and that a promise will constitute a contract where it (i) is reciprocated by a requested act of performance; or (ii) is reciprocated by a promise; or (iii) is intended to, and does, induce reasonable reliance or expectation on the part of the promisee; or (iv) is in a deed.

Is the definitional question merely academic?

1.17   It might be thought that definitional puzzles are of academic interest only. In practice, it might be thought, it cannot matter whether a contract is conceived of in terms of promise, agreement, bargain, or whatever. If a transaction meets the stipulated doctrinal requirements of offer and acceptance, consideration, and so on, it is a contract; if it does not, it is not. Surely, it is as simple as that.

By and large, it is probably correct to think that the puzzle about defining a contract is more of academic than practical interest. On occasion, however, the way in which we conceive of a contract does have a practical bearing. Consider, again, Mrs Carlill's purchase of the smoke ball from the chemist. No one doubts that this transaction was contractual; and, moreover, no one doubts that it was contractual because it satisfied the requirements laid down by the law for the formation of a contract. The difficulty in *Carlill* was whether Mrs Carlill also had a contract with the manufacturers of the smoke ball. This, however, was not a philosophical difficulty: the puzzle was a technical-legal one of finding a way of fitting the facts into the matrix stipulated by the law so that a contractual remedy could be given to the plaintiff. Suppose, though, that a modern day Mrs Carlill's transaction with the chemist was for a medicine prescribed by her general practitioner, under the terms of the National Health Service, and for which she paid the standard charge. If Mrs Carlill's relationship with the chemist was contractual when she purchased the smoke ball, would it also be contractual when (in our hypothetical case) she obtained the medicine for the standard NHS prescription charge? According to the House of Lords in *Pfizer Corpn v Ministry of Health*[1], such a transaction would not constitute a contract.

The background to *Pfizer* was that the Government decided that, in order to reduce the costs to the National Health Service, it would obtain certain patented drugs from sources other than the patentees or their licensees. With a view to protecting its new suppliers from patent infringement and royalty payments, the Government purported to exercise certain reserve powers under Patents Act 1949, s46. *Pfizer* was primarily a test case on the scope and interpretation of s46. However, one of the questions that arose in the case was precisely how to characterise a transaction where drugs were supplied under NHS prescription for (what was then) a nominal charge of two shillings. Although their Lordships were divided on some aspects of the interpretation of section 46, they were unanimous that the transaction was not a sale (ie, was not a contract). Giving the leading speech, Lord Reid, having identified 'agreement' as essential for a contract, said that there was no room (nor need) for agreement where, on the one side, there was a statutory right to demand the drug on payment of the standard charge and, on the other side, a statutory obligation to supply[2]. Lord Reid also pointed out that there was no scope for bargaining and that the charge was in no sense a market price.

Nevertheless, could it not be argued that the transaction was consensual, at least in the sense that a prescription-holder elects to acquire the drug? Lord Pearce exposed the weakness in this line of thinking[3]:

> [The prescription-holder's] choice is not whether he will or will not buy the drugs; it is merely a choice whether he will or will not exercise his statutory right to acquire it with a corresponding statutory obligation to pay a small uniform charge which bears no relation to its value. And the Minister or his agent has no choice whether to supply or not.

If, then, the transaction was not contractual, and neither was it a gift (because a charge was made), what precisely was it? According to Lord Upjohn, the transaction was one that was *sui generis*: it was, said his Lordship, simply 'the creature of statute'[4].

Their Lordships' remarks in *Pfizer* suggest that contracts are distinguished by: (i) a threshold level of voluntariness; (ii) an element of agreement; (iii) an element of bargaining; and (iv) a close correlation between price and value. Taking these elements in reverse order, how important are they to the existence of a contract? The fourth element (close correlation between price and value) surely cannot be taken seriously, for one of the distinctive features of English contract law is that, as a general rule, it refuses to inquire as to the adequacy of consideration[5]. No one would argue that Mrs Carlill had no contract with the manufacturers of the smoke ball because the promised payment of £100 was wholly disproportionate to the minor inconvenience that she suffered in using the preparation. The third element (bargaining), too, seems dubious. Routine retail sales, in chemists or any other kind of store, generally involve no bargaining: customers face a take-it-

or-leave-it deal; but no one thinks that this militates against the sales counting as contracts. The second element (agreement) is more plausible. However, as we have seen already, the initial difficulty with the notion of agreement is that it can mean several different things. In *Pfizer*, what Lord Reid seems to have in mind is that, to some extent, the terms of a contract will be settled (agreed upon) by the parties themselves. This looks like a point well taken: it is implicit, surely, in our understanding of a contract that one of the parties at least has some control over the substance of the transaction. Finally, the first element (voluntariness) also has a ring of plausibility. For, there is a distinction between the chemist who cannot refuse to supply an NHS prescription-holder and the chemist who can tell Mrs Carlill to buy her smoke balls elsewhere; and this distinction seems to be material to our conception of a contract.

1   [1965] AC 512.
2   [1965] AC 512 at 535–536.
3   [1965] AC 512 at 548.
4   [1965] AC 512 at 552.
5   See eg *Thomas v Thomas* (1842) 2QB 851.

1.18   More recently, the elements of voluntariness and control were treated as critical in *Norweb plc v Dixon*[1], where the Divisional Court applied *Pfizer* in ruling that the relationship between a public electricity supplier and a tariff customer was not contractual[2]. As Dyson J put it, 'the legal compulsion both as to the creation of the relationship and the fixing of its terms is inconsistent with the existence of a contract[3]'. With regard to the former (compulsion as to the creation of the relationship), the electricity company was under a statutory obligation to supply if so requested; and, with regard to the latter (compulsion as to the fixing of the terms of supply), the principal terms, including the tariff, were set in accordance with the statutory scheme. Moreover, the statutory scheme, by allowing for special supply agreements—where what 'is contemplated is a negotiated agreement to meet the particular requirements of a consumer'[4]—only served to confirm the view that the relationship between public electricity suppliers and their tariff customers is to be characterised as statutory rather than contractual.

1   [1995] 3 All ER 952. See, too, *W v Essex County Council* [1998] 3 All ER 111, at 128, where Stuart Smith LJ, rejecting the argument that a specialist foster care agreement (made between a council and foster parents) is contractual, followed *Norweb* in saying: 'A contract is essentially an agreement that is freely entered into on terms that are freely negotiated. If there is a statutory obligation to enter into a form of agreement the terms of which are laid down, at any rate in their most important respects, there is no contract.'
2   The question of whether the relationship was contractual arose in the context of of the Administration of Justice Act 1970 s 40(1) (as amended), under which

an offence of unlawful harassment can arise where money is claimed from
another 'as a debt due under a contract'.

3　[1995] 3 All ER 952 at 959.
4　[1995] 3 All ER 952 at 959.

1.19　The import of *Pfizer* and *Dixon* is twofold. First, these cases
illustrate how our deeper conceptions of contract sometimes can have
a practical bearing. Secondly, they highlight the importance of both
some degree of control and an element of voluntariness to our
understanding of contract. Certainly, if we were to return to our cluster
concept definition of contract, we would have to adopt these elements
as part of the unstated background to that definition.

The essential ethic of contract

1.20　Although tradition dictates that contract must be defined before
all else, it is arguable that the nature of contract is more tellingly
disclosed by uncovering its underlying ethic. What kind of ethic
distinguishes contract? If we follow modern thinking in treating
bilateral transactions as the paradigm[1], then the framework of contract
law might be informed by one of three ethics as follows:

(i)　prioritisation of self-interest (in which a contractor puts its own
interests above the interests of a fellow contractor);
(ii)　equality of interest (in which a contractor treats its own interests
and the interests of a fellow contractor as of equal weight); or
(iii)　prioritisation of the interests of others (in which a contractor
puts the interests of a fellow contractor above its own interests).

We can call the first of these ethics, the ethic of individualism,
the second, the ethic of co-operativism, and the third, the ethic of
altruism. If we disregard altruism, as characteristic of fiduciary rather
than contractual relationships, which of the remaining two ethics is
distinctive of contract? To some extent, the answer to this question
depends on whether we are looking at transactional practice (contract
in action) or the presuppositions of contract doctrine (contract in the
books).

1　Cf Atiyah *Essays on Contract* (1986) pp 11–13.

1.21　Ever since Stewart Macaulay carried out his pioneering
empirical research in Wisconsin, it has been recognised that, in
practice, at least some (and, probably, a great deal of) business
contracting is conducted on a basis that fits better with an ethic of co-
operativism than one of individualism[1]. Twenty years on from his initial

work, Macaulay underlined the contrast between the individualistic ethic apparently informing contract doctrine and the ethic of accommodation and compromise actually guiding business[2]:

> Academic writers [in line with the classical model] often make individualistic assumptions. Their theories rest on worlds of discrete transactions where people respond to calculations of short-term advantage. However, people engaged in business often find that they do not need contract planning and contract law because of relational sanctions. There are effective private governments and social fields, affected but seldom controlled by the formal legal system. Even discrete transactions take place within a setting of continuing relationships and interdependence. The value of these relationships means that all involved must work to satisfy each other. Potential disputes are suppressed, ignored, or compromised in the service of keeping the relationship alive.

Although Macaulay's observations have been confirmed in stable business networks where the parties have developed a relationship of trust and confidence over some years, and where relationships are thought of in terms of mutual dependence and partnership[3], it would be a mistake to assume that contract in action always, and everywhere, is driven by co-operative thinking.

It might also be a mistake to assume that every instance of co-operative contracting in practice reflects a deeply-held moral concern for one's fellow contractors. Rather, it might be the case that contractors treat one another as having equal interests as a matter of enlightened self-interest, as a matter perhaps of long-term rather than short-term prudential calculation. So much can be conceded. Purists will want to distinguish between co-operation that is based on prudence and co-operation that is based on moral principle; and, as a philosphical issue, this is a matter of some importance. However, if the practical ethic is one of co-operation, it matters little whether it is rooted in moral principle or a settled calculation of self-interest[4].

1   Macaulay 'Non-Contractual Relations in Business' 28 American Sociological Review (1963) 55; see, too, 'Elegant Models, Empirical Patterns, and the Complexities of Contract' 11 Law and Society Review (1977) 507.
2   Macaulay 'An Empirical View of Contract' Wisconsin LR (1985) 465.
3   See eg Beale and Dugdale 'Contracts between Businessmen: Planning and the Use of Contractual Remedies' 2 British Journal of Law and Society (1975) 45; and Lorenz 'Neither Friends nor Strangers: Informal Networks of Subcontracting in French Industry' in Thompson, Frances, Levacic and Mitchell (eds) *Markets, Hierarchies and Networks* (1991) 183.
4   Cf Brownsword 'From Co-operative Contracting to a Contract of Co-operation' in Campbell and Vincent-Jones (eds) *Contract and Economic Organisation* (1996) 14. See, too, Bernstein 'Opting Out of the Legal System: Extralegal Contractual Relations in the Diamond Industry' (1992) 21 Journal of Legal Studies 115 at 157, for a nice anecdotal reflection on the difference between viewing truth and

trust as the only basis on which decent people do business in contrast with viewing them strategically as the basis for profitable business.

1.22 If we turn from practice to doctrine, the individualism that Macaulay takes to be characteristic of contract law clearly underlies the so-called 'classical' model of contract[1]. According to this view, contractual transactions must be free from the more egregious forms of coercion, and they must not be induced by fraud; however, subject to such limited constraints, it is permissible for one party to take advantage of the other's vulnerability. Nowhere is contract law more clearly portrayed as a licence for self-interested dealing than in *Smith v Hughes*[2]—a case which, for one reason or another[3], commentators have seen as of seminal importance. In *Smith v Hughes*, the defendant, a racehorse trainer, wanted old oats, but the plaintiff, a farmer, delivered new oats. The defendant refused to pay, and refused to accept further deliveries. The plaintiff sued for the price of the oats delivered, as well as for damages for the defendant's refusal to accept further deliveries. The jury found in favour of the defendant. On appeal, however, it was held that the judge had misdirected the jury. Assuming that the plaintiff had not described the oats that he was offering for sale as 'old' oats, the judge had advised the jury that they should nevertheless find for the defendant if they thought that the defendant mistakenly assumed that he was contracting for old oats, and the plaintiff was aware of the defendant's mistake[4]. The defect in this direction, however, was that it failed to discriminate between two kinds of mistake: a mistake as to the terms of the contract, as opposed to a mistake as to the nature of the oats themselves. Only if the defendant's mistake was of the former kind was there a good defence.

The distinction between these two kinds of mistake is fine but important. If the defendant misunderstood the terms of the contract, and the plaintiff realised this, then the plaintiff could not hold the defendant to the contract (as the plaintiff understood it). However, if the defendant simply mistook the nature of the oats that he had agreed to buy, even though the plaintiff seller realised this, this would not affect the validity of the contract and the plaintiff could hold the defendant to the bargain. For, it is axiomatic within the classical law that the seller has no duty to disclose to the buyer facts which are material to the buyer (such as the nature of the oats), but which do not directly concern the terms of the contract.

The individualist ethic underpinning the classical law, and dictating the reasoning of the court in *Smith v Hughes*, was underlined by Lord Cockburn CJ in the following terms:

> The question is not what a man of scrupulous morality or nice honour would do under such circumstances. The case put of the purchase of

an estate, in which there is a mine under the surface, but the fact is unknown to the seller, is one in which a man of tender conscience or high honour would be unwilling to take advantage of the ignorance of the seller; but there can be no doubt that the contract for the sale of the estate would be binding.[5]

In fact, as we have seen already, the question is not simply what 'a man of scrupulous morality or nice honour' would do. In practice, contractors cannot be divided into either self-interested predators or men of scrupulous morality; they are at least as likely to be guided by enlightened self-interest. Thus, even if the farmer in *Smith v Hughes* was not a man of scrupulous morality, he would still have corrected the racehorse trainer's mistake if he had been concerned to develop a long-term trading relationship with the latter. Lord Cockburn CJ also assumes too quickly that morality would dictate disclosure in the hypothetical case of the purchase of the estate. However, whether or not morality would dictate disclosure depends on the particular standards employed, as well as a number of unspecified variables in the hypothetical case (for example, concerning the way in which the purchaser came to have the knowledge in question). Nevertheless, even if Lord Cockburn CJ's remarks now seem a touch superficial, they point unequivocally to the ethic of individualism.

The individualist thinking in *Smith v Hughes* is by no means exceptional, or a phenomenon confined to the nineteenth century. For example, in the same period that he was trumpeting the cause of consumer protection in *Donoghue v Stevenson*[6], Lord Atkin was laying down a thoroughly individualist regime in such leading cases as *Bell v Lever Bros Ltd*[7] and *Arcos Ltd v EA Ronaasen and Son*[8]; and, even in the late twentieth century, when the common law of contract has been modernised in a variety of ways, echoes of classical individualism are still to be heard—most strikingly perhaps in *Walford v Miles*[9], where Lord Ackner said that a doctrinal recognition of a duty to negotiate in good faith would be 'inherently repugnant to the adversarial position of the parties'[10].

Just as it would be a mistake, however, to think that the *practice* of contract is entirely co-operative, so it would be a mistake to assume that contract *doctrine* is wholly predicated on an individualist ethic. For example, Recital 16 to the EC Directive on Unfair Terms in Consumer Contracts[11], provides that the requirement of good faith (as it appears in the general test of fairness in Article 3.1 of the Directive[12]) 'may be satisfied by the seller or supplier where he deals fairly and equitably with the other party whose legitimate interests he has to take into account.' In the implementing Regulations, the letter of this Recital is not completely followed, but its spirit is preserved by providing that, in determining whether a business contractor has acted in good faith, regard shall be had to 'the extent to which the seller or supplier has dealt fairly and equitably with the consumer'[13]. Moreover, as we have seen already—in cases as different as *Blackpool and Fylde Aero Club Ltd v Blackpool Borough Council*[14], *Carlill v Carbolic Smoke Ball Co*[15] and *Williams v Roffey Bros & Nicholls (Contractors) Ltd*[16]—the courts are sometimes ready to manipulate orthodox doctrine so that reasonable expectations are protected. So, for example, in *Scally v Southern Health and Social Services Board*[17], the House of Lords held that the defendant employers had an implied obligation to look after the interests of their plaintiff doctor employees by drawing to their attention the existence of a limited opportunity to purchase 'added years' so that they would make up the full 40 years' contributions required for full entitlement under the applicable pension scheme. Judged by the orthodox standard for implied terms (ie, a test of necessary implication)[18], the House took a bold view. However, this was thought to be no ordinary contract of employment; rather it was one that fell within a special category where a more liberal approach to implication of terms was appropriate. According to Lord Bridge, the distinguishing features were: (i) that the contractual terms were not negotiated with individual employees but resulted from negotiation with a representative body or were otherwise incorporated by reference; (ii) that the contractual terms made available to employees a valuable right but one which was contingent upon employees taking action to avail themselves of the benefit; and (iii) that employees could not, in all the circumstances, reasonably be expected to be aware of such contractual terms unless they were drawn to their attention[19]. In other words, where the relationship is such that the parties reasonably expect disclosure or some other co-operative act, then (whether this is in the context of consumer contracts, employment contracts, or commercial contracts) doctrine will sometimes be manipulated to reflect such expectations by channelling contractors towards taking the interests of the other party into account[20].

1   For the defining characteristics of the classical law, see paras 2.3 and 2.4.
2   (1871) LR 6QB 597.
3   Often, the case is thought to be important for Lord Blackburn's articulation of an 'objective' approach to contractual agreement. Famously, Lord Blackburn said (at 607):
      If, whatever a man's real intention may be, he so conducts himself that a reasonable man would believe that he was assenting to the terms proposed by the other party, and that other party upon that belief enters into a contract with him, the man thus conducting himself would be equally bound as if he had intended to agree to the other party's terms.
4   This rather complicated question seems to derive from William Paley's *The Principles of Moral and Political Philosophy* (1809) p 126 et seq. Paley cites the example of the tyrant Temores who promised the inhabitants of Sebastia that, if they surrendered to him, no blood would be shed. In the event, Temores

kept his promise by burying the inhabitants alive. Not surprisingly, Paley considered this exploitation of a known misunderstanding to be wrong. He therefore proposed that promises should be interpreted in the sense in which the promisor believed that the promisee accepted the promise: p 126.

5   (1871) LR 6QB 597, 603–604.
6   [1932] AC 562.
7   [1932] AC 161. Here, Lord Atkin, taking a line on non-disclosure every bit as uncompromising as that in *Smith v Hughes*, considered that the validity of a contract was rarely affected simply because one or both parties were ignorant of the true facts. Most pointedly, his Lordship said (at 224):

> A. buys a roadside garage business from B. abutting on a public thoroughfare: unknown to A., but known to B., it has already been decided to construct a byepass road which will divert substantially the whole of the traffic from passing A.'s garage. Again A. has no remedy. All [such] cases involve hardship on A. and benefit B. ... [but] it is of paramount importance that contracts should be observed, and that if parties honestly comply with the essentials of the formation of contracts ... they are bound, and must rely on the stipulations of the contract for protection from the effect of facts unknown to them.

8   [1933] AC 470. In this case, Lord Atkin was party to the unanimous House of Lords' view that sellers who failed to deliver goods corresponding precisely to the contractual description had no cause for complaint if buyers then rejected the goods purely for their own economic advantage.
9   [1992] 2AC 128.
10 [1992] 2AC 128 at 138. Similarly, see eg Slade LJ in *Banque Financière de la Cité SA v Westgate Insurance Co Ltd* [1989] 2 All ER 952, 1013; and May LJ in *Bank of Nova Scotia v Hellenic Mutual War Risks Association (Bermuda) Ltd, The Good Luck* [1989] 3 All ER 628, 667. See further section F below for the tendencies of the modern law.
11 93/13/EEC.
12 See Brownsword, Howells and Wilhelmsson 'Between Market and Welfare: Some Reflections on Article 3 of the EC Directive on Unfair Terms in Consumer Contracts' in Willett (ed) *Aspects of Fairness in Contract* (1996) 25.
13 Unfair Terms in Consumer Contracts Regulations 1994, SI 1994/3159, reg 4(3) and Sch 2(d).
14 [1990] 3 All ER 25.
15 [1893] 1QB 256.
1   [1990] 1 All ER 512.
17 [1992] 1AC 294. Although cf *Reid v Rush and Tompkins Group plc* [1989] 3 All ER 228.
18 See *Liverpool City Council v Irwin* [1977] AC 239.
19 [1992] 1AC 294, 307.
20 Cf Burrows 'Contractual Co-operation and the Implied Term' (1968) 31 MLR 390; Collins 'Implied Duty to Give Information During Performance of Contracts' (1992) 55 MLR 556; Collins *The Law of Contract* (3rd edn, 1997) ch 15. See further chapters 5 and 6.

1.23   The complexity of contract doctrine and its relationship with practice is brought into sharp relief by the division of opinion in the House of Lords in *L Schuler AG v Wickman Machine Tool Sales Ltd*[1]. The question in *Schuler* was whether a single breach of a visiting obligation, described in the particular contract between a German manufacturer and its English agent as a 'condition', would justify termination of the agency. Technically, this turned on how the word 'condition' was interpreted. The majority Law Lords declined to read the visiting obligation as a condition in the strict sense because they thought that the contractors could not have intended the German manufacturer to have such a draconian power. By contrast, in an uncompromising dissenting speech, Lord Wilberforce said:

> [T]o call the clause arbitrary, capricious or fantastic, or to introduce as a test of its validity the ubiquitous reasonable man (I do not know whether he is English or German) is to assume, contrary to the evidence, that both parties to this contract adopted a standard of easygoing tolerance rather than one of aggressive, insistent punctuality and efficiency. This is not an assumption I am prepared to make, nor do I think myself entitled to impose the former standard upon the parties if their words indicate, as they plainly do, the latter.[2]

If we want to polarise the rival views in *Schuler*, we can treat Lord Wilberforce's dissent as an endorsement of individualism and the majority's view as an expression of co-operativism. How well, though, would these views fit with the practice of business contractors in Germany and England?

There is good evidence[3] to suggest that German business contractors have a relatively strong preference for long-term trading relationships; that the kind of termination clause at issue in *Schuler* is a relatively common feature of contracts used by German firms; that German firms are less likely than their British or Italian counterparts 'to take legal action for breach of contract, even to recover debts'[4]; and that British firms associate the forgiveness of occasional faults (breaches) more with trust than their German and Italian counterparts (for whom the association between contract adherence and trust is correspondingly higher)[5]. We can infer from this not only that Schuler would have been acting out of type if they had sought to terminate the contract for a single breach by Wickman, but also that Wickman would not have equated a single breach with a breakdown in the relationship. We might conclude, therefore, that the majority view fitted the parties' expectations rather more closely than the robust individualism evinced in Lord Wilberforce's dissent. However, such a conclusion would be too swift. The fact of the matter was that, by the time of the purported termination, Wickman had actually breached the visiting obligation on a great number of occasions. In defence of Lord Wilberforce, therefore, we might argue that Schuler were not acting out of type; that Wickman could not reasonably expect Schuler to continue indefinitely to indulge their non-adherence to the contract; and that the reservation of the right to terminate for a single breach eased any evidential difficulties that Schuler might otherwise have faced in establishing the precise extent of its agent's non-compliance with its visiting obligations.

These remarks invite a more subtle conclusion. At one level, the majority were right: neither party intended, nor expected, that an isolated breach of the visiting obligation would lead to termination of the contract. Yet, at another level, Lord Wilberforce was right: Schuler apparently did attach considerable importance to contract compliance and there was no reason to question their reservation of the right to terminate. Placed in the broader picture of contracting practice, however, neither view seems entirely satisfactory. The majority's position, whilst it is in line with the parties' expectation that the option to terminate would be invoked only exceptionally, can be criticised as giving too much weight to British tolerance of breach and as failing to locate the significance of a single breach in a contractor's overall record of performance and breach. By contrast, whilst Lord Wilberforce's position arguably accords rather better with the parties' expectations at the time of the breach in question, his Lordship's rhetoric of robust individualism seems rather at odds with practice.

1   [1974] AC 235.
2   [1974] AC 235 at 263.
3   See Arrighetti, Bachmann, and Deakin 'Contract Law, Social Norms and Inter-Firm Cooperation' (1997) 21 Cambridge Journal of Economics 171.
4   (1997) 21 Cambridge Journal of Economics 171, 187.
5   See Burchell and Wilkinson 'Trust, Business Relationships and the Contractual Environment' (1997) 21 Cambridge Journal of Economics 217.

1.24   Drawing together these threads, it is clear that the contrast between the ethic of individualism and that of co-operativism is one of the keys to contract doctrine; that it is also a key to understanding contract practice; and that, insofar as contract doctrine takes its lead from contract practice (via doctrines of reasonableness, reasonable expectation, good faith, and the like), it is a distinction that is central to the moulding of doctrine. These are matters to which we will return on several occasions.

The function of contract law

1.25   There are a number of angles from which we might inquire as to the function of contract law. We might ask, for example, what function contract law is intended to have, or what function it actually does have, or what function it ideally ought to have. In principle, different accounts of the function of contract law might follow from the differing ways in which the question is posed. For instance, we might say that the *intended* function of the law of contract is to establish the ground rules for trading between free and equal individuals; that, *in practice*, where the parties are free and equal, they make little use of contract law and, where the parties are not free and equal, contract law functions as a licence for one party to exploit the vulnerability of the other; and that, *ideally*, contract law ought to function as a platform for developing relationships built on trust and solidarity rather than legitimating short-term advantage-taking—in other words, contract law ought to re-inforce and reflect a co-operative rather than an individualist ethic[1].

1   Cf Brownsword 'Contract Law, Co-operation, and Good Faith: the Movement from Static to Dynamic Market-Individualism' in Deakin and Michie (eds) *Contracts, Co-operation and Competition: Inter-Disciplinary Perspectives* (1997) 255; and, for an overview, see Milne *Making Markets Work* (1997).

1.26   If our angle of inquiry is the intended function of contract law, we must allow for the possibility of some deviation in practice (ie, in relation to the actual function of contract law) and we must not assume that the specified intended function will correspond with everyone's idea of the ideal function. However, we can avoid begging too many questions by saying that the core purpose of contract law is to set out a regulatory framework within which exchange can take place. Furthermore, if this regulatory framework is to be at all adequate, we can take it that it must prescribe what counts as a contract, that it must determine when contractual obligation arises and how contracts are to be interpreted, and (crucially) that it must provide for a remedial regime of some kind. As Wolfgang Friedmann put it, it is 'the sanctions of contract [that] enable the hirer of services, the manufacturer of goods, the speculator in land or the purchaser of shares, to engage in calculated economic risks[1].' Yet, insurance against calculated economic risks (or security against non-performance or defective performance) is only one of four elements that Friedmann associates with the social function of contract in the formative period of modern industrial and capitalist society, the other three elements being freedom of movement, freedom of will, and equality between parties[2].

1   Friedmann *Law in a Changing Society* (2nd edn, 1972) p 121.
2   Friedmann *Law in a Changing Society* (2nd edn, 1972) pp 119–129.

1.27   According to Friedmann, contract functions as a legal instrument for the free circulation of goods and labour, thereby signalling the movement away from societies characterised by status and immobility. Again, we can accept this as a statement of the intended function of contract without begging too many questions. However, when we move on to the elements of freedom of will and equality between the parties, Friedmann warns that we are dealing with expressions of particular political and social ideologies. In the case of freedom of will, we are taking on board the ideology of freedom of contract; and, as Friedmann explains, the ideology of equality is its partner in crime:

To some extent, the concepts of freedom and equality in contract are interchangeable. Lack of freedom to make or unmake a contract, or to bargain on its terms, also implies lack of equality. As long as we restrict both concepts to the limited meaning which the orthodox theory of contract gives them, one usually implies the other. In so far as a person is free from physical restraint or other direct compulsion to make and unmake a contract, he is also assumed to be in a position of equality. Because the law will impartially award damages or an injunction according to the same principles of corrective justice to the employer and to the employee, it is not generally concerned with the inequality resulting from the fact that one may be a corporation controlling the entire oil or chemical industry of the country, and the other a worker on weekly wage and notice.[1]

As Friedmann himself observes, the practice of contracting and, concomitantly, the law of contract itself has been transformed by such factors as the standardisation of contracts, collective bargaining, programmes of welfare and consumer protection, and the realignment of the relationship between the public and private spheres. In due course, we will look more carefully at the modern view of freedom and sanctity of contract[2], of inequality of bargaining power[3], and of fairness and reasonableness[4], as well as at the ideological tensions that persist in the law[5]. In anticipation of that discussion, we can highlight three broad objectives that might serve to guide our thinking about the intended, actual, and ideal functions of the modern law of contract[6].

1 Friedmann *Law in a Changing Society* (2nd edn, 1972) p 124.
2 See chapter 2.
3 See chapter 3.
4 See chapter 4.
5 See chapter 6.
6 Generally, cf Llewellyn 'The Normative, the Legal, and the Law-Jobs: The Problem of Juristic Method' (1940) 49 Yale LJ 1355.

1.28   First, it is widely accepted that contract law aims to facilitate exchange. Exchange is not normally compulsory; but, for those who wish to exchange, contract law attempts to put in place a secured framework that facilitates dealing with a degree of confidence and trust. Contract law lays down the transactional ground rules; contractors know where they stand; whether parties deal with friends or strangers, at home or away, they trade in the shadow of the sanctioning apparatus of the law. To this extent, contract law channels parties towards performance.

Secondly, it is recognised that contract law has a protective function. At one level, this function is relatively uncontroversial, the idea being that contract law must be compatible with the public interest in general. Thus, parties must not be encouraged or permitted to draw on the sanctioning apparatus of contract law where their agreement is illegal or, in some other sense, is antithetical to the public interest. More controversially, however, it is arguable that the intent underlying much of the modern law is to protect parties who are relatively vulnerable. Certainly, it is widely agreed that one of the distinctive functions of the modern law of contract is to put in place a protective regime for routine consumer dealing.

Thirdly, where contracts give rise to disputes, it is accepted that one of the objectives of contract law is to put in place machinery for the resolution of such disputes[1]. Indeed, some commentators would argue that the distinctive feature of the modern law is that the *courts* have increasingly taken their function to be that of private dispute-settlement rather than that of general channelling or rule-setting— and one might see as one of the corollaries of this thesis a tendency for the body of contract doctrine to reflect this change by becoming more flexible, open-textured, and discretionary[2]. Whether or not contract law actually succeeds in practice in delivering on its facilitative, protective, and dispute-resolving objectives, is a matter for the kind of empirical inquiry to which we have already adverted (including inquiry into the accessibility of the institutions through which the law is administered)[3]. Whether or not contract law ought to adopt such functions, and in what sense and how it ought to adopt such functions, are matters that need further analysis.

1   Or, to respect the machinery put in place by the contracting parties. In line with this objective, the modern law of arbitration has moved ever closer to accepting the principle that, in general, where the parties have agreed to provide their own machinery for settling disputes, court intervention should be minimised—a principle strongly accepted by the Arbitration Act 1996.

2   See, eg PS Atiyah *From Principles to Pragmatism* (1978); Treitel *Doctrine and Discretion in the Law of Contract* (1981); and Friedman *Contract Law in America: A Social and Economic Case Study* (1965).

3   See para 1.7. Cf Collins 'The Sanctimony of Contract' in Rawlings (ed) *Law, Society and Economy* (1997) 63; and, generally on access to justice, see Cappelletti 'Alternative Dispute Resolution Processes within the Framework of the World-Wide Access-to-Justice Movement' (1993) 56 MLR 282.

1.29   On the face of it, the function of facilitating exchange is unproblematic. However, once we begin to debate the more detailed features of the regulatory regime, we run into the question of what kind of exchange relationship the law of contract should aim to facilitate. Should it be self-interested exchange, based on the ethic of individualism; or should it be exchange that is guided by co-operative thinking? Moreover, there is another major question concealed by the bland statement that contract law aims to facilitate exchange. In principle, contract law could be seen as a free-standing framework for exchange or as one that is deeply connected with existing trading practices. On the former view, contract law is, so to speak, imposed *ab extra*; whereas, on the latter view, contract law largely tracks existing practice and simply formalises transactional norms that are already recognised by traders. To put the point more sharply, did Lord Goff speak for the ideal function of contract law generally when he said of the work of the Commercial Court: 'We are there to help businessmen, not to hinder them: we are there to give effect to their transactions, not to frustrate them: we are there to oil the wheels of commerce, not to put a spanner in the works, or even grit in the oil'[1]? This is a question to which we will return[2].

The second function of the modern law of contract is, as we have noted already, a matter of some controversy. Whilst, at one extreme, free marketeers might argue that it is quite wrong for the law to assume any kind of protective function, at the opposite extreme, it will be argued that the law should offer comprehensive protection to those who are damaged by the deals that they make, and various shades of opinion will be expressed in the middle. There will also be debates about whether, if protection is to be offered, the law of contract is the best instrument for achieving this purpose (as against, say, the use of criminal law, administrative regulation, or redistributive taxation). And, there will be debates about whether protectivism can be distinguished from paternalism and consumerism; and, if so, whether a defensible protectivism can be prosecuted in practice without also adopting elements of paternalism and consumerism. Again, these are matters to which we will return[3].

Finally, if the commentators are right in detecting more flexibility and discretion in the law, then there is likely to be less calculability in the law, and a familiar puzzle arises. Namely, should contract law prioritise its commitment to facilitation of exchange (to certainty, predictability, and bright line rules) or should it prioritise its commitment to fairness in dispute resolution? Frequently, this is the issue that divides the courts; and the accommodation of these competing functions is often reflected in the particulars of doctrine—for example, by structuring and confining what might otherwise be open-ended discretions. Indeed, whether one thinks that the function of contract law is primarily about constituting a market in accordance with sharply defined rules, or whether one thinks that it is primarily about achieving fair and reasonable settlements of disputes arising from transactions, this is one of the major ideological questions for contract lawyers. It is another large issue to which we will have to return[4].

1   The Rt Hon Sir Robert Goff 'Commercial Contracts and the Commercial Court' (1984) Lloyd's MCLQ 382, 391. See, too, Lord Devlin 'The Relation between Commercial Law and Commercial Practice' (1951) 14 MLR 249, 266:

   [T]he law might go further than it does towards meeting the business attitude. In particular a more generous admission into contract of custom and trade practice would be entirely in keeping with the basic principles of the law merchant and with the traditions which lie at the heart of the common law.

2   See chapter 6.
3   See chapter 3
4   See chapter 6

The classification of contracts and contractors

1.30   Contracts can be classified in many different ways. English law, as we have said already, classifies contracts as unilateral, bilateral, or formal. In effect, this trichotomy operates with two variables, whether or not the contract is in a deed, and whether (in the case of non-deed contracts) the transaction is in the form of a promise for a promise or a promise for an act. In principle, however, many other variables and resulting classifications might be used. For example, we might classify contracts according to their subject-matter (sales, employment, construction, charterparty and so on), or their type (whether they are standard form or individually negotiated contracts), or their consequences (whether they are void, voidable, or unenforceable); or we might classify according to the capacity in which the parties contract (particularly, whether they deal as consumers or as business contractors) or according to whether or not they deal with one another regularly, and so on. No doubt, there are other variables that might be suggested for a classificatory scheme. However, there is little point in piling one classification on top of another simply for its own sake. In what follows, therefore, we will comment only briefly on a number of the leading classificatory ideas.

1.31   The threefold classification between unilateral, bilateral, and formal contracts is a helpful way of mapping the general terrain of contract. Because formal contracts (promises in deeds) are subject to their own legal regime[1], contract lawyers (and contract texts) generally focus on transactions that fit either the form of a unilateral or a bilateral contract. Given that different rules apply to these contractual forms, it is a matter of some importance to determine whether a particular transaction is unilateral or bilateral; and, on occasion, this can be the subject of a dispute. For instance, in *United Dominions Trust (Commercial) Ltd v Eagle Aircraft Services Ltd*[2], the question of whether a transaction was characterised as unilateral or bilateral was critical. There, the defendants, Eagle Aircraft Services, sold a Viking aircraft to a finance company, UDT, who then sold the plane on hire-purchase terms to Orion Airways. The defendants also entered into a repurchase (recourse) agreement with UDT to cover the possibility of the hire-purchase agreement (with Orion) being terminated. In due course, a compulsory winding-up order having been made against Orion, UDT terminated the hire-purchase agreement and, some five months after termination, UDT called on Eagle to repurchase the aircraft. Eagle declined to repurchase arguing, first, that UDT had failed to call on Eagle to repurchase within a reasonable period after termination and, secondly, that UDT had failed to comply with an express provision in the recourse agreement under which UDT were required to notify Eagle of any payment defaults by Orion within seven days of such default. At trial, the recourse agreement was treated as a bilateral contract, as a result of which Eagle's arguments could succeed only if it could be shown that UDT's failures were of a kind that gave Eagle the option of discharging themselves from their obligation to repurchase. Widgery J ruled that it could not be so shown. On appeal, however, the repurchase contract was treated as unilateral; UDT's failures were not treated as breaches, but as failed conditions precedent to the crystallisation of Eagle's obligation; and Eagle's defence succeeded.

1   See BCLS: CL (1999) ch 2, paras 2.100 and 2.101.
2   [1968] 1 All ER 104.

1.32   If we classify contracts by reference to criteria (variables) given *explicitly* in contract doctrine, then there are many possible classificatory schemes—and, as we have just seen in relation to the distinction between unilateral and bilateral contracts, the way in which we classify a particular transaction can be both a disputed and an important question. Thus, it may matter a good deal whether we classify a particular transaction as, say, a sale (rather than a contract for work and materials, or as some other kind of contract)[1]; and, in relation to the kind and extent of remedial relief, it may matter whether a contract of sale is classified as a business contract or as a consumer contract. Similarly, where a contract has a defect of some kind, doctrine will dictate whether it is rendered void (eg in the event of mistake, frustration, or illegality), or voidable (eg in the event of misrepresentation, duress, undue influence, or incapacity); and, in the same way, doctrine will dictate whether a contract is enforceable or unenforceable (eg where the relevant limitation period has expired). However, important though these doctrinally given classifications are for the application of contract law and for the resolution of particular disputes, they do not in themselves throw very much light on the general nature of contract.

1   Cf *Esso Petroleum Ltd v Customs and Excise Comrs* [1976] 1 All ER 117, where Esso's liability to pay purchase tax on promotional World Cup coins (advertised as free with the purchase of four gallons of petrol) turned on whether the coins were transferred to motorists under a contract of sale.

1.33   Just as a number of classifications are given explicitly by contract law, we might detect a number of *implicit* classifications, that is, classifications not openly recognised by doctrine but influential nevertheless in resolving disputes. To take an obvious example, long before the distinction between consumer and business contracts was explicitly recognised in contract doctrine, initially in the Unfair Contract Terms Act 1977 and subsequently in a stream of doctrine either anticipating or shaped by European Union Directives[1], commentators suspected that different rules were being applied to business and consumer contracts[2]. Similarly, we might believe that the extent to which a particular contract displays 'relational'[3] elements—whether in the sense that the parties are repeat dealers[4] or are economically integrated[5]—operates as an unstated factor of some significance. Again, however, although an appreciation of the classifications embryonically present in the law is important if we are to anticipate doctrinal developments, such classifications do not as such add to our understanding of the general nature of contract law.

1   See chapter 7 below. Cf Beale 'The "Europeanisation" of Contract Law' in Halson (ed) *Exploring the Boundaries of Contract* (1996) 23, 25–32.
2   In relation to the incorporation of terms, cf eg *Thornton v Shoe Lane Parking Ltd* [1971] 2QB 163 (a consumer case) and *British Crane Hire Corpn Ltd v Ipswich Plant Hire Ltd* [1975] QB 303 (a contract between two businesses).
3   Seminally, see Macneil 'The Many Futures of Contract' (1974) 47 Southern California LR 691, and 'Contracts: Adjustment of Long-Term Economic Relations under Classical, Neo-Classical and Relational Contract Law' (1978) 72 Nw ULR 854. The term 'relational' is used broadly to cover both cases where there is a close trading relationship between the parties and cases where the particular contract is of a long-term kind: see eg Bell 'The Effect of Changes

in Circumstances on Long-Term Contracts' in Harris and Tallon (eds) *Contract Law Today* (1989) 195.

4   Indeed, the fact that parties are repeat dealers is explicitly recognised doctrinally in the previous dealing exception to the ordinary rules concerning the incorporation of terms by notice: see eg *Hardwick Game Farm v Suffolk Agricultural etc Association* [1969] 2AC 31; and *Hollier v Rambler Motors (AMC) Ltd* [1972] 2QB 71.

5   Cf *New Zealand Shipping Co Ltd v AM Satterthwaite and Co Ltd, The Eurymedon* [1975] AC 154, where two of the principal litigants were companies within the same corporate group (namely a parent company and its wholly-owned subsidiary). This line of reasoning applied a fortiori in *London Drugs Ltd v Kuehne and Nagel International Ltd* [1993] 1 WWR 1: see Adams and Brownsword 'More Answers than Questions: The London Drugs Case' (1991) 55 Saskatchewan LR 441, and 'Privity of Contract—That Pestilential Nuisance' (1993) 56 MLR 722.

1.34   What, then, can we say about classifications of contracts and contractors? First, the fact that contract law involves classifications, explicit and implicit, tells us something about the systematic nature of legal reasoning. This may seem obvious, but it is by no means insignificant. The fact that we take it for granted that contract law is a rational enterprise, in at least this sense, offers a vantage point from which to gather together a whole range of ideas about contract[1]. Secondly, the fact that we recognise classifications based on the status of contracting parties is testament to an important development in the modern law, namely that we no longer treat all parties as undifferentiated contractors[2]. It matters whether parties deal as business or as consumer contractors; and, on occasion, it matters whether a party is perceived to be an exceptionally vulnerable contractor— whether in the sense that they are easily taken advantage of, that they have a lot to lose, or that they qualify for protection as 'poor and ignorant persons'[3]. Thirdly, the utility of particular classifications depends on our particular cognitive interest. Where our interest is in the general nature of contract law, classifications recognised within contract doctrine offer only a limited insight. Rather, to grasp the general nature of contract law, we need to explore the more general considerations underlying the law—considerations such as the importance of the autonomy of the parties and freedom of contract; the promotion of fairness, reasonableness, and good faith in contract in a context of unequal bargaining strength; and, ultimately, the aspiration to go beyond mere ideology to put contract law on a solid rational basis. It is to considerations of this order that we can now turn.

1   Generally, cf Adams and Brownsword, *Key Issues in Contract* (1995). See further chapter 9.
2   See eg Wilhelmsson *Critical Studies in Private Law* (1992).

3   See eg *Ingram v Little* [1961] 1QB 31 (elderly ladies easily taken advantage of); *Lloyds Bank Ltd v Bundy* [1975] QB 326 (farmer with a lot to lose); and *Cresswell v Potter* [1978] 1 WLR 255n (for modern application of the 'poor and ignorant persons' doctrine).

CHAPTER 2

Freedom of Contract

The classical law of contract

2.1 Modern thinking about contract often defines itself by way of opposition to (or, as a counterpoint to) the so-called 'classical law' of contract—a constellation of doctrine, presupposition, and ideology, at the heart of which is the idea of 'freedom of contract'. Accordingly, if we are to understand the idea of freedom of contract, we should first set it in the context of the classical law.

2.2 The classical law can be viewed in two different ways, either as a definite historical phenomenon, located at some period in the eighteenth and nineteenth century[1], or as an ideal-type (a paradigm not necessarily instantiated in practice during any particular period of English legal history). For those who are interested in charting the history of law or the history of ideas, it is of course a matter of some importance whether (and, if so, precisely when and why) the classical model took hold at a particular time in the development of English contract law. For present purposes, however, it matters little which view we take. The classical law, whether viewed as an historical fact or as a theoretical construct, serves as a significant point of contrast with the modern law of contract (which, again, can be viewed either as historical fact or as an ideal-type) as well as supplying the context for the idea of freedom of contract[2].

1   The definitive historical study is Atiyah *The Rise and Fall of Freedom of Contract* (1979). There, the period 1770–1870 is treated, so to speak, as the golden age of freedom of contract and, concomitantly, of the classical law. It should not be thought, however, that this was a period free of legislative intereference (see BCLS: CL (1999) ch 16). Nor should it be thought that the Judiciary of this period was of a single mind in relation to freedom of contract. At the one

extreme, Atiyah identifies Baron Bramwell as 'something of a fanatic' in his pursuit of individualism and freedom of contract (p380); while, at the other extreme, Sir John Byles is picked out as being 'years ahead of his time' in his rejection of laissez-faire together with his support for legislative protection for weaker contracting parties (p 382). Although neither of these judges was representative of general judicial opinion, Atiyah suggests that 'in the middle third of the century, the majority of the judges would have inclined more to Bramwell's position, though in the latter half of the century, opinion may have begun to moderate slightly' (p 383).

2   See Collins *The Law of Contract* (3rd edn, 1997) ch 2.

2.3 In his authoritative historical study, Patrick Atiyah traces the development of the classical law through to 1870, by which time it 'had arrived at its mature form[1]'. In this mature form, Atiyah suggests that the classical law had evolved into a general law of contract with two principal characteristics:

> The first was that the model of contract was based on the economic model of the free market transaction; and the second was that contract was seen primarily as an instrument of market *planning*, that is to say, the model was that of the wholly executory contract ... Above all, of course, the model was suffused with the notion that the consequences of the contract depended entirely on the intention of the parties, and were not imposed by the Courts. The Courts did not make contracts for the parties, nor did they adjust or alter the terms agreed by the parties. The fairness and justice of the exchange was irrelevant[2].

Spelling this out rather more fully, we can say that the doctrinal landmarks of the classical law are founded upon a handful of key ideas: in particular, an adversarial ethic (this being presupposed by 'the economic model of the free market transaction')[3]; the primacy of the contractors' intentions; the centrality of exchange; and the protection of the expectation interest (the executory promise of future performance being treated, so to speak, as a matter of present entitlement)[4]. These ideas dictate that the existence of a contract is predicated on a common intention by the parties to enter into such an arrangement[5]; that questions of construction, interpretation, or implication in relation to the agreement are governed by the parties' common intentions (and not by external standards of fairness, justice, or reasonableness)[6]; that exchange is a necessary ingredient of a contract (together with the related idea that strangers to the exchange are barred from enforcing the contract); and that the object of compensation is to put the innocent party in the same position as if the contract had been performed.

1   Atiyah *The Rise and Fall of Freedom of Contract* p 681.
2   Atiyah *The Rise and Fall of Freedom of Contract* p 681.
3   Atiyah *The Rise and Fall of Freedom of Contract* at pp 402–403, where Atiyah includes arm's length dealing and self-reliance in his list of the principal features

of the classical model. Thus (at p403): '[N]either party owes any duty to volunteer information to the other, nor is he entitled to rely on the other except within the narrowest possible limits.'

4   Cf Fuller and Perdue 'The Reliance Interest in Contract Damages' (1936) 46 Yale LJ 52 and 373.

5   For Baron Bramwell's firm adherence to the principle that a contract cannot come into existence without the mutual assent of the parties, see Atiyah *The Rise and Fall of Freedom of Contract* at p376.

6   The robust individualism underpinning the classical approach is clearly brought out by Atiyah (*The Rise and Fall of Freedom of Contract* at p 403):
     [T]he content of the contract, the terms and the price and the subject-matter are entirely for the parties to settle. It is assumed that the parties know their own minds, that they will calculate the risks and future contingencies that are relevant, and that all these enter into the bargain. It follows that unfairness of the bargain—gross inadequacy or excess of price—is irrelevant, and once made the contract is binding.

2.4 If, however, we probe a little deeper into the foundations of the classical law, we find a number of less obvious, but no less significant, presuppositions. According to Atiyah, there are four such presuppositions, namely: the idea that contract law is about what parties intend, not about what they do; the treatment of a contract as a thing; the assumption that the function of the courts is to encourage parties to perform their contracts rather than to settle disputes; and the view that it makes sense to conceive of a general law of contract, rather than a fragmented law of contracts[1].

As we have indicated already, the first of these presuppositions is important in determining both whether there is a contractual relationship and how a particular agreement is to be read. However, Atiyah draws out another implication from the classical law's emphasis upon the parties' intentions rather than their actions. This is that, in classical thinking, contract itself is distinguished from the tortious and restitutionary threads of the common law of obligations by its focus on intention and by their focus on action[2].

The second presupposition, that contract is a thing, involves a distinctive reification of contracts. No doubt, some contracts have a thing-like existence where the agreement is embodied in a written document. However, the significance of treating contract as a thing is not simply that it again divides contract from tort and restitution, where matters are not conceived of in thing-like terms. Rather, this facet of classical thought reinforces respect for the autonomy of the contractors (in the sense of the contractors having control over their own transactional affairs) and the tangible product (the agreement) of their autonomous wills.

Thirdly, Atiyah makes a point that we have encountered already when discussing the function of contract[3]. On the classical view, '[t]he purpose of contract law is to encourage people to pay their debts, keep their promises, and generally be truthful in their dealings with each other[4]. Thus, the function of contract law is what Atiyah calls 'deterrent or hortatory'[5] and, to this extent, the classical view sees contract law in much the same terms as criminal law or property law.

Finally, we come to the presupposition that contract law is of general application. According to this view, although contracts may be of many different types, they all belong to the one general species and they are all susceptible to the same (classical) principles of regulation. Such an imperialistic philosophy, Atiyah suggests, was not shaped by an approach that sought to commercialise all human relationships and to commodify all spheres of social life. Rather, the deeper thinking was that it was seen as:

> desirable that men should learn to order their lives according to some definite plan, that they should be encouraged to aim for particular goals, that they should co-operate with others in attempting to seek those goals, that those who let down their fellows should be made to pay the cost of doing so; [it was] thought desirable that men should be free to develop their skills and ambitions, and [it was] accepted [as a] natural corollary that some would rise and some would sink.[6]

Contract, in other words, was the vehicle through which autonomy and rational planning could be simultaneously promoted, the former by respecting the parties' free choices, and the latter by channelling the parties towards performance by holding those in breach responsible for letting down their fellow contractors. Or, to put this in terms that marry the classical law with the foundational ideas of freedom of contract and sanctity of contract, contract serves autonomy by adopting the principle of freedom of contract, and contract underpins rational planning by adopting the principle of sanctity of contract.

1   Atiyah *Essays on Contract* (1986) pp 13–17.
2   Cf chapter 8.
3   See paras 1.25–1.29.
4   Atiyah Essays on Contract p 15.
5   Atiyah Essays on Contract p 15.
6   Atiyah Essays on Contract p 16.

2.5   As we move on to look more carefully at the idea of freedom of contract, it is helpful to distinguish between freedom of contract in a broad sense and freedom of contract in a narrow sense. In a broad sense, freedom of contract embraces three related ideas: freedom to contract (or party freedom), freedom of contract (or term freedom), and sanctity of contract. In a narrow sense, freedom of contract (term freedom) emphasises that the law should recognise the importance of respecting the parties' own choices and preferences as expressed in the kinds of transactions they enter upon and the particular terms to which they agree. It follows that freedom of contract in the narrow sense argues for a minimalist (ie, light regulatory) approach both to the categories of transaction that are treated as illegal and to the kinds of terms that are black-listed as void and unenforceable[1].

1 See Brownsword '"Remedy-Stipulation" in the English Law of Contract—Freedom or Paternalism?' (1977) 9 Ottawa LR 95, 96–99.

Freedom of contract

2.6 According to Lord Devlin, it is axiomatic within the classical view that free dealing is fair dealing[1]. Thus, in *Printing and Numerical Registering Co v Sampson*[2], Sir George Jessel MR famously said:

> [I]f there is one thing which more than another public policy requires it is that men of full age and competent understanding shall have the utmost liberty of contracting, and that their contracts when entered into freely and voluntarily shall be held sacred and shall be enforced by Courts of justice. Therefore, you have this paramount public policy to consider—that you are not lightly to interfere with this freedom of contract.[3]

Sir George's remarks suggest that respect for freedom of contract involves two related forms of legislative and judicial restraint. First, freedom of contract enjoins that the parties shall have 'the utmost liberty of contracting', in the sense that they are left free to set their own terms. It follows that legislatures and courts should be slow to limit the kinds of transactions, or the kinds of terms, that the parties can agree upon within the domain of contract. An over-restrictive approach disallows options that should be available to the parties and, to this extent, illegitimately trims the parties' autonomy[4]. Secondly, freedom of contract enjoins that the parties' freely-made agreements shall be enforced by the courts. Courts might be tempted to release parties from hard bargains, but where agreements have been freely made such a temptation must be resisted: even well-meaning paternalism betrays a lack of respect for a person's autonomy. To mark these two aspects of freedom of contract (in the broad sense), we can call the first form of restraint the ideal of 'term freedom' (that is, freedom of contract in the narrow sense) and the second the ideal of 'sanctity of contract'.

1 Devlin *The Enforcement of Morals* (1965) p 47.
2 (1875) LR 19 Eq 462.
3 (1875) LR 19 Eq 462 at 465.
4 In the modern case law, see eg *Suisse Atlantique Société d'Armement Maritime SA v NV Rotterdamsche Kolen Centrale* [1967] 1AC 361, 399 (Lord Reid); and *Photo Production Ltd v Securicor Transport Ltd* [1980] AC 827, 848 (Lord

Diplock). In *Federal Commerce and Navigation Co Ltd v Tradax Export SA, The Maratha Envoy* [1978] AC 1, 8, Lord Diplock echoed Sir George Jessel's remarks as follows:

> It is not part of the function of a Court of justice to dictate to charterers and shipowners the terms of the contracts into which they ought to enter on the freight market. [W]hen occasion arises for a Court to enforce the contract … the fact that the members of the Court themselves may think that one of the parties was unwise in agreeing to assume a particular … risk or unlucky in its proving more expensive to him than he expected, has nothing to do with the merits of the case or with enabling justice to be done. The only merits of the case are that parties who have bargained on equal terms in a free market should stick to their agreements. Justice is done by seeing that they do so or compensating the party who has kept his promise for any loss he has sustained by the failure of the other to keep his.

2.7 Absolute term freedom implies a licence to write contracts with any content, that is, an absence of legal restriction upon the kinds of bargains, or the types of contractual provision, that the parties can agree upon. A legal system guided by the ideal of term freedom will limit such a licence only where it has good reason. Of course, what constitutes 'a good reason' will depend upon the background philosophy of the particular legal order. Thus, if a legal system is guided by utilitarian (or by wealth maximising) thinking, countervailing good reasons will involve disutilities (or wealth losses) occasioned by term freedom; whereas, in a legal system that is guided by an individual rights-led morality, the right of freedom of contract will be abridged only where more important rights are at stake[1].

Bearing in mind the important caveat that different views can be taken about what constitutes a good reason for limiting term freedom, we can say that, in principle, arguments for a restriction upon term freedom might be based on one or more of the following four grounds: (i) that the terms (or the general purpose of the contract) are harmful to the interests of third parties (e g, where the purpose of an agreement is to kill an innocent third party); (ii) that the terms (or the general purpose of the contract) are harmful to the public interest (e g, where the purpose of an agreement is to evade liability under a justifiable tax regime)[2]; (iii) that the transaction is harmful to the interests of one of the contracting parties (e g, a sale at undervalue, a usury agreement, or a contract of enslavement might be seen as falling into this category); and (iv) that the transaction is harmful to the interests of both the contracting parties (eg, some might argue that gaming and wagering agreements, or contracts for sexual favours fall into this category). In some instances, of course, the arguments against term freedom overlap. For example, it might be argued that the parties' freedom to make surrogacy contracts should be restricted on a variety of grounds—that such agreements are harmful to third parties (the surrogate children), to the broader public interest (by commodifying reproduction), to the surrogate mother (whose dignity is violated), and to the commissioning parents (who might find themselves exploited)[3].

In this light, it is interesting to look back at the basis of the (unsuccessful) argument for restriction on term freedom in *Printing and Numerical Registering Co v Sampson*. The agreement in that case was one in which an inventor assigned a patent to a company. Under the agreement, the vendor undertook to enter into a covenant with the company for the assignment of any future patents acquired (in the United Kingdom and various other places) in relation to the particular invention in question (or any similar invention). The vendor subsequently argued that this undertaking was contrary to the public interest in that it discouraged both inventors and the bringing forward of inventions into the public domain. The Master of the Rolls, however, was unconvinced. In his opinion, it was perfectly reasonable for the company to contract for this covenant; there was no compelling evidence of damage to the public interest; and this was no more than a case of the vendor trying to escape from the consequences of a sound commercial bargain. Suppose, though, the vendor of the patent had been in a weak bargaining position as a result of which the agreement struck was unreasonably one-sided in favour of the company. Would Sir George have appealed so strongly to the principle of freedom of contract? In fact, he probably would. For, in *Bennet v Bennet*[4], he upheld a moneylending agreement entered into at rates of 60 per cent, saying that borrowers can agree to pay 100 per cent if they so choose, that '[t]here is no reason why a man should not be a fool', and that the law does not prevent men from being fools[5]. Term freedom, therefore, countenances the possibility that parties—at any rate, as Sir George put it, 'men of full age and competent understanding'—should be given the utmost liberty to make improvident and foolish contracts.

1   Generally, see Trebilcock *The Limits of Freedom of Contract* (1993); and Collins *The Law of Contract* (3rd edn, 1997), pp 96–101.
2   Cf Lord Atkin's remark in *Fender v St John-Mildmay* [1938] AC 1, 12, that the public interest restriction on freedom of contract 'should only be invoked in clear cases in which the harm to the public is substantially incontestable, and does not depend upon the idiosyncratic inferences of a few judicial minds'. Similarly, see Simon Brown LJ in *Lancashire County Council v Municipal Mutual Insurance Ltd* [1996] 3 All ER 545, 555–556: 'contracts should only be held unenforceable on public policy grounds in very plain cases'.
3   Cf Collins The Law of Contract pp 105–106.
4   (1876) 43LT 246n.
5   (1876) 43LT 246n at 247.

2.8   Closely related to the ideal of term freedom, is the ideal of sanctity of contract. Whereas term freedom sets up a presumption against unnecessary restrictions on the kinds of agreements that parties can make, sanctity of contract emphasises that parties are to be held to the agreements that they have freely made[1]. This general idea can be deployed in more than one context. Most obviously, it applies in the context of hard cases and improvident contracts. In a legal system that subscribes to the principle of sanctity of contract, there will be no jurisdiction to grant paternalistic relief where a party is simply trying to avoid the consequences of a bargain that is now regretted. Accordingly, in *Printing and Numerical Registering Co v Sampson*, if the court had felt that the company had contracted for a greater protection than it really needed, and if the contract had subsequently worked a significant hardship upon the vendor-inventor, then sanctity of contract would treat such considerations as irrelevant—contracts, as Sir George said, are sacred; and the justification for their enforcement originates in free agreement, not in some calculus of sympathy and antipathy in relation to the parties. In addition to this obvious application, sanctity of contract can have a bearing on the renegotiation or variation of contracts. In this context, sanctity of contract does not preclude a party waiving the right to hold a fellow contractor to the agreed terms of the bargain, but it does encourage courts to take a hard look at renegotiated agreements apparently showing benefit to just one side—particularly a hard look at whether the renegotiation was free and fully consensual[2].

Where the express terms of a freely agreed bargain quite clearly cover a disputed situation, an appeal to the ideal of sanctity of contract is relatively straightforward (although, of course, not uncontroversial). However, where the express terms of the contract either (i) do not clearly apply or (ii) make no provision for the disputed situation (which has not been anticipated), then an appeal to sanctity of contract is more problematic. In the former case, arguably, an appeal to sanctity of contract is premature: until the meaning of the express provisions has been settled, it is surely unhelpful to invoke the rhetoric of enforcing the bargain according to its terms[3]. In the latter case, because an appeal to sanctity of contract no longer seems to rest on respect for the parties' autonomous decision-making (because, in the absence of express contractual provision, there is apparently no relevant decision), it might be thought to have no application. The position, however, is not quite so clear-cut.

1   Generally, see Parry *The Sanctity of Contract* (1965); Baker, 'From Sanctity of Contract to Reasonable Expectation?' (1979) 32 CLP 17.
2   Cf *Williams v Roffey Bros & Nicholls (Contractors) Ltd* [1990] 1 All ER 512; and see para 1.14.
3   Cf the discussion of *L Schuler AG v Wickman Machine Tool Sales Ltd* [1974] AC 235, in para 1.23.

2.9 Where a contract fails to make express provision for an unanticipated situation, there are two dimensions in which such a failure might be plotted. One dimension concerns the nature or the type of risk; the other dimension concerns the extent or degree of the particular risk. For example, in *Davis Contractors Ltd v Fareham UDC*[1], the leading English authority on the doctrine of frustration, the building contractors were caught out by a combination of shortages in relation to both materials and labour (primarily the latter). Without doubt, risks of this type (the first dimension of risk) were within the parties' general field of contemplation. For, the building contractors said (in a covering letter) that their tender was 'subject to adequate supplies of material and labour being available as and when required to carry out the work within the time specified'; and the local authority's conditions of contract (in conjunction with an Appendix to the tender document) dealt with price variation in respect of goods and materials provided directly by the building contractors[2]. What we cannot be certain about, however, is the second dimension of risk. What degree of price fluctuation or shortage might the parties have contemplated on a scale running from best to worst case scenario? Let us suppose, for example, that the parties in *Davis v Fareham* regarded fluctuations in the price of materials of up to 10% as normal, and had known prices to fluctuate by as much as 50% (although they regarded such fluctuations as exceptional). Suppose, moreover, that although the parties had experienced shortages of skilled labour, shortages of unskilled labour were unheard of. Now, on such assumptions, and in the absence of express contractual provision for price fluctuations or labour shortages[3], what sense can we make of an appeal to sanctity of contract in the following situations:

(i) materials are in short supply, as a result of which the builder has to pay 10% more than estimated;

(ii) materials are in short supply, as a result of which the builder has to pay 50% more than estimated;

(iii) there is an unprecedented shortage of materials, as a result of which the builder has to pay 200% more than estimated; and

(iv) there is a shortage of unskilled labour?

In situation (i), the type of risk (price fluctuation because of shortage of materials) is well-known to the parties and the extent of the risk falls within the range of what the parties themselves regard as normal risk. In the absence of express provision, a plausible reading of the contract is that the parties intended that the builder should bear such a risk. If the contract is so read, then sanctity of contract demands that the contract should be so enforced. Additionally, though, the rhetoric of sanctity of contract might be invoked in an extended sense as a principle of interpretation rather than as one purely of enforcement, the contention being that the contract *should be* so read (ie, as allocating the risk to the builder where the type of risk is known and the degree of risk is within the range that the parties treat as normal). Such an interpretative principle might be defended on more than one ground. However, to keep faith with the spirit of freedom of contract, as well as the core idea of sanctity of contract, the argument must be that, in more cases than not, such an interpretative principle will reflect the unexpressed expectations of the parties.

Situation (ii), like situation (i), involves a known type of risk. However, in situation (ii), the extent of the risk lies well beyond what the parties would count as normal and is, in their terms, exceptional. Here, it is less plausible surely to take the absence of express provision as an indication that the parties intended to allocate such a risk to the builder. If, however, this reading is adopted, then sanctity of contract argues for enforcement in such terms. Is it intelligible, though, to appeal to sanctity of contract (in an extended sense) for the argument that the contract *should be* so read? In *Davis v Fareham*, Lord Radcliffe quite rightly pointed out that there is a serious problem with attributing all contractual consequences to the will of the parties, express or implied. For, as his Lordship said, 'there is something of a logical difficulty in seeing how the parties could even impliedly have provided for something which ex hypothesi they neither expected nor foresaw[4].' No doubt there is room for argument about how far implied expectation can be taken into the realm of the unanticipated. However, in situation (ii), the rhetoric of sanctity of contract—deployed as an argument that the express terms should be taken at face value, and without reference to changed circumstances, even where the parties regard the contingency as exceptional—is less convincing.

In situation (iii), the risk is still of a known type but the extent of the risk is well beyond previous experience. To this extent, the risk is unanticipated and any argument that rests on the parties' unexpressed expectations must allow for the fact that the risk, albeit of a known kind, lies beyond the contemplation of the parties. In other words, such an argument must attribute to the parties three degrees of expectation in relation to known types of risks: expectations in relation, respectively, to normal, exceptional, and (in situation (iii)) hitherto uncontemplated levels of risk. It is possible that the parties will have clear (although unexpressed) expectations in relation to all three tiers of risk. However, common sense suggests that, the less likely the risk, the less likely it is that the parties will have clear expectations—in which case, if the contract is read in situation (iii) as allocating the risk to the builder, the link with the parties' expectations, and concomitantly with respect for their autonomy, is stretched to breaking point. It follows that an appeal to sanctity of contract, whether in the context of interpretation or that of enforcement, no longer rings true. It is one thing to argue that contracts should be interpreted and enforced in accordance with the parties' agreed allocations of risk (whether express or implied); it is quite another matter to argue that contracts should be interpreted and enforced in a particular manner where the risk lies beyond the terms of the parties' agreement.

Finally, in situation (iv), the risk (shortage of unskilled labour) is of a type that has not been anticipated. In principle, the parties might have unexpressed expectations about the allocation of risks of an unanticipated type—just as, in situation (iii), the parties might have unexpressed expectations in relation to hitherto unprecedented levels of a known type of risk. So far as sanctity of contract is concerned, therefore, the analysis of situation (iii) applies mutatis mutandis to situation (iv): in short, an appeal to sanctity of contract can carry little conviction because it has lost contact with its paradigm, namely the situation where the contracting parties have addressed a particular issue and have freely agreed that it shall be dealt with in a certain way.

1   [1956] AC 696.
2   In the event, neither the reservation in the covering letter nor the price variation provisions assisted the building contractors, the former because the letter was held not to be incorporated, and the latter because the provisions were construed as having no application to the general question of the availability of labour and materials.
3   See note 2.
4   [1956] AC 696, 728.

2.10   The third element of freedom of contract (in the broad sense), it will be recalled, is party freedom. This is the right to choose one's contracting partners which, in practice, means the right to refuse to deal with a particular person. It is, of course, axiomatic within the general idea of freedom of contract that there is a threshold freedom to decline an offer (even an offer that, in practice, no rational person would refuse)[1]. However, party freedom constitutes a licence to discriminate against a particular person or particular types of person by excluding such persons from one's contracting activities for whatever reason or whim one likes. This is not to say that those who actually make offers may then pick and choose amongst acceptors who are eligible relative to the scope of the offer: if the offer is open to everyone, anyone may accept; if the offer is open to any member of a particular class, anyone within that class may accept; if the offer is open to all save for a particular restriction, anyone not excluded by that restriction may accept, and so on. However, what party freedom does mean is that offerors may restrict their offers in the first place (by specifying who is and who is not eligible to accept); that offerees may decline to accept offers because they do not want to deal with particular offerors; and that, in both cases, the grounds that offerors and offerees have for so doing are not subject to legal regulation or judicial scrutiny.

1   Cf Kennedy, 'Distributive and Paternalist Motives in Contract and Tort Law, with Special Reference to Compulsory Terms and Unequal Bargaining Power' (1982) 41 Maryland LR 563, 568:
        'People are free *not* to make agreements É You don't have to contract. This means there are the following rules: (i) The state will not punish you for refusing to enter agreements within the domain, no matter how much your potential partner wants you to and no matter how obvious it may be É that you *ought* to.'

The decline of freedom of contract

2.11 The modern law of contract may be contrasted with the classical law in terms either of a change of kind or simply a change of degree. Whether or not the movement from classical to modern (viewed either as historical fact or as theoretical construct) involves a change of kind (and, if so, what kind of change it might be) is a moot point. However, it is widely agreed that legislators in particular see the need to regulate more densely the classical licence to deal and from this it is tempting to infer that the modern law of contract pays less heed than the classical law to the ideal of freedom of contract[1].

1   See eg Fridman 'Freedom of Contract' (1967) 2 Ottawa LR 1, 22:
        The tendency of modern law, therefore, is away from the principle of freedom of contract. It may be that there is a long way to go before utter regulation of contractual relationships is the rule, rather than the exception. But the signs to be found in the cases, it is suggested, point to a movement towards such a situation.
    For judicial recognition of the scale (and appropriateness) of *legislative* restriction upon freedom of contract, see *National Westminster Bank plc v Morgan* [1985] AC 686, 708 (Lord Scarman) (cited at para 3.11). Generally, see Collins *The Law of Contract* (3rd edn, 1997) ch 2.

2.12 Writing in 1959, Sir David Hughes Parry highlighted a number of instances of what he perceived to be legislative and judicial curtailment of freedom of contract[1]. Although Hughes Parry's survey leaves no doubt that, freedom of contract notwithstanding, contractors enjoy no more than a qualified licence to make binding agreements, the general impression is not one of a sea-change taking place in the legal framework of contract. To some extent, the snapshot taken by Hughes Parry lacks an obvious black and white contrast because many of his examples have a legal pedigree pre-dating the turn of the twentieth century. Moreover, where curtailment has a clear economic public policy rationale (such as the regulation of contracts in restraint of trade, or restrictive practices and monopolies), or where curtailment protects those who are not yet 'of full age and competent understanding' (such as the regulation of minors' contracts), there is no sense that freedom of contract is under threat. For the law to confront freedom of contract head-on, it has to be prepared to say (at any rate, with regard to term freedom) that particular contractual provisions, despite having been agreed upon by parties of full and competent understanding, cannot be enforced. In Hughes Parry's survey, perhaps the closest that twentieth-century legislation comes to taking such a stance is in the Hire-Purchase Acts of 1938 and 1954, which sought to ensure that credit purchasers understood the extent of their financial undertakings. Even here, though, the law stopped short of fully curtailing freedom of contract.

> Obviously the legislature's objective was the protection of hire-purchasers in the lower income groups. Instead of declaring certain types of such agreements 'absolutely void,' it sought to provide for such disclosure of certain vital terms of the contract as directly to influence the terms of hire-purchase agreements generally and to open the eyes of the hirer to see the full implications of his bargain. Restrictions were imposed by these ... modern statutes on the freedom of contract in the interests of fair dealing between parties and to protect persons whose acquisitive instincts may be greater than their economic resources.[2]

It will be appreciated that, by taking such an approach, the law went only so far in protecting persons against foolish and improvident bargains (the price that the classical law was prepared to exact for the enjoyment of freedom of contract): rather than declaring certain kinds of agreements off bounds, the legislative strategy was to improve the chances of the purchaser giving an *informed* consent to the agreement and to channel sellers away from using oppressive terms (because such terms would need to be disclosed). In other words, the law regulated the bargaining process without directly regulating the bargain itself[3].

1 Parry *The Sanctity of Contract* (1965) pp 24–66. Under the heading of legislative curtailment, Hughes Parry cites the regulation of contracts entered into on a Sunday, gaming and wagering contracts, infants' contracts, the Truck Acts, the Moneylenders Acts, the Hire-Purchase Acts, and labour and trade union legislation. Under the heading of curtailment by the courts, the examples given are implied terms, impossibility of performance, contracts contrary to law or morality, contracts in restraint of trade, monopolies and restrictive practices (even though this largely centres on the Restrictive Trade Practices Act 1956), and executive arrangements (as in *The Amphitrite* [1921] 3KB 500).

2 Parry *The Sanctity of Contract* p 32.

3 Cf Atiyah *Essays on Contract* (1988) p 362, for the view that there is nothing contrary to the ideology of freedom of contract in ensuring that moneylending

and credit agreements are accompanied by 'the full consent and understanding of the consumer'. Indeed, Atiyah suggests that 'the giving of information about true rates of interest available from suppliers of credit can be justified as an aid to the competitive market'.

2.13   To readers familiar with the evolution of the English law of contract in the second half of the twentieth century, there is one particularly striking omission from Hughes Parry's discussion. By mid-century, the most troublesome pressure point with regard to freedom of contract was the use of exclusion clauses in standard form consumer contracts[1]. Even as Hughes Parry was delivering his Hamlyn Lectures, the courts were responding to the perceived unfairness of such provisions in such a contracting context, by developing the dual doctrines of fundamental term and fundamental breach. The intended effect of these doctrines was to make liability for breach of the ostensible core obligations of a contract non-excludable, not merely as a rule of construction (that is, as a presumption of contractual intention) but as a substantive rule of law. Thus, in *Karsales (Harrow) Ltd v Wallis*[2], which concerned the validity of exclusionary provisions in a hire-purchase contract for a car, Denning LJ said that, if the vendor was in breach of its obligations 'in a respect which goes to the very root of the contract'—the vendor's obligations being determined 'apart from the exempting clauses'—the vendor could not then rely on the exemptions[3]. The development of such radical ideas left the courts in something of a quandary. On the one hand, there was support for a protective approach in standard form consumer contracting; on the other hand, such an approach threatened the calculability of risk allocation in commercial contracts as well as flying in the face of established ideas of freedom of contract[4]. In the landmark case of *Suisse Atlantique Société d'Armement Maritime SA v NV Rotterdamsche Kolen Centrale*[5], the House of Lords sought to re-establish the importance of respecting the parties' agreed decisions by declaring that the new doctrines were not to be treated as substantive rules but, rather, as modern articulations of established rules of construction. The rhetoric of *Suisse Atlantique*, therefore, was classical; the guiding principle continued to be freedom of contract. As Viscount Dilhorne, for instance, put it:

> In my view, it is not right to say that the law prohibits and nullifies a clause exempting or limiting liability for a fundamental breach or breach of a fundamental term. Such a rule of law would involve a restriction on freedom of contract ...[6]

The reality, however, was rather different. For one thing, the rules of construction permitted a protective approach to be employed in the name of effectuating the parties' agreement[7]; and, furthermore, moves were soon to be made to legislate substantive rules for unfair contractual terms.

1 Seminally, see, Kessler 'Contracts of Adhesion: Some Thoughts about Freedom of Contract' (1943) 43 Columbia LR 629. In his concluding remarks, Hughes Parry notes that 'an increasing number of contracts is now entered into by the acceptance of standard forms containing many terms which the acceptor often never reads and often also which, if he did read, he could not fully comprehend' (The Sanctity of Contract at pp 75–76). Quite rightly, Hughes Parry suggests that such a practice is likely to dilute respect for such standard form obligations. However, he does not expressly relate this suggestion to the use of exclusion clauses.

2 [1956] 2 All ER 866.

3 [1956] 2 All ER 866 at 869.

4 It was also famously argued that Lord Denning's approach to exemption clauses overlooked the traditional role of exclusions as a drafting device for the more precise specification of a party's general obligation under a contract. See Coote *Exception Clauses* (1964).

5 [1967] 1AC 361.

6 [1967] 1AC 361 at 392.

7 See eg Lord Denning MR in *Gillespie Bros v Roy Bowles Transport Ltd* [1973] QB 400, 415:

> The judges have, then, time after time, sanctioned a departure from the ordinary meaning. They have done it under the guise of 'construing' the clause. They assume that the party cannot have intended anything so unreasonable. So they construe the clause 'strictly'. They cut down the ordinary meaning of the words and reduce them to reasonable proportions.

Generally, see further chapter 4.

2.14 Growing pressure to regulate the framework of consumer contracting led to a number of important legislative initiatives in the years following the *Suisse Atlantique*. Of these initiatives, the most significant was the Unfair Contract Terms Act 1977 (UCTA)[1]. Under UCTA 1977, a wide range of exclusionary provisions are either black-listed (that is, declared to be void[2]) or placed on a grey-list (that is, declared to be valid only if they satisfy a test of reasonableness). In this latter category, UCTA 1977, s 3 has a particularly broad sweep, applying to exclusions in consumer contracts as well as to contracts concluded on a party's 'written standard terms of business' (whether a consumer or a commercial contract). The Act, as Patrick Atiyah says, is 'a highly paternalistic measure'[3]; and its paternalism can be seen as operating at three levels.

First, and most obviously, the Act constrains the power of the parties to enforce certain terms even though they might have been freely agreed. Thus, for example, even though parties might willingly contract on the basis that there should be no liability for negligence resulting in death or personal injury, or that a seller's statutory implied obligations as to title should be excluded, the Act renders such terms

void. Moreover, under the Fair Trading Act 1973, civil law non-
enforcement can be (and occasionally has been) backed up by criminal
offences where terms and conditions in contracts are so adverse to the
economic interests of consumers as to be inequitable[4]. No doubt, many
will be puzzled as to why anyone should freely wish to deal on terms
that accept risks that contractors typically wish to avoid. Such
puzzlement, however, is precisely what freedom of contract enjoins
the law to put to one side.

Secondly, because the Act compels business contractors to accept
certain kinds of risk, such contractors effectively operate as insurers
against the risks in question. In other words, as part of the contractual
package, the customer gets the benefit of various rights irrespective
of whether such rights are wanted—or, more pointedly, even if the
customer would prefer to contract without such protected rights and
at a lower price. As Atiyah asks:

> Why should we prevent these buyers from exercising their freedom
> of choice? This is on the face of it pure paternalism: the law tells the
> buyer that he does not know what is in his own best interest, and that
> if he wants to buy certain goods or services he must buy certain rights
> as a sort of compulsory extra.[5]

According to Atiyah, the best that can be said in favour of such pure
paternalism is that the cost of restricting the freedom of choice of the
minority (who, idiosyncratically, prefer to contract without insurance)
is outweighed by the benefit to the majority who prefer the protected
deal[6].

Thirdly, the Act apparently adds another layer of paternalism when
it contemplates questionable terms being ruled invalid as unreasonable.
The position, here, however, is rather more complex. Freedom of
contract is challenged head-on where the law provides that, even though
a party has freely agreed to a term, the term is invalid. If the Act
authorised the courts to strike out terms as unreasonable where, despite
the free agreement of the parties, the terms were judged to be contrary
to the parties' best interests, then freedom of contract would be directly
compromised. In fact, the reasonableness requirement in UCTA 1977,
s 11—at least, when read in conjunction with the guidelines in Sch
2[7]—does not give the courts this kind of jurisdiction. According to
Sch 2, the factors which weigh against the reasonableness of a term
include: (a) that the parties are of unequal bargaining strength (where
the party in the stronger bargaining position has imposed the term on
the party in the weaker bargaining position); and (b) that the supplier
is in a monopoly position in relation to the customer—that, for the
customer, it is essentially a case of 'take it or leave it'. On the other
side, factors which weigh in favour of the reasonableness of a term

include: (a) that an inducement is offered for acceptance of the term (eg a price reduction for a limitation of liability); (b) that the customer has other options; and (c) that the customer knows, or ought reasonably to know, about the term[8]. Seemingly, these balancing factors do not relate *directly* to the reasonableness of particular terms so much as to the context in which a contract has been formed. In other words, this level of protection in UCTA is largely concerned with whether the terms of the contract are transparent, with whether a particular contract resulted from the parties' genuine negotiation, in short with whether the parties came to terms on a free and informed basis—and, to this extent, the Act replicates the kind of approach that Hughes Parry detected in the earlier Hire-Purchase Acts[9].

1   See, too, the Misrepresentation Act 1967, the Fair Trading Act 1973, and the Consumer Credit Act 1974 (esp s137(1) which regulates extortionate credit bargains).
2   As is the case, for example, with clauses which purport to exclude or restrict liability for death or personal injury resulting from negligence (s 2(1)), clauses which purport to exclude the implied obligations as to title under s12 of the Sale of Goods Act (s 6(1)), and clauses in consumer contracts that purport to exclude or restrict liability for breach of the implied obligations under ss 13, 14, and 15 of the Sale of Goods Act 1979 (s 6(2)).
3   Atiyah *Essays on Contract* (1988) p 364.
4   See Fair Trading Act 1973, ss 17(2)(d), 22, and 23; and the Consumer Transactions (Restrictions on Statements) Order 1976, SI 1976/1813, as amended by SI 1978/127.
5   Atiyah Essays on Contract p 375.
6   Atiyah Essays on Contract p 376. Where the law adopts a paternalistic policy by laying down safety standards for products (eg prescribing that car manufacturers must fit safety belts to their vehicles), one justificatory argument might be that, in many cases, the increased cost of incorporating safety features is marginal; or that, in the case of mass produced goods, costs would be increased even more if the manufacturer were to produce two lines of goods, one with the safety feature, the other without it. Following Atiyah, however, perhaps the best that can be said in favour of a paternalistic move towards safety is that the risk-averse preferences of the majority outweigh idiosyncratic minority preferences.
7   Although the guidelines in Sch 2 relate explicitly only to the reasonableness test as it arises under UCTA, ss 6 and 7, judicial practice is to regard the guidelines as generally applicable. See eg *Stag Line Ltd v Tyne Shiprepair Group Ltd, The Zinnia* [1984] 2 Lloyd's Rep 211; *Rees-Hough Ltd v Redland Reinforced Plastics Ltd* (1984) 2 Con LR 109; and *Phillips Products Ltd v T Hyland and Hamstead Plant Hire Co Ltd* [1987] 2 All ER 620.
8   Schedule 2 of UCTA also lists 'whether the goods were manufactured, processed or adapted to the special order of the customer'. Presumably, where goods are so manufactured, processed or adapted, this factor tends to weigh in favour of the reasonableness of a term.
9   Cf the Office of Fair Trading's Report *Photocopier Selling Practices* (March 1994) for a similar emphasis on transparency in the context of leasing photocopiers. As the Director General put his approach in the Foreword to the Report (at p 4):

The guiding principle should be transparency, so that the main terms and conditions of all leases, including the terms on which early settlement may be made, are set out overtly and without ambiguity. In short, I am calling for full disclosure of terms and conditions rather than for control of them.

2.15 At the same time that the legislature was encroaching upon term freedom, it was also placing restrictions on party freedom. During this period, the most notable constraints on this aspect of freedom of contract were the Sex Discrimination Act 1975[1] and the Race Relations Act 1976[2]. Of course, restrictions on party freedom were not unprecedented. Indeed, the common law had long regulated the freedom of some tradespersons—common carriers and innkeepers are the standard examples—to choose their customers[3]. So, in the notorious modern case of *Constantine v Imperial Hotels Ltd*[4], the Imperial Hotel in London was held to be in breach of its common law duty when, without sufficient excuse, it refused to accommodate a well-known West Indian cricket player. Following the example of *Constantine*, the legislation of the 1970s renders it unlawful to discriminate on the grounds of sex or race in the provision (or non provision) of accommodation[5]. However, this is just one instance of the many applications of the legislation, the scope of which extends well beyond the common law principles in confining the opportunities for contractors to deal on the basis of their prejudices. Not surprisingly, therefore, the mid-1970s is seen as something of a watershed in the evolution of the modern law of contract.

1   Parts II, III, and VII. See esp s29, which deals with discrimination in the provision of goods, facilities, or services.
2   Parts II, III, and VIII. See esp s29, which deals with discrimination in the provision of goods, facilities, or services.
3   See 5(1) Halsbury's Laws of England (4th edn) para 402 (for common carriers), and para 1113 et seq (for innkeepers). There is also a suggestion that, at one time, blacksmiths might have been similarly restricted: see 5(1) Halsbury's Laws of England (4th edn) para 1116, note 2, and *Johnson v Midland Rly Co* (1849) 4 Exch 367, 372–373 (Baron Parke).
4   [1944] KB 693. In fact, the plaintiff had a contract with the defendants for the reception of his wife, his daughter, and himself at the hotel. However, the action was brought in tort (on the case) rather than in contract.
5   See Sex Discrimination Act 1975, s29(2)(b); and Race Relations Act 1976, s20(2)(b).

2.16 What are we to conclude, then, about the supposed decline of freedom of contract? In one sense, there is no doubt that contract in general, as well as in specific contexts such as employment and housing, has become more densely regulated in the twentieth century. There is also no mistaking the bifurcation of commercial and consumer contracting, with the latter attracting its own tailored regime of protective law. Understandably, developments of this kind encourage the view that the classical law has been displaced or that, at the very least, freedom of contract is not as highly valued as it once was. However, before we write off freedom of contract, three points should give us pause. First, as we saw when discussing *Norweb plc v Dixon*[1], where the relationship between a public electricity supplier and a tariff customer was held to be statutory rather than contractual, the idea that contract involves voluntariness and control over the transaction is deeply embedded even in the modern legal consciousness. Freedom of contract, in other words, is not just an ideal for contract law; it speaks to the essence of what a contract is. Secondly, although statutes such as the Unfair Contract Terms Act 1977 do directly regulate term freedom, much of the regulation of consumer contracts is designed to ensure that informed consent is given; and, to this extent, such regulation is compatible with freedom of contract[2]. Thirdly, the degree of respect (or disrespect) for freedom of contract can be measured either by asking whether there is still a presumption in favour of freedom or by considering whether the 'good reasons' for curtailing freedom are now understood in a way that more readily gives the green light to intervention. If we ask whether transactional freedom is still regarded in a favourable light, the answer is surely in the affirmative. If we ask whether our understanding of 'good reasons' has changed, this is a much more complex question—because, as it was emphasised earlier, the nature of such good reasons is governed by the overall legal-moral theory in which freedom of contract has its place[3]. Thus, if utilitarianism provides the basic setting, and if our reasons for limiting contractual freedom continue to be utilitarian reasons, then our respect for freedom of contract has not diminished even though our reasoning now requires more tinkering with the legal ground rules. If, on the other hand, our background framework is rights-led, and if we believe that freedom of contract follows from, say, a right to autonomy, then in one sense we take freedom of contract more seriously: for, an individual's right to autonomy and the concomitant right to freedom of contract cannot then be limited for simple utilitarian reasons[4]. We must also accept, however, that the right to freedom of contract can be limited where its exercise is incompatible with the background regime of individual rights. Accordingly, the limitations imposed on party freedom by the race relations and sex discrimination legislation will almost certainly be required by the background regime of individual rights (that is, by the background regime which itself supports freedom of contract). In this example, as in many other instances, the suggestion that freedom of contract is in decline invites further analysis and needs to be approached with some caution[5].

1   [1995] 3 All ER 952. See para 1.18.
2   For the logic of taking freedom of contract (informed consent) seriously in the context of standard form contracting, see Rakoff 'Contracts of Adhesion: An Essay in Reconstruction' (1983) 96 Harv LR 1174.
3   See para 2.7.
4   Cf Dworkin *Taking Rights Seriously* (1978). On the utlitarian justification for the use of standard forms, see eg Kessler 'Contracts of Adhesion: Some Thoughts about Freedom of Contract' (1943) 43 Columbia LR 629. On the concept of autonomy in the context of contract, see Collins *The Law of Contract* (3rd edn 1997) pp 28–34; Brownsword 'Liberalism and the Law of Contract' in Bellamy (ed) *Liberalism and Recent Legal and Social Philosophy* (ARSP Beiheft 36) (1989) p 86; and generally see Raz *The Morality of Freedom* (1986).
5   Cf Collins The Law of Contract pp 261–265.

The coherence of freedom of contract

2.17   Freedom of contract, as we have seen, is an idea that can be taken broadly or narrowly (in which case, its focus is term freedom). It is also an idea that can be seen as attractive from more than one moral perspective. From a utilitarian perspective, there is considerable sense in the idea that welfare will be maximised if the law permits individuals to transact according to their own preferences; and, from a rights perspective, there is good sense in respecting the choices of autonomous individuals. If there is a stable core idea in these variations on the theme of freedom of contract, it must be that other things being equal the products of free dealing are to be respected. Yet, is this a coherent idea? What are the necessary and sufficient conditions for free (and, thus, on the classical approach, fair) dealing?

2.18   Typically, accounts of free dealing focus on two factors: how much pressure there is to deal (raising questions of duress and undue influence, and the like); and to what extent accurate information is denied or disclosed, or made available (raising questions of fraud, misrepresentation, non-disclosure, mistake and so on). If freedom of contract is to be a coherent idea, it has to take a decisive position on these conceptual questions. This, however, is where the contested nature of freedom threatens to undermine the classical project; for, as Duncan Kennedy has pointed out, the concept of voluntariness is elastic:

> [W]ithout doing violence to the notion of voluntariness as it has been worked out in the law, [we] could adopt a hard-nosed self-reliant, individualist posture that shrinks the defenses of fraud and duress almost to nothing. At the other extreme, [we] could require the slightly stronger or slightly better-informed party to give away all his advantage ... If we cut back the rules far enough, we would arrive at

something like the state of nature—legalized theft. If we extended them far enough, we would jeopardize the enforceability of the whole range of bargains that define a mixed capitalist economy ... In either extreme case, we would have departed from freedom of contract—the concept has some meaning and imposes some loose limits.[1]

If we accept this analysis, there seem to be two responses. First, it might be conceded that free dealing is an idea that occupies no fixed point on, so to speak, the spectrum of voluntariness. As Kennedy portrays the matter, freedom of contract excludes the extremes but allows itself room for manoeuvre in between the outer limits of the scale. On this view, as we have seen, there is no problem in reconciling many of the modern protective interventions with freedom of contract; but, of course, it does involve admitting that there is some indeterminacy in the essential idea. The alternative response is to give free dealing a definite location on the spectrum of voluntariness. The problem with this response, however, is that there is no obvious reason why freedom of contract should settle on one location rather than another.

This latter point leads on to what Kennedy sees as the underlying issue uncovered by the looseness of the idea of freedom of contract. Thus:

> Confronted with a choice, [we] will have available two sets of stereotypical policy arguments. One 'altruist' set of arguments suggests that [we] should resolve the gap, conflict, or ambiguity by requiring a party who injures the other to pay compensation, and also that [we] should allow a liberal law of excuse when the injuring party claims to be somehow not really responsible. The other 'individualist' set of arguments emphasizes that the injured party should have looked out for himself, rather than demanding that the other renounce freedom of action, and that the party seeking excuse should have avoided binding himself to obligations he couldn't fulfill.[2]

Expressing this in terms of the conflict between the ethic of individualism and the ethic of co-operativism[3], whereas an individualist will tend to equate freedom with the absence of fraud and the most naked forms of coercion, a proponent of co-operativism will tend to equate freedom with the absence of disinformation and economic pressure; and, whereas an individualist will rarely accept uncontemplated events as an excuse for non-performance, a proponent of co-operativism will argue for some sharing of unanticipated risks. In other words, the ideas of freedom of contract and sanctity of contract are contested concepts, the interpretation of which turns on the particular ethical base from which the interpreter begins[4].

1   Kennedy 'Distributive and Paternalist Motives in Contract and Tort Law, with Special Reference to Compulsory Terms and Unequal Bargaining Power' (1982) 41 Maryland LR 563, 582.

2   Kennedy (1982) 41 Maryland LR 563 at 581.
3   See para 1.20.
4   Much the same might be said about the related idea of consent. A person's consent only carries normative force where it is free and informed, where the consenting party 'know[s] the relevant facts and act[s] without being under pressure' (see Fletcher *Basic Concepts of Legal Thought* (1996) 112. But, what precisely do we mean by these conditions of informed consent? See further, eg Barnett 'A Consent Theory of Contract' (1986) 86 Columbia LR 269, esp at 300–319. As Barnett concedes, '[t]he hard work facing any legal system based on entitlements includes determining what constitutes "valid" title and what acts constitute "consent"' (at p 307). Whilst linguistic and legal conventions can settle 'the meaning of one's freely chosen words or conduct' (at p 303), and thus what counts as 'consent' for the purposes of contractual transfers, the defensibility of such conventions and the concomitant models of freedom upon which they rely is where the hard work really has to be undertaken.

2.19   If analysis of the idea of voluntariness takes us back to the contested ethics of contract law, a further question about the coherence of freedom of contract may be raised. Much of the modern interest in a co-operative ethic has been prompted by reflections (both empirical and economic) on contracting practice in long-term or relational contexts[1]. In such contexts, the parties want a framework for their dealing, but it does not always suit their interests to make detailed provision for future contingencies in the initial contract documents. What such contractors need is an agreement that allows for ongoing adjustment, revision, and flexibility, rather than one that has performance obligations and allocations of risk written in stone. How much sense does it make, then, to apply notions of sanctity of contract in such a transactional setting? Nagla Nassar, writing about long-term international commercial transactions, contends that the classical ideals no longer fit the practical needs of contractors[2]. For, in relational dealing:

> the goal of contract law is not limited to ensuring enforceability, certainty and delimiting rights and duties. Rather '[c]ontract law is there to provide for the continuity of relationships through resolution of conflicts and correcting for market changes and failures that may arise during the course of performance. Solutions adopted under contract law primarily should be concerned with furthering all the different interests involved. This is usually attainable through the articulation of legal standards which, contrary to technical rules, are inherently flexible. Fairness and good faith, defined in reference to best efforts, become the backbone of contract law through which mutual trust between the contracting parties is promoted' The aim of contract law should be the protection of the contractual relationship and the balancing of the involved interests, not the protection of individually acquired positions.[3]

In short, the maxim *pacta sunt servanda* (at any rate, if applied in a literal and mechanical fashion), like the ideal of freedom of contract,

is out of place where the parties' relationship is ongoing, evolving, and dynamic rather than fixed by a particular contractual agreement at a single point in time. Plainly, if freedom of contract no longer accords with the needs and expectations of those who deal in the heartland of commerce, its coherence is challenged in a way that calls for urgent attention.

1   See eg Campbell and Harris 'Flexibility in Long-Term Contractual Relationships: The Role of Co-operation' (1993) 20 Journal of Law and Society 166; and Brownsword 'From Co-operative Contracting to a Contract of Co-operation' in Campbell and Vincent-Jones (eds) *Contract and Economic Organisation* (1996) 14. On relational contracting, seminally, see Macneil, 'The Many Futures of Contract' (1974) 47 Southern California LR 691, and 'Contracts: Adjustment of Long-Term Economic Relations under Classical, Neo-Classical and Relational Contract Law' (1978) 72 Northwestern University LR 854. The term 'relational' is used broadly to cover both cases where there is a close trading relationship between the parties and cases where the particular contract is of a long-term kind: see eg Bell 'The Effect of Changes in Circumstances on Long-Term Contracts' in Harris and Tallon (eds) *Contract Law Today* (1989) 195. For relational contracts and good faith, see eg Eisenberg, 'Relational Contracts' in Beatson and Freedman (eds) *Good Faith and Fault in Contract Law* (1995) 291.
     An excellent example of this approach underlies the Model Form of (Lump Sum) Contract (3rd edn, 1995) drafted by the Institution of Chemical Engineers, the basic philosophy of which is said to be 'the view that the parties should co-operate to achieve the mutual objective of a successful project rather than regarding the contract as the basis for an adversarial relationship' (at p 1).
2   Nassar *Sanctity of Contracts Revisited* (1995).
3   Nassar *Sanctity of Contracts Revisited* pp 24–25.

Synthesis

2.20 Two signal developments in the modern law and practice of contracting place serious questionmarks alongside the appropriateness of freedom of contract[1]. These are, first, the development of a mass consumer market—now being established across Europe[2]—and, with it, a tailored protective regime of contract law[3]; and, secondly, the growing recognition that relational commercial dealing needs its own regulatory framework. With regard to the former, two of the key ideas lending support to the articulation of a protective framework of consumer law have been that consumer contractors suffer from an inequality of bargaining power when dealing with business contractors, and that standard form consumer contracts often contain terms that are not reasonable. In the next two sections, we can look more closely at these important ideas of inequality of bargaining power[4] and reasonableness[5]. With regard to long-term commercial dealing, freedom of contract can be seen as problematic where its licence for

one-sided advantage-taking impedes the cultivation of more productive economic relationships. In this light, Pt II of the Housing Grants, Construction and Regeneration Act 1996 is an interesting case in point. On the face of it, Pt II, which applies deep in the commercial sector, adopts a surprisingly restrictive approach to freedom of contract (by curbing, inter alia, the abuse of 'set-off' and 'pay when paid' provisions). However, the underlying rationale for such inroads into freedom of contract is to lay the legal foundations for better relationships in the construction industry[6]. Freedom of contract can also be problematic where it imports doctrinal requirements that do not fit with the way that the contractors want to plan and arrange their business. For instance, the classical doctrinal requirement of certainty of terms can prove a hindrance to long-term dealers who prefer not to agree every detail at the outset[7]. Above all, where the spirit in which contractors relate to one another is that of good faith co-operation rather than self-interested opportunism, the adversarial culture implicit in freedom of contract makes it, quite simply, the wrong starting point. In later sections, we will look at the arguments concerning the incorporation of a general principle of good faith[8] before mapping out the way in which modern contract law is beginning to move with the shape and standards of the modern marketplace[9].

1   Cf Friedman 'Some General Considerations' in *International Encyclopedia of Comparative Law* Vol VII, 3, esp at pp 5–6, and 11–17 (on the development of the modern law of contract).
2   See chapter 7.
3   See Brownsword, Howells and Wilhelmsson 'Between Market and Welfare: Some Reflections on Article 3 of the EC Directive on Unfair Terms in Consumer Contracts' in Willett (ed) *Aspects of Fairness in Contract* (1996) 25. See also chapter 7.
4   See chapter 3.
5   See chapter 4.
6   Generally, for reflections on the way in which contract law can play a background role in shaping co-operative relationships, see Deakin and Michie (eds) *Contracts, Co-operation, and Competition* (1997).
7   Cf Williamson 'Transaction-Cost Economics. The Governance of Contractual Relations' (1979) 22 Journal of Law and Economics 233.
8   See chapter 5.
9   See chapter 6.

CHAPTER 3

Inequality of Bargaining Power

Inequality of bargaining power: from the classical to the modern view

3.1 Within the classical law of contract, the relative bargaining strength of the contractors is not a question for judicial inquiry. As Patrick Atiyah says:

> The Court's function [on the classical view] is to ensure procedural fair play: the Court is the umpire to be appealed to when a foul is alleged, but the Court has no substantive function beyond this. It is not the Court's business to ensure that the bargain is fair, or to see that one party does not take undue advantage of another, or impose unreasonable terms by virtue of superior bargaining position. Any superiority in bargaining power is itself a matter for the market to rectify.[1]

The modern view, however, is rather different[2]. Although a doctrine of inequality of bargaining strength is not recognised as such[3], the relative bargaining power of the parties is often a relevant consideration, particularly where the issue concerns the validity of exemption clauses in standard form contracts.

It will be recalled that, prior to the enactment of the Unfair Contract Terms Act 1977, the courts were becoming increasingly concerned about the use of standard form exemptions, particularly in consumer contracts. The essence of this concern was captured in Lord Reid's speech in the *Suisse Atlantique*[4]:

> Exemption clauses differ greatly in many respects. Probably the most objectionable are found in the complex standard conditions which are now so common. In the ordinary way the customer has no time to read them, and if he did read them he would probably not understand

them. And if he did understand or object to any of them, he would
generally be told he could take it or leave it. And if he then went to
another supplier the result would be the same. Freedom to contract
must surely imply some choice or room for bargaining.

At the other extreme is the case where parties are bargaining on
terms of equality and a stringent exemption clause is accepted for a
quid pro quo or other good reason.

Following the decision in the *Suisse Atlantique*, which, it has been
suggested, formally upheld freedom of contract while informally
permitting regulation via an aggressive use of the rules of construction[5],
Lord Reid's remarks about equality (and inequality) of bargaining
power foreshadowed three major doctrinal developments.

1   Atiyah *The Rise and Fall of Freedom of Contract* (1979) p 404.
2   See eg Reiter 'The Control of Contract Power' (1981) 1 OJLS 347.
3   See *National Westminster Bank plc v Morgan* [1985] 1 All ER 821.
4   *Suisse Atlantique Société d'Armement Maritime SA v NV Rotterdamsche Kolen
     Centrale* [1967] 1AC 361, 406. See, too, Donaldson J in *Kenyon, Son and
     Craven Ltd v Baxter Hoare and Co* [1971] 2 All ER 708, 720: 'If [the exemption
     clause] occurred in a printed form of contract between parties of unequal
     bargaining power, it would be socially most undesirable ...'.
5   See para 2.13.

3.2 The first development was the accentuation of the already incipient
bifurcation in the law between the rules applicable to consumer
contracts and those applicable to commercial contracts. Moreover, it
was widely accepted that the justification for this regulatory dichotomy
lay in the differential bargaining power of the contractors. Quite simply,
so the reasoning runs, whereas the parties to commercial contracts
tend to be of roughly equal bargaining strength, the parties to consumer
contracts tend to be of unequal bargaining strength—consumers
ordinarily being reliant on the skill and expertise of business
contractors, as well as having less choice and control in relation to
particular transactions, and generally having fewer resources at their
disposal[1]. Legislative endorsement of this distinction (and its underlying
rationale) followed in enactments such as the Unfair Contract Terms
Act 1977 (UCTA) and the Sale and Supply of Goods Act 1994, where
one stream of provisions deals with consumer contracts and another
stream provides for commercial contracts, as well as in dedicated
consumer protection legislation, such as the Unfair Terms in
Consumer Contracts Regulations 1994[2]. For the modern law of
contract, therefore, the transactional world is to be viewed as class-
divided; on the one hand, there are commercial contracts, on the other,
consumer contracts; and relative strength of bargaining position is
treated as the basis for this division as well as being the key to a
contractor's class membership[3].

1 A good example is the contrast between the approach of the Court of Appeal (with regard to the incorporation of standard terms) in the commercial case of *British Crane Hire Corpn v Ipswich Plant Hire Ltd* [1974] 1 All ER 1059 and the consumer case of *Hollier v Rambler Motors (AMC) Ltd* [1972] 2QB 71. In the former case (at 1061–62), Lord Denning MR remarked: 'The plaintiff [in *Hollier*] was not of equal bargaining power with the garage company which repaired the car. The conditions were not incorporated. But here the parties were both in the trade and were of equal bargaining power'.

2 SI 1994/3159, implementing Directive 93/13/EEC.

3 This characterisation is not uniquely English. The impact of the idea of relative bargaining strength has been felt across Europe: see Beale 'Inequality of Bargaining Power' (1986) 6 OJLS 123; and for the Nordic countries, see Wilhelmsson, 'The Philosophy of Welfarism and its Emergence in the Modern Scandinavian Contract Law' in Brownsword, Howells and Wilhelmsson (eds) *Welfarism in Contract Law* (1994) 63.

3.3 The second application of the idea of relative bargaining strength can be seen in the statutory regimes that nowadays regulate the validity of exclusion clauses. Where the validity of a controlled exemption clause is at issue, the statutory guidelines make the relative bargaining strength of the parties a relevant factor. So, for example, guideline (a) in UCTA Sch 2 (which, in principle, applies to both consumer *and commercial* contracts) refers to 'the strength of the bargaining positions of the parties relative to each other, taking into account (among other things) alternative means by which the customer's requirements could have been met.' We find a similar provision, albeit with exclusive application to consumer contracts, in the Unfair Terms in Consumer Contracts Regulations 1994. There, according to the general test in reg 4(1), a term is unfair if 'contrary to the requirement of good faith, it causes a significant imbalance in the parties' rights and obligations arising under the contract, to the detriment of the consumer'; and the guidelines on whether the requirement of good faith has been satisfied mirror the UCTA approach by stating that regard shall be had, inter alia, to 'the strength of the bargaining positions of the parties'[1].

To the extent that relative bargaining strength is made a relevant consideration in the context of consumer contracts, this simply reinforces the initial (protective) separation of consumer contracts from commercial contracts[2]. However, where, as in UCTA, relative bargaining strength is made a relevant consideration, too, with regard to *commercial* contracts, this can cause some tensions—particularly between those judges who are disposed to take it on trust that commercial contracts (unlike consumer contracts) are normally the outcome of bilateral negotiation and those who wish to satisfy themselves in each case that the contract has not been unilaterally imposed by a party in a dominant bargaining position. The logic of the former view is that the UCTA guidelines should not be construed as an invitation to discriminate case-by-case on the basis of relative bargaining strength—and, on one reading at least, this is precisely how we might interpret Lord Wilberforce's well-known post-UCTA plea for judicial restraint in *Photo Production Ltd v Securicor Transport Ltd*[3]:

> After this Act [ie, UCTA], in commercial matters generally, when the parties are not of unequal bargaining power, and when risks are normally borne by insurance, not only is the case for judicial intervention undemonstrated, but there is everything to be said, and this seems to have been Parliament's intention, for leaving the parties free to apportion the risks as they think fit and for respecting their decisions.[4]

By contrast, in *George Mitchell (Chesterhall) Ltd v Finney Lock Seeds Ltd*[5] the House of Lords seemed to treat a case-by-case approach as appropriate. On this view, although it might generally be true that commercial contractors deal on a roughly equal footing, the point of the statutory guidance is to check the bargaining position in each particular case. Moreover, in the evolving jurisprudence of the reasonableness test in UCTA, we can certainly find support for the view that, where parties are presented with 'take it or leave it' conditions of dealing, then inequality of bargaining strength is likely to be a material factor (weighing against the validity of the conditions) even in commercial disputes[6].

1 See reg 4(3), and Sch 2, guideline (a).
2 Cf *Smith v Eric S Bush* [1989] 2 All ER 514.
3 [1980] AC 827. On another reading, the emphasis of Lord Wilberforce's remark is not on 'commercial matters generally' but on the qualifier 'when the parties are not of unequal bargaining power'. This reading puts Lord Wilberforce much closer to the view that favours a case-by-case monitoring of the parties' relative bargaining position.
4 [1980] AC 827 at 843.
5 [1983] 2 AC 803.
6 See eg *Phillips Products Ltd v T Hyland and Hamstead Plant Hire Co Ltd* [1987] 2 All ER 620; *St Albans City and District Council v International Computers Ltd* [1995] FSR 686; and, generally, see Adams and Brownsword 'The Unfair Contract Terms Act: A Decade of Discretion' (1988) 104 LQR 94, and *Key Issues in Contract* (1995) Ch 8.

3.4 Thirdly, Lord Reid's observations presaged a more general recognition of the significance of inequality of bargaining power, stretching beyond consumer contracts, and beyond exemption clauses. So, for example, in *Schroeder Music Publishing Co Ltd v Macaulay*[1], a case involving restraint of trade provisions in a standard form contract made between a music publishing house and a young songwriter, Lord Reid himself underlined the importance of relative bargaining strength.

In favour of the contractual provisions, it was argued that they had stood the test of time and caused no obvious injustice. Responding to this, however, Lord Reid said that, whilst there might be good reason for respecting contracts 'made freely by parties bargaining on equal terms'[2] or 'moulded under the pressure of negotiation'[3], there was no evidence in the instant case that the contract fitted any such description. Pursuing this theme, Lord Diplock drew a distinction between those standard forms that have been negotiated for use in a particular trade by parties 'whose bargaining power is fairly matched'[4], and those standard forms that have been negotiated in a one-sided way. In relation to the latter, his Lordship said:

> The terms of this kind of standard form of contract have not been the subject of negotiation between the parties to it, or approved by any organisation representing the interests of the weaker party. They have been dictated by that party whose bargaining power, either exercised alone or in conjunction with others providing similar goods and services, enables him to say: 'If you want these goods or services at all, these are the only terms on which they are obtainable. Take it or leave it.'
>
> To be in a position to adopt this attitude toward a party desirous of entering into a contract to obtain goods or services provides a classic instance of superior bargaining power.[5]

The force of this distinction is that, where contracts are the outcome of negotiations that are not manifestly one-sided, there is a presumption in favour of treating the terms as fair and reasonable; where, on the other hand, contracts are dictated in a one-sided way, there is no such presumption. This is not to say that a party who presents terms of this dictated kind, and who can afford to tell the other party that this is the only offer on the table, necessarily takes advantage of the situation to drive an unconscionable bargain. However, in such a case, Lord Diplock enjoins the courts to be especially vigilant in ensuring that a superior bargaining position has not been abused.

The line of reasoning in *Schroeder v Macaulay* could be generalised to express a general principle for the protection of those who are vulnerable by dint of their relative bargaining position. Indeed, in a famous judgment handed down in *Lloyds Bank Ltd v Bundy*[6], Lord Denning MR drew on a number of strands of authority (in the case-law dealing with duress of goods, unconscionable transactions, undue influence, undue pressure, and salvage agreements) to argue precisely for a general doctrine of inequality of bargaining power:

> Gathering all together, I would suggest that through all these instances there runs a single thread. They rest on 'inequality of bargaining power.' By virtue of it, the English law gives relief to one who, without independent advice, enters into a contract upon terms which are very

unfair or transfers property for a consideration which is grossly inadequate, when his bargaining power is grievously impaired by reason of his own needs or desires, or by his own ignorance or infirmity, coupled with undue influences or pressure brought to bear on him by or for the benefit of the other.[7]

Applying this principle to the facts of *Bundy*—where an elderly farmer, acting without independent advice, had charged the full value of his house in favour of a bank as security for an overdraft facility extended to his son's plant hire company—Lord Denning thought that this was an eminently suitable case to intervene. Sir Eric Sachs and Cairns LJJ, too, agreed with Lord Denning that the bank should not be allowed to enforce the transaction against Mr Bundy. However, they rested their reasoning on the established principle of undue influence rather than the freshly minted doctrine of inequality of bargaining power.

In the event, the doctrine of inequality of bargaining power, as articulated in *Bundy*, was to prove to be one of Lord Denning's less successful attempts to synthesise a new overarching principle from a number of accepted doctrinal elements. However, before we discuss the subsequent rejection of any such overarching principle, we need to examine more carefully what we mean by relative bargaining strength, what the idea of inequality of bargaining power might amount to, and why precisely the law might contemplate intervening in cases where there is such an inequality.

1   [1974] 1 WLR 1308. For discussion, see Trebilcock 'The Doctrine of Inequality of Bargaining Power: Post-Benthamite Economics in the House of Lords' (1976) 26 U Toronto LJ 359.
2   [1974] 1 WLR 1308 at 1314, citing Lord Pearce in *Esso Petroleum Co Ltd v Harper's Garage (Stourport) Ltd* [1968] AC 269, 323. And, by analogy, it might be argued that where the parties are each 'large sophisticated commercial organisations' there is good reason for respecting the remedial regime that the parties would expect to be applied to a breach: see Lord Hoffmann in *Co-operative Insurance Society Ltd v Argyll Stores* (Holdings) Ltd [1997] 3 All ER 297, 307.
3   [1974] 1 WLR 1308 citing Lord Wilberforce in the *Esso* case [1968] AC 269, 332–333.
4   [1974] 1 WLR 1308 at 1316.
5   [1974] 1 WLR 1308 at 1316.
6   [1975] QB 326.
7   [1975] QB 326 at 339.

Relative bargaining strength and inequality of bargaining power

3.5 Because the ideas of relative bargaining strength and inequality of bargaining power have largely emerged in English contract law in the context of a coalescence of concerns about standard form dealing, exclusion clauses, small print, and consumer contracting, it is not easy to take an uncluttered look at these concepts. Nevertheless, if we could extract these ideas from their customary context, what would we mean by, and how would we identify, relative bargaining strength or inequality of bargaining power? And, why should inequality of this kind give us a reason for interfering with the ordinary enforcement of contracts?

Starting afresh, any plausible doctrine of inequality of bargaining power should have answers to the following three questions:

(i) What do we mean by 'bargaining power'? What sorts of things does it cover?

(ii) Relative to whom (or relative to which benchmark) is a contractor's bargaining strength judged to be weak or strong, resulting in inequality of bargaining power?

(iii) Is inequality of bargaining power to be read as a 'defendant-sided' or as a 'plaintiff-sided' doctrine[1]? That is, is the basis for relief defendant-sided, in the sense that the stronger bargaining party has taken unfair advantage of the weaker, or is it plaintiff-sided, in the sense that the weaker party has not given a free and informed consent to the transaction?

1   For this terminology, see Birks and Yin 'On the Nature of Undue Influence' in Beatson and Friedmann (eds) *Good Faith and Fault in Contract Law* (1995) 57. The authors say that, where the emphasis is put on:
    wrongful abuse or exploitation by the stronger party É we call that a defendant-sided analysis. It is convenient to refer to the party against whom relief for undue influence is sought as the defendant, even though in some configurations it is in fact the plaintiff in the action who is obliged to resist a defence based on undue influence: a defendant-sided analysis is one which explains the relief in terms of the bad conduct of the party against whom the relief is sought (at 58). See, too, Bigwood 'Undue Influence: "Impaired Consent" or "Wicked Exploitation"?' (1996) 16 OJLS 503 for some questionmarks against the Birks and Yin distinction.

3.6   The first of these questions, as Hugh Beale has pointed out, has been relatively neglected[1]. It really ought to be a pretty straightforward inquiry, and yet we soon run into trouble. Consider the position of old Mr Bundy, supposedly the paradigm of a person suffering from unequal bargaining power. In what respect was Mr Bundy's bargaining power deficient? As Lord Denning tells the story, Mr Bundy trusted the bank to look after his financial affairs, he relied on its advice, and in consequence he entered into a ruinous transaction for a grossly inadequate consideration. As all three judges characterise the situation, Mr Bundy was acting under the undue influence of the bank; on all fronts, he was vulnerable to persuasion. What is paradoxical about such accounts, however, is that the more it is emphasised that Mr Bundy charged his property to the bank in a setting of implicit trust and confidence, the less appropriate it seems to talk about relative 'bargaining' power—for settings of trust and confidence are ones in which, *ex hypothesi*, bargaining simply does not take place. *Bundy* notwithstanding, therefore, a focused doctrine of inequality of bargaining power must centre on situations where negotiation and bargaining is the order of the day. In such situations, it is suggested, we can conceive of each party dealing, so to speak, with its own bargaining hand, the strength or weakness of its hand determining its bargaining power. The answer to the first question, therefore, will be an inventory of the kinds of bargaining cards that can be carried into a contractual negotiation—in particular, cards concerning knowledge (or ignorance), need to deal, and negotiating skill[2].

1   Beale 'Inequality of Bargaining Power' (1986) 6 OJLS 123. And, see further, Beale, Harris, and Sharpe 'The Distribution of Cars: A Complex Contractual Technique' in Harris and Tallon (eds) *Contract Law Today* (1989) 301.

2   Cf Beale (1986) 6 OJLS 123 at 125; and Beale, Harris, and Sharpe 'The Distribution of Cars: A Complex Contractual Technique' in Harris and Tallon (eds) *Contract Law Today* (1989) 301 at 307–309. Such factors must then be placed in the context of a particular market. It might be, for instance, that one contracting party has a monopoly on the supply of particular goods or services. See para 3.7.

3.7 If factors of this kind constitute a party's bargaining power, then we can address the second question: how do we determine the strength or weakness of a particular contractor's bargaining position? Generally, the rhetoric of bargaining power involves the idea of *relative* bargaining strength, implying that the matter is to be judged entirely inter-personally. Following this approach, Smith can be in a strong position relative to Jones (who is in a weak position relative to Smith); Jones can be in a strong position relative to Hughes (who is in a weak position relative to Jones); and Smith, Jones, and Hughes might all be in a weak position relative to Davis[1]. The crucial consideration, in other words, is how one stands relative to one's fellow contractor, not how one stands relative to some third party or some other benchmark of bargaining power[2].

Proceeding in this way, we need to build up a statement of relative bargaining power one step at a time. Importantly, we must proceed one party at a time; it is not simply a matter of treating each party's strength or weakness as a correlative of the other party's strength or weakness. Just because a business contractor may be able to tell a consumer customer to take-it-or-leave-it, it does not follow that the former's (potential) bargaining strength translates into the latter's (actual) bargaining weakness. The latter might be perfectly happy to leave it or, at any rate, to take their trade elsewhere. Similarly, just because a particular consumer customer is desperately keen to buy, it does not entail that the customer's (potential) bargaining weakness translates into a seller's (actual) bargaining strength. For example, if the latter does not know about the former's eagerness to buy, he cannot take advantage of the buyer's vulnerability. To construct a picture of relative bargaining power, we need to build a profile of each party's bargaining position, first independently of one another, and then in conjunction with one another in a particular negotiating context.

Accordingly, let us suppose that Smith is a car dealer, whose business is quite seasonal: there are certain times of the year when demand for cars is high; but, equally, there are times when demand is rather flat; and inbetween times demand is steady. If Smith is negotiating to sell a car to Jones, we can say quite a lot about the strength of Smith's bargaining position without knowing anything at all about Jones's particular circumstances. For, we can say whether Smith is trading at one of the peaks or in one of the troughs of his annual business cycle, or whether it is a time of steady demand somewhere between the extremes; and, in this sense, we can characterise Smith's bargaining position as strong, middling, or weak *independent of Jones's position.* We might then analyse Jones's particular circumstances. Perhaps Jones sometimes buys cars when he needs them fairly urgently; at other times, he is under no pressure to buy so that he can, if he wishes, walk away from a deal; and sometimes he buys when there is some pressure to do so but without it being a matter of urgency. Again, relative to these considerations we can characterise Jones's bargaining position as strong, middling, or weak *independent of Smith's position.* Finally, it is only when we put together Smith's position (independently evaluated) with Jones's position (independently evaluated) that we can form a view about the relative bargaining strength of the parties.

Using the variables just mentioned, there are nine permutations, each producing its own distinctive bargaining situation. Assuming that Smith's bargaining register is comparable to that of Jones, then, in three of the situations, the parties are evenly matched, each party negotiating from the equivalent position on its own bargaining scale (whether it be strong, middling, or weak). In the remaining six situations, however, there is a disparity of bargaining power, in the sense that the parties are not dealing from equivalent positions. These six situations of inequality of bargaining power are as follows:

(i) Smith is trading at a peak (strong position); Jones needs to buy but without it being a matter of urgency (middle position);

(ii)   Smith is trading at a peak (strong position); Jones urgently needs to buy (weak position);

(iii)   Smith is trading at a time of steady demand (middle position); Jones is under no pressure to buy (strong position);

(iv)   Smith is trading at a time of steady demand (middle position); Jones urgently needs to buy (weak position);

(v)   Smith is trading in a trough (weak position); Jones is under no pressure to buy (strong position);

(vi)   Smith is trading in a trough (weak position); Jones needs to buy but without it being a matter of urgency (middle position).

In situations (i), (ii), and (iv), Smith has the superior bargaining position; conversely, in situations (iii), (v), and (vi), Jones has the superior bargaining positon. Other things being equal, the hardest bargains are likely to be driven in situations (ii) and (v), for it is here that the relative inequality is at its greatest. In situation (ii), Jones will have to pay a top-of-the market price for the car; and, if Smith is aware that Jones is in urgent need of the car, Smith may be able to extract a premium price from Jones. Conversely, in situation (v), Jones can adopt a take-it-or-leave-it attitude and, irrespective of whether Jones is aware of Smith's trading situation, Jones may succeed in snapping up the car at a bargain price.

If a doctrine of inequality of bargaining power is to apply to situations in which there is some distance between the parties' bargaining situations, then the greater the distance the more tempting it is to apply the doctrine. Accordingly, in relation to the above bargaining situations, the temptation is at its strongest in cases (ii) and (v). Nevertheless, two considerations might be thought to militate against treating such inequality as constituting sufficient reason to trigger relief from the contract struck in such situations. First, contractors routinely deal with bargaining cards of differing strengths. Unless there is something out of the ordinary about the situation, inequality of bargaining strength arguably does not warrant intervention[3]. Secondly, regardless of whether the situation is routine or exceptional, it might be argued that there is not sufficient reason for relief unless there is either some unconscionable conduct by the party in the dominant position[4] or a failure of free and informed consent on the part of the weaker contractor. We can deal with these reservations in turn.

In *Bundy*, Lord Denning said that the general rule is that '[n]o bargain will be upset which is the result of the ordinary interplay of forces'[5]. At common law, Lord Denning observed, there could be many a hard case—the homeless person who agrees to pay a high rent to a landlord, the hard-pressed debtor who borrows at a high rate of interest, and the like. Presented in this way, the doctrine of inequality of bargaining power is an exception to the general rule, dealing with those special cases 'when the parties have not met on equal terms—when the one is so strong in bargaining power and the other so weak—that, as a matter of common fairness, it is not right that the strong should be allowed to push the weak to the wall'[6]. The problem with such a formulation, however, is that a workable doctrine of inequality of bargaining power must be able to explicate the idea of a party being 'so strong' or 'so weak' in terms of bargaining power that a reasonably bright line can be drawn between the standard and the exceptional cases[7].

For the sake of illustration, we can reconsider hypothetical situation (ii), where Smith has a significantly superior bargaining position to Jones. What might take this inequality out of the normal? Consider, first, Smith's bargaining hand. In principle, we could strengthen Smith's position by assuming an even better set of bargaining cards. For example, Smith might be the sole distributor (in the town, region, country) for a particular make of vehicle; or he might be an especially skilled negotiator; and so on. Similarly, we could weaken Jones's position by assuming an even weaker set of bargaining cards. For example, given that Jones urgently needs to buy a car, we could further weaken his position by supposing that Jones must close the deal within the hour, that he must buy a particular model (which becomes a serious point of vulnerability if Smith is sole distributor of the model in question), and that the consequences of Jones failing to buy will be ruinous rather than merely inconvenient. If we combine these assumptions, while Smith is dealing from the position of a monopolist, Jones is dealing from circumstances of dire necessity (as in the most urgent kind of salvage or rescue case). From whichever side we view the transaction, therefore, we are likely to agree that this inequality of bargaining strength is exceptional.

Unfortunately, although we can imagine a bargaining situation where it is generally agreed that the case is now exceptional, the question is whether we can agree at which point precisely the line between the usual and the exceptional is crossed. Without being able to settle this question, the putative doctrine apparently suffers from serious indeterminacy.

Even if the line between usual and exceptional bargaining inequality can be drawn, and even if a particular bargaining situation clearly falls on the exceptional side of the line, there was, it will be recalled, a second reservation to be set against intervention. This reservation is to the effect that something more is required: that what is crucial is not so much the disparity between the bargaining power of the parties as that the stronger party takes unfair advantage of the weaker party or that the weaker party is in no position to give a proper consent to the transaction. This second reservation is another way of expressing our third general question: namely, whether the doctrine of inequality of bargaining power is to be viewed as a defendant-sided or as a plaintiff-sided principle.

1   Of course, once the parties begin the bargaining process, *if they are to contract*, they will need to work towards an equilibrium position in which, from both sides, the terms are judged to be acceptable.
2   For a contrast between weakness relative to one's fellow contractor, and weakness relative to some external minimum level of bargaining power, see Brownsword 'The Philosophy of Welfarism and its Emergence in the Modern English Law of Contract' in Brownsword, Howells and Wilhelmsson (eds) *Welfarism in Contract Law* (1994) 21.
3   Cf Thal 'The Inequality of Bargaining Power Doctrine: The Problem of Defining Contractual Unfairness' (1988) 8 OJLS 17. Thal, having said that exploitation only becomes a problem for the law where 'one party has an incredibly strong bargaining position in a particular market' (at 29) or when 'one party is in an incredibly weak bargaining position' (at 29), then differentiates between strength-based and weakness-based inequality. An inquiry into strength-based inequality focuses on the contestability of the particular market; an inquiry into weakness-based inequality requires an analysis of the individual transaction. Dealing with the latter, Thal says (at 30):
    [A] party can not call the inequality of bargaining power doctrine into aid merely because he or she is in an inferior bargaining position. For the doctrine to be relevant, it is essential that the inequality arise because of unusual weakness of bargaining power on one side of the transaction.
    Thal concludes by suggesting imperfect information (eg with regard to the value of the subject-matter of the transaction, or the nature of the obligation), an absence of bargaining alternatives, and trust as relevant forms of weakness.
4   For sustained insistence upon this reservation, see Cartwright *Unequal Bargaining* (1991).
5   [1975] QB 326, 336. See, too, *Alec Lobb (Garages) Ltd v Total Oil GB Ltd* [1985] 1 All ER 303, 313: 'Inequality of bargaining power must anyhow be a relative concept. It is seldom in any negotiation that the bargaining powers of the parties are absolutely equal' (per Dillon LJ).
6   [1975] QB 326 at 336–337.
7   Cf Thal, note 3. Without more, simply to rely on characterising a particular party's bargaining power as 'incredibly strong', or 'incredibly weak', invites the question: incredibly strong or weak, relative to what?

3.8 It is possible to ask of any relieving principle whether it is a defendant-sided or a plaintiff-sided doctrine. In principle, this is a question that we might ask, for example, of duress, undue influence, misrepresentation, mistake, and so on. Thus, in the seminal Australian case of *Commercial Bank of Australia v Amadio*[1], Deane J draws the following contrast:

The equitable principles relating to relief against unconscionable dealing and the principles relating to undue influence are closely related. The two doctrines are, however, distinct. Undue influence, like common law duress, looks to the quality of the consent or assent of the weaker party [plaintiff-sided] ... Unconscionable dealing looks to the conduct of the stronger party in attempting to enforce, or retain the benefit of, a dealing with a person under a special disability in circumstances where it is not consistent with equity or good conscience that he should do so [defendant-sided].[2]

So, too, we should clarify the basis of relief in relation to the doctrine of inequality of bargaining power. Is the basis for relief that the defendant (sic)[3] in the stronger bargaining position, has acted improperly, by taking unfair advantage of the plaintiff? Or, is the basis of the doctrine that the plaintiff's weakness of bargaining position is such as to vitiate consent?

In *Bundy*, it is not at all clear whether Lord Denning was thinking in plaintiff-sided or defendant-sided terms. The various authorities that he relied on to ground the master exception of inequality of bargaining power involve both types of analysis, some speaking of the need for free and voluntary agency (as in plaintiff-sided thinking), others talking in terms of the unconscientious use of power by the strong over the weak (as in defendant-sided thinking). Lord Denning's synthesising statement of the principle also suffers from the same ambivalence. As we have seen, he regarded it as unfair if 'the strong should be allowed to push the weak to the wall[4]'—which could be read as implying a defendant-sided analysis. However, against this, he denied any suggestion that 'the principle depends on proof of any wrongdoing', saying that '[t]he one who stipulates for an unfair advantage may be moved solely by his own self-interest, unconscious of the distress he is bringing to the other'[5]. If Lord Denning was not taking a defendant-sided approach, was he adopting a plaintiff-sided analysis? On the face of it, he was not, for he said that he had 'avoided any reference to the will of the one being "dominated" or "overcome" by the other'[6]. However, this is not conclusive: one could be concerned with the quality of the consent without conceiving of the issue in terms of dominated (undominated) or overborne (non-overborne) will. For instance, Lord Denning might have thought that if Mr Bundy was under unusual pressure to guarantee his son's overdraft, his assent to the guarantee and charge was unreliable even though there was no suggestion that his will had been overborne at the time.

Whatever Lord Denning's thinking in *Bundy*, a choice must be made between a plaintiff-sided or a defendant-sided basis for a doctrine of inequality of bargaining power. Whichever way we go, though, further difficulties lie ahead. If we opt for a plaintiff-sided analysis, we hold that the plaintiff is to be granted relief where the inequality of bargaining power is such as to undermine the conditions for free and informed consent—which takes us back to the problem that we have already encountered of how we define the conditions of voluntariness[7]. If we opt for a defendant-sided analysis, we hold that the plaintiff is to be granted relief where the defendant has knowingly taken unfair advantage of the plaintiff's situation. The difficulty with this is twofold: first, this doctrine involves an inquiry into the defendant's state of mind; and, secondly, relative to whose (or which) standards are we to draw the line between fair and unfair advantage-taking? Both difficulties are ones that we will find recurring in our discussion in later sections.

1   (1983) 151 CLR 447.
2   (1983) 151 CLR 447 at 474.
3   Cf para 1.59 note 1.
4   [1975] QB 326, 336–337.
5   [1975] QB 326 at 339. Lord Denning also pointed out that the bank manager 'acted in the utmost good faith and was straightforward and genuine' ([1975] QB 326 at 340). However, this was stated in relation to a holding based on the doctrine of undue influence. For further analysis of the relationship between *Bundy* and (defendant-sided) unconscionability, cf Waddams 'Unconscionability in Contracts' (1976) 39 MLR 369.
6   [1975] QB 326 at 339.
7   See para 2.18.

Rejection of a general doctrine of inequality of bargaining power

3.9 Despite Lord Denning's qualifying remarks, his judgment in *Bundy* encouraged contracting parties who agreed to terms under pressure, and who subsequently regretted such agreement, to plead the general exception of inequality of bargaining power. Any such encouragement was swiftly removed, however, first by the Privy Council in *Pao On v Lau Yiu Long*[1] and then by the decision of the House of Lords in *National Westminster Bank plc v Morgan*[2], in both of which cases it fell to Lord Scarman to hand down the key opinion.

1   [1980] AC 614.
2   [1985] AC 686.

3.10 *Pao On* was a case involving the renegotiation of a contract. Put shortly, the parties in *Pao On* entered into a principal contract under which the plaintiffs took as consideration shares in the defendants' company. It was agreed that, to avoid destabilising the price of shares in the defendants' company, the plaintiffs would retain 60% of their newly acquired shares for a year. To cover the risk of the value of the shares falling during the period that the contractual bar against sale applied, a subsidiary agreement was entered into. All that the plaintiffs needed was an indemnity to cover any fall in the value of the shares. However, the subsidiary agreement, while protecting the plaintiffs against a fall in value by requiring the defendants to buy back the shares at the indemnity price, allowed the latter to buy back at the same price (and, thus, at a profit) in the event of the shares *rising* in value. As soon as the plaintiffs realised this, they threatened that they would not perform the principal agreement unless the subsidiary agreement was cancelled and replaced with a simple indemnity. Fearing delays and a loss of public confidence in their public company, the defendants acceded to the plaintiffs' demands. In due course, the defendants refused to honour the indemnity and one of the arguments pleaded was to the effect that they should be relieved because of the plaintiffs' unfair use of a dominant bargaining position. However, the basis of this defence was rejected in no uncertain terms:

> Their Lordships' conclusion is that where businessmen are negotiating at arm's length it is unnecessary for the achievement of justice, and unhelpful in the development of the law, to invoke such a rule of public policy. It would also create unacceptable anomaly.[1]

Why, though, was the doctrine of inequality of bargaining power thought to be unnecessary, unhelpful and anomalous?

First, why was the doctrine judged to be unnecessary? According to Lord Scarman:

> It is unnecessary because justice requires that men, who have negotiated at arm's length, be held to their bargains unless it can be shown that their consent was vitiated by fraud, mistake or duress. If a promise is induced by coercion of a man's will, the doctrine of duress suffices to do justice.[2]

This, it will be appreciated, presupposes a plaintiff-sided analysis, with inequality of bargaining power being equated with duress, and with both being conceived of as raising questions about the voluntariness of the supposed consent. It follows, as Lord Scarman says, that a legal order that already has a doctrine of duress—and that goes as far as it thinks fairness requires with its doctrine of duress—does not need a doctrine of inequality of bargaining power.

Secondly, Lord Scarman said that the doctrine would be unhelpful 'because it would render the law uncertain.'[3] He continued: 'It would become a question of fact and degree to determine in each case whether there had been, short of duress, an unfair use of a strong bargaining position.'[4] Here, Lord Scarman apparently switches to a defendant-sided analysis. Viewed from this perspective, it might be thought that, if anything, Lord Scarman understates the potential uncertainty of such a doctrine. Questions of fact and degree typically characterise decisions that have to be made in a grey area lying between clear cases on either side. Whether or not a particular bargaining position in the grey area falls on one side of the line or the other must involve some uncertainty. However, there is also the question of whether the particular use of a strong bargaining position is unfair; and, unless standards of fair dealing are settled and calculable, this, too, is likely to involve some uncertainty.

Thirdly, in what sense would the adoption of a doctrine of inequality of bargaining power create an unacceptable anomaly? In the light of the foregoing, it might be thought anomalous that a legal system should contemplate having two relieving doctrines dealing with coercion or pressure, one (duress) going so far, and the other (inequality of bargaining power) going further. Of course, if one doctrine is defendant-sided and the other plaintiff-sided, we might be able to make some sense of these overlapping doctrines. Lord Scarman, however, does not have anomalies of this kind in mind. Rather, his point is that anomaly would flow from a doctrine of inequality of bargaining power if it were to render a contract void. Thus:

> It would be strange if conduct less than duress could render a contract void, whereas duress does no more than render a contract voidable.[5]

On the face of it, this would be anomalous: in circumstances of extreme pressure (duress) the contract is merely voidable, yet in circumstances of less pressure (inequality of bargaining power) it is void. However, this anomaly could be removed without rejecting the very idea of a doctrine of inequality of bargaining power—most straightforwardly, perhaps, by substituting voidability for voidness as the legal consequence of such inequality. The problem with this, though, is that the closer the doctrine moves into line with duress, the less reason there seems to be for having it.

1   [1980] AC 614, 634.
2   [1980] AC 614, 634.
3   [1980] AC 614, 634.
4   [1980] AC 614, 634.
5   [1980] AC 614, 634.

3.11 The situation in the second case, *National Westminster Bank plc v Morgan*[1], was much closer to that in *Bundy* itself. In *Morgan*, as in *Bundy*, a house was charged to a bank as security to refinance the existing building society mortgage on the property as well as to cover Mr Morgan's business liabilities to the bank. Without independent legal advice, Mrs Morgan (who owned the home jointly with her husband) signed the agreement with the bank. Subsequently, Mrs Morgan argued that the agreement had been obtained by undue influence[2]. Although counsel for Mrs Morgan did not rely on the *Bundy* doctrine of inequality of bargaining power, Lord Scarman took the opportunity to underline his earlier rejection of any such general exception:

> The doctrine of undue influence has been sufficiently developed not to need the support of a principle which by its formulation in the language of the law of contract is not appropriate to cover transactions of gift where there is no bargain ... And even in the field of contract I question whether there is any need in the modern law to erect a general principle of relief against inequality of bargaining power. Parliament has undertaken the task—and it is essentially a legislative task—of enacting such restrictions upon freedom of contract as are in its judgment necessary to relieve against the mischief: for example, the hire-purchase and consumer protection legislation of which the Supply of Goods (Implied Terms) Act 1973, Consumer Credit Act 1974, Consumer Safety Act 1978, Supply of Goods and Services Act 1982 and Insurance Companies Act 1982 are examples. I doubt whether the courts should assume the burden of formulating further restrictions.[3]

In the opening part of these remarks, Lord Scarman rightly observes that an exception for inequality of bargaining power only makes sense in contractual situations. In gift situations, the doctrine of undue influence does the work. But, then, less persuasively perhaps, Lord Scarman suggests that, in contractual situations, any problems arising from the mischief of bargaining inequality are best left to Parliament. To be sure, a stream of modern consumer protection legislation can be cited as an adequate response to the structural imbalance between business contractors and consumer contractors. However, it is arguable that such legislation fails to tackle two significant cases of bargaining inequality[4].

1   [1985] AC 686.
2   Although Lord Scarman's remarks on the doctrine of inequality of bargaining power remain authoritative, it should be noted that *Barclays Bank plc v O'Brien* [1994] 1AC 180 now sets the framework for dealings between creditor banks, debtor husbands, and wives who charge their property in order to secure finance for businesses run by their husbands.
3   [1985] AC 686, 708.
4   Other cases where inequality of bargaining power might be argued to have a role to play are cases of unequal bargaining skill and unequal information. In both cases, though, mere adoption of a doctrine of inequality of bargaining power would not assist with fundamental questions of principle: namely, in which circumstances the less skilful should be protected against the more skilful, and the better-informed should be required to share their knowledge with the less well-informed.

3.12 First, it can be argued that, if we have good reason to protect consumers in their dealings with business contractors, then we have equally good reason to protect small business contractors in their dealings with larger, more powerful, commercial contractors[1]. For example, where smaller businesses service the needs of a major manufacturer, the more powerful contractor will probably be in a position to dictate terms to all those parties (commercial and consumer alike) that trade in its economic network. Thus, as Stewart Macaulay remarked of the contractual relationships formed by automobile manufacturers in the United States:

> [I]n order for rationalized economic plans to work, parts suppliers, dealers and automobile buyers, must surrender important amounts of control of their own destinies and enter relationships of dependency on large and relatively impersonal organizations.[2]

So much for systemic inequality of bargaining strength where small business contractors are locked-in to, and reliant upon, the patronage of a major manufacturer; but business contractors might be vulnerable, too, on an occasional basis. After all, the notorious rule in *L'Estrange v Graucob Ltd*[3] originated in a case where an unskilled business contractor was caught out by the small print employed by a standard form dealer[4].

To some extent, small business contractors (like many other contractors) are already protected under UCTA: for, relative bargaining strength is a relevant consideration in assessing the validity of terms that are subject to the reasonableness test. Nevertheless, even allowing for occasional judicial attempts to expand the scope of UCTA[5], the legislative (and common law) protection of small businesses is limited[6]. If the vulnerability of small business contractors were thought to require a protective regime of the kind put in place for consumer contractors, how should this be achieved? Here, Lord Scarman is surely right in suggesting that treatment of the mischief would be best left to Parliament, for such a dedicated regulatory regime would have to start either by defining (inevitably, in a somewhat rough and ready fashion) what counts as a small business or by putting in place a bespoke regime for a particular commercial sector[7].

Secondly, Lord Scarman's remarks are directed at the problem of inequality of bargaining power at the time of formation of a contract. However, where there is a delay between the time of formation and the time for performance, the balance of bargaining power might alter. Sometimes, initial inequality of bargaining strength might even out; at other times, the initial inequality might be reversed, the stronger party at formation becoming the weaker party during the contract. As several cases from *Pao On* onwards have highlighted, pressure to renegotiate (typically, in relation to commercial contracts) can take place at the point of performance in a setting of extreme inequality of bargaining power[8]. Moreover, the party applying the pressure can, at worst, engineer the situation to demand renegotiation at precisely the time that the other party is most vulnerable[9]. Parliament has not addressed this mischief; but, of course, as Lord Scarman himself indicated in *Pao On*, this is where the doctrine of (economic) duress has its most important application.

The rejection of a general doctrine of inequality of bargaining power suggests two fundamental difficulties with the proposed principle. On the one hand, the doctrine makes sense only where the parties are bargaining with one another. In gift situations, or in contractual situations coloured by trust and confidence, *ex hypothesi*, the doctrine has no application. On the other hand, where the doctrine might have some application (because bargaining is taking place), not only does it suffer from conceptual uncertainty, its relationship with other relieving doctrines, particularly undue influence and economic duress, needs to be clarified[10].

1   Cf Furmston 'Unidroit General Principles for International Commercial Contracts' (1996) 10 JCL 11 at 12: 'It is indeed one of the common oversimplifications of debate on modern contract law to equate the need to protect the consumer with inequality of bargaining power'—this remark being in the context of Article 3.10 of the UNIDROIT Principles for International Commercial Contracts.

2   Macaulay, 'The Standardized Contracts of United States Automobile Manufacturers' in *International Encyclopedia of Comparative Law* Vol VII, 18, at p 32. See, too, Macaulay's comment at pp 30–31: 'Generally, the automobile manufacturer has great power and the market does not prevent him from writing a contract to serve his own interests whether the other party is a supplier, dealer or new car buyer.'

3   [1934] 2KB 394.

4   In fact, it is not unknown for large business to be caught out in the same way. For example, in the Office of Fair Trading's Report *Photocopier Selling Practices* (March 1994), it is reported that even the purchasing officers of some major companies were thought to have acted in an 'unbusinesslike' fashion at one time, allowing themselves to be taken in by the salesmen from the photocopier leasing companies.

5   See Adams and Brownsword *Key Issues in Contract* (1995) pp 269–281.

6   Cf Beale, Harris and Sharpe 'The Distribution of Cars: A Complex Contractual Technique' in Harris and Tallon (eds), *Contract Law Today* (1989) 301, 312–318.

7   For legislative attempts to protect the interests of car dealers in the United States, see Macaulay 'The Standardized Contracts of United States Automobile Manufacturers' in *International Encyclopedia of Comparative Law* Vol VII, 18.

8   See eg *B & S Contracts and Design Ltd v Victor Green Publications Ltd* [1984] ICR 419; *Atlas Express Ltd v Kafco (Importers and Distrubutors) Ltd* [1989] QB 833; and *Vantage Navigation Corpn v Suhail and Saud Bahwan Building Materials Inc, The Alev* [1989] 1 Lloyd's Rep 138.

9   See eg *D and C Builders v Rees Ltd v Rees* [1966] 2QB 617. In the US case law, nice examples are *Headley v Hackley* 45 Mich 569, 8NW 511 (1881)

(pressure to reduce contract sum as in *D and C Builders*); and *Alaska Packers Association v Domenico* 117F 99 (9th Cir 1902) (pressure to increase contract sum, as in the cases cited in note 8).

10 A similar point might be taken against other proposed general relieving principles, such as unconscionability or good faith, at least where they operate in a legal system that already has specific doctrines designed to address unfair dealing. See further chapter 5.

Correcting bargaining inequality: between collapse and reconstruction

3.13 A concern with relative bargaining strength is widely thought of as a modern qualification to the approach of the classical law of contract. Certainly, the modern approach recognises that contractors rarely negotiate from positions of equal bargaining strength. Having recognised this, however, the dilemma is to find a way of correcting bargaining inequality without adjusting practically every contract struck in the market[1]. Even if the law treats a doctrine of unequal bargaining power as an exception, it needs to prevent the exception swallowing up the general rule of enforcement of contracts. The dilemma, in other words, is to find a way of correcting bargaining inequality without precipitating a collapse of the institution of contract itself.

The response of English law has four main strands. First, to prevent collapse, it has rejected a general doctrine of unequal bargaining power. Secondly, to correct for the structural inequality in the mass market for consumer goods and services, it has black-listed those provisions which a well-advised consumer almost always would refuse to accept in an equal bargaining situation. Thirdly, to correct for occasional inequality it has grey-listed terms that a well-advised contractor (consumer or commercial) would normally prefer not to accept—although, here, the validity of the term does not hinge upon proof of equality of bargaining power so much as some semblance of negotiation. Fourthly, where there is pressure to renegotiate a contract (typically in commercial cases), situational monopoly is regulated by a doctrine of economic duress.

So long as such protective measures are seen as preserving free and informed consent as the foundation of contract, the thread of principle linking modern corrective intervention with the classical ideal of freedom of contract is maintained. In other words, so long as any doctrinal application of unequal bargaining power takes a plaintiff-sided approach, the modern law can be viewed as a restatement of classical principles. However, if concerns about relative bargaining strength express themselves either as principles militating against unconscionable advantage-taking by the stronger party (as in a defendant-sided analysis), or as concerns that bargained outcomes should be intrinsically fair or balanced, then the modern law is taking on a major reconstruction of the institution of contract[2].

1 Cf Collins *The Law of Contract* (3rd edn, 1997) ch 8.
2 In this light, *Crédit Lyonnais Bank Nederland NV v Burch* [1997] 1 All ER 144 is a striking example of the Court of Appeal emphasising that the jurisdiction to relieve against unconscionable transactions is 'in good heart and capable of adaptation to different transactions entered into in changing circumstances' (per Nourse LJ at 151). However, the circumstances in *Burch* were exceptional; relief was available under the doctrine of undue influence; and the court's remarks about having the transaction set aside directly as an unconscionable bargain were obiter.

CHAPTER 4

Reasonableness

Reasonableness: four steps from the classical to the modern law

4.1 If the classical law has come to be associated with the values of freedom of contract[1], the modern law has become a byword for reasonableness in contract. For, wherever one looks in the modern law of contract, the notion of reasonableness seems to be at the core of its doctrinal operations. Yet, how might the law evolve from an intention-based model (such as the classical law of contract) to a paradigm in which reasonableness is a pervasive concern? We can sketch such an evolutionary process by identifying four key steps.

1   See chapter 2.

4.2 In its purest form, an intention-based model of contract has no need for the concept of reasonableness. The parties' intentions (interpreted in accordance with a subjective 'meeting of minds' or will theory)[1] govern whether there is a contract; and, if there is, how the particular contract is to be interpreted and enforced. The only test of the fairness of the deal is whether it was freely made. The cornerstones of the law, free agreement and sovereign intention, serve to exclude (or, some might say, answer) questions about the reasonableness of the deal or its enforcement. Subject to one caveat—namely, that it operates with an objective rather than a subjective test of intention— this is the model of the classical law. However, the caveat is significant, for whichever version of the objective test the law adopts, it involves building the concept of reasonableness into its interpretative standpoint. For example, if we ask on the facts of *Carlill v Carbolic Smoke Ball Co*[2] whether the company's advertisement in the *Pall Mall Gazette* was intended seriously as a contractual offer (rather than as mere promotional publicity), an objective test will focus on how the company would reasonably expect readers of the *Gazette* to understand the advertisement[3], or how readers of the *Gazette* would reasonably understand the company's intentions[4], or how some third party would reasonably understand the advertisement[5]. Accordingly, even if we start with the classical law, there are already seeds of reasonableness in what is otherwise a model dedicated to giving effect to the parties' intentions.

The first step away from the classical law comes with the employment of the idea of reasonableness in cases where there is scope for argument about how the parties intended their agreement to be read. Such argument might arise where the express terms of the contract are vague or ambiguous in some respect; or where the implication of a term is contested, or where the contract is silent on some matter, and so on. In its classical articulation, the law will avoid having recourse to the concept of reasonableness in order to handle these difficulties. Rather, it will treat uncertainty as a reason for non-enforcement; it will treat silence as an indication that the contract is to be performed according to its (express) terms; and it will insist that terms are to be implied only where strictly necessary (in the sense that the parties must have intended their implication).

The second step occurs when reasonableness is employed as more than a supplementary principle to cover those cases where the parties' intentions under-determine the question. Here, albeit covertly, reasonableness is employed to override even tolerably clear expressions of contractual intention. Where the law is at this stage of its evolution, reasonableness is not openly used to challenge the intentions of the contractors; instead, considerations of reasonableness are wrapped up in the classical language of what the parties must have intended[6]. There is, however, a limit to the corrective power of reasonableness at this second stage. If the parties' intentions are expressed in wholly unequivocal language, the contract must be so interpreted and enforced.

The third step removes the limit on reasonableness that is accepted at the second step. Accordingly, even if the terms of the contract are pellucid, they will be enforced only insofar as they are judged to be reasonable. However, as at the second stage, employment of reasonableness is not yet officially declared. Unofficially, by the third stage, it will be an open secret, if not something of a scandal, that the basis of contract law has changed.

The fourth step simply makes explicit and open the position taken at the third step. Respect for the parties' intentions, however plainly expressed, is not the overriding principle of contract law. In principle, the progression from intention to reasonableness can take place on a narrow or a broad front. At its broadest, when the fourth step has been comprehensively taken, all contract doctrines are subject to the overriding proviso of reasonableness. Whether we are looking at questions concerning formation, interpretation, discharge, or remedies, contract law must be guided by the canon of reasonableness[7].

1   Cf Dalton 'An Essay in the Deconstruction of Contract Doctrine' (1985) 94
    Yale LJ 997, 1042:
      'A standard history of contract doctrine represents that, from the sixteenth
      to the early nineteenth century, contract formation depended upon a
      subjective "meeting of the minds." Despite the accordance of this subjective
      theory with the nineteenth-century "will theory" of contract, by the middle
      of the nineteenth century "the tide had turned in favour of an objective
      theory of contract" [here, quoting Farnsworth "'Meaning' in the Law of
      Contracts" (1967) 76 Yale LJ 939, 945].'
2   [1893] 1QB 256.
3   Such a focus might be invited by the company's (alleged) deposit of £1,000
    with the Alliance Bank, 'shewing our sincerity in the matter' (as the
    advertisment put it); cf Lindley LJ, [1893] 1QB 256 at 261–262.
4   Cf Bowen LJ, [1893] 1QB 256 at 266: 'It seems to me that in order to arrive
    at a right conclusion we must read this advertisement in its plain meaning, as
    the public would understand it. It was intended to be issued to the public and
    to be read by the public. How would an ordinary person reading this document
    construe it?'
5   Cf [1893] 1 QB 256, at 273, where A L Smith LJ says that he at least cannot
    read the advertisment as a 'mere expression of confidence' in the product.
    However, the particular version of the objective test presupposed in this
    judgment is not entirely clear.
6   Cf Atiyah 'Judicial Techniques and the English Law of Contract' (1968) 2
    Ottawa LR 337, 339:
      Even the merest tyro will soon learn ... that it is not much use arguing against
      a particular construction of a written contract on the ground that it would
      produce unjust or inconvenient results for his client; but he will equally soon
      learn that it is perfectly permissible to present the same argument in the
      form that 'the parties could not have intended' the contract to bear the
      meaning argued against because of the results which would follow.
7   In principle, even the core terms concerning price and the like would be subject
    to a reasonableness test. The story of modern English law, however, is one of
    limited adoption of a reasonableness regime. See further para 4.3 note 9.

4.3 Although the move from step three to step four involves an important issue of general adjudicative principle[1], it is the move from step one to step three (via step two) that marks the sea-change in contract law. At step one, the use of reasonableness occurs only interstitially, in the gaps left by the parties' intentions. At step three, however, the parties' intentions no longer limit recourse to reasonableness; on the contrary, it is reasonableness that limits the parties' intentions. At step one, freedom of contract rules; at step three, freedom of contract rules only so far as freedom is exercised reasonably. The significance of this transition from first step to third step thinking is nicely illustrated in *Gillespie Bros v Roy Bowles Transport Ltd*[2], a case turning on the interpretation of an indemnity clause in a commercial contract. Adopting first step language, Buckley LJ outlined his approach to the interpretation of contracts thus:

> It is not in my view the function of a court of construction to fashion a contract in such a way as to produce a result which the court considers that it would have been fair or reasonable for the parties to have intended. The court must attempt to discover what they did in fact intend. In choosing between two or more equally available interpretations of the language used it is of course right that the court should consider which will be likely to produce the more reasonable result, for the parties are more likely to have intended this than a less reasonable result.[3]

According to Lord Denning MR, however, some judges have seen their function in more active (second step) terms, hiding behind the traditional language of construction and intention to displace the ordinary reading of contractual provisions in favour of reasonable terms. Thus:

> What is the justification for the courts ... departing from the ordinary meaning of the words? If you examine all the cases, you will ... find that at bottom it is because the clause ... is unreasonable, or is being applied unreasonably in the circumstances of the particular case. The judges have, then, time after time, sanctioned a departure from the ordinary meaning. They have done it under the guise of 'construing' the clause. They assume that the party cannot have intended anything so unreasonable. So they construe the clause 'strictly'. They cut down the ordinary meaning of the words and reduce them to reasonable proportions. They use all their skill and art to this end.[4]

On this view, there is a running battle between the draftsmen and the courts, the former trying to write their contracts in such a way that they are so clear as to be 'judgeproof'. This invites the question: what happens when the skill and art of the judges can no longer find a toehold for 'construing' unreasonable provisions? What are the courts to do when they run out of 'tortuous constructions'[5]? In *Gillespie*, Lord Denning MR had no hesitation in saying that this is where the law moves on to steps three and four: when control under the guise of construction is no longer feasible, the courts must rely directly on the principle of reasonableness to ensure that freedom of contract is not abused[6]. The general principle, reflecting the pre-eminence of reasonableness, can be expressed as follows:

> When a clause is reasonable, and is reasonably applied, it should be given effect according to its terms. ... It should be given its ordinary meaning, that is, the meaning which the parties understood by the clause and must be presumed to have intended. The court should

Mandeep Laun Many

GET THE OFFICIAL DVSA LEARNING MATERIALS

ONLINE

USE CODE LD20
FOR **20% OFF**

www.**dvsalearningzone**.co.uk

OTHER FORMATS

USE CODE LD20
FOR **20% OFF**

www.**safedrivingforlife**.info

MOBILE

ONLY OFFICIAL THEORY TEST KIT APP

The OFFICIAL
DVSA THEORY
TEST KIT

FOLLOW US ON

INS 51T   DVSA 001   An executive agency of the Department for Transport

Discount offer excludes ebooks and smartphone apps.
The marketing of products published by TSO is funded by TSO, tso.co.uk The Stationery Office Limited is registered in England No. 3049649 at 55 Wells Street, London, W1A 3AE

MIX
Paper from
responsible sources
FSC® C002151

Driver & Vehicle
Standards
Agency

WANT TO PASS YOUR THEORY TEST FIRST TIME?

LEARN FROM THE PEOPLE WHO SET THE TESTS

give effect to the clause according to that meaning—provided always ... that it is reasonable as between the parties and is applied reasonably in the circumstances of the particular case.[7]

Three years on from *Gillespie*, the Unfair Contract Terms Act 1977, while not providing for a general (overarching) reasonableness proviso[8], certainly endorsed the open application of reasonableness criteria in relation to a variety of contractual terms thereby confirming at least a limited movement in English law from step three to step four[9].

As we have said, the most important step in the transition from intention to reasonableness comes when reasonableness limits rather than merely supplements intention. We must look more carefully at reasonableness in these two roles, first as a supplementary principle and then as a limiting principle.

1   See section I for the argument that rational law requires there to be a congruence between doctrine as declared and doctrine as actually administered.
2   [1973] QB 400.
3   [1973] QB 400 at 421.
4   [1973] QB 400 at 415. Cf Simon Brown LJ in *Lancashire County Council v Municipal Mutual Insurance Ltd* [1996] 3 All ER 545, 552: 'The principles governing the construction of commercial contracts are not in doubt: the more unreasonable the result of a given construction, the readier should the court be to adopt some less obvious construction of the words.'
5   Cf *Robophone Facilities Ltd v Blank* [1966] 3 All ER 128, 142:
      The court has no general jurisdiction to reform terms of a contract because it thinks them unduly onerous on one of the parties—otherwise we should not be so hard put to find tortuous constructions for exemption clauses, which are penalty clauses in reverse; we could simply refuse to enforce them (per Diplock LJ).
6   In so saying, Lord Denning relied on his remarks in an earlier indemnity case, *John Lee and Son (Grantham) Ltd v Railway Executive* [1949] 2 All ER 581, 584.
7   [1973] QB 400, 416.
8   Importantly, neither the Unfair Contract Terms Act 1977 nor the Unfair Terms in Consumer Contracts Regulations 1994, SI 1994/3159 expose the central core of a contract (the agreed price) to review on the grounds of (un)reasonableness.
9   Cf eg *Levison v Patent Steam Carpet Cleaning Co Ltd* [1978] QB 69, 79 (where Lord Denning MR treated a maximum value limitation clause and an 'owner's risk' clause in a cleaning contract as void for unreasonableness); and *Multiservice Bookbinding Ltd v Marden* [1978] 2 All ER 489, 502, where Browne-Wilkinson J (as he then was) declined to review the reasonableness of an index-linked money obligation in a mortgage agreement:
      [I]n order to be freed from the necessity to comply with all the terms of the mortgage, the plaintiffs must show that the bargain, or some of its terms, was unfair and unconscionable; it is not enough to show that, in the eyes of the court, it was unreasonable.
      In my judgment a bargain cannot be unfair and unconscionable unless one of the parties to it has imposed the objectionable terms in a morally reprehensible manner, that is to say, in a way which affects his conscience.

Reasonableness as a supplementary principle

4.4 If reasonableness is to operate as a supplementary principle, the assumption is that the law falls back on this standard in cases where the express terms of the contract (in conjunction with any settled implied terms) fail to offer clear guidance as to the parties' intentions. This presupposes a two-stage procedure: first, the contract is construed, in accordance with recognised interpretative conventions, with a view to ascertaining the parties' intentions; then, if, and only if, this first-stage procedure fails to determine the parties' intentions does the court embark on a second-stage inquiry with reasonableness as the criterion for whatever decision is to be made. This picture of reasonableness as a supplementary principle might be thought to gloss over two questions. One question concerns the extent to which ideas of reasonableness are already built into the first-stage 'recognised interpretative conventions'; and, the other question concerns the reference point for reasonableness at the second-stage—in other words, whose idea of reasonableness is it that is applied? We can consider each of these questions in turn.

4.5 First, where the meaning of an express term of a contract is contested, what conventions of interpretation apply? Certainly, so far as the reading of exemption clauses is concerned, the most important general rule is the so-called contra proferentem principle. This common law principle dictates that any lack of clarity in the drafting of the terms should be read against the party who seeks to rely on the exemption. What this means is that the contract is construed strictly, the court doing nothing to assist the party in whose favour the terms have been drafted[1]. This general approach has a number of specific applications, one of the most important of which arises where a defendant purports to rely on a contractual provision to shield itself against the consequences of its own negligence. Typically, this will involve reliance on a contractual provision which the defendant presents either as an exemption from liability for negligence or as an indemnity shifting the risk of negligence to a fellow contracting party. In cases of this kind, a recognised set of interpretative conventions applies. One of the leading statements of these conventions is in *Canada Steamship Lines Ltd v R*[2], a case in which the Crown, having leased a freight shed in Montreal to the company, sought to avoid the consequences of the negligence of its servants by relying on both an exemption and an indemnity clause in the contract. The Privy Council, in an opinion given by Lord Morton, set out three basic rules for the construction of such provisions[3]. First, if the clause expressly states that it covers negligence, then effect must be given to such unequivocal language. Secondly, if the clause does not expressly refer to negligence, then the question is whether the language is wide enough to cover negligence. If a doubt arises at this point, it must be resolved against the party seeking to rely on the clause. Thirdly, if the clause does not expressly refer to negligence, but the language is wide enough to cover negligence, then the question is whether the provision can be given an intelligible meaning without applying to negligence. In short, is there a head of liability other than negligence to which the clause might apply? If so, the clause will be read as applying to that other head of liability rather than to negligence[4].

What should we make of these rules of interpretation? Quite clearly, as a set, the three rules reflect a bias against exemption or indemnity clauses being construed as covering negligence. Unless the clause explicitly and unmistakably refers to negligence, the rules militate against it being so read. Under the proviso to the second rule, where there is a doubt about whether the language is broad enough to cover negligence, the doubt will be resolved against the clause being wide enough; and, under the third rule, even though the language of the clause is acknowledged to be wide enough to cover negligence, the conventions require the courts to hunt around for an alternative reading. These are not neutral rules; they are rules that, in some sense[5], reflect an underlying concern about the unreasonableness of exemptions and indemnities against negligence[6]. As Lord Morton put it in the *Canada Steamship* case, the Crown's interpretation of the indemnity provision 'imposes a very remarkable and burdensome obligation on the company[7].'

Further evidence of the bias built into the *Canada Steamship* rules can be seen in *Smith v South Wales Switchgear Ltd*[8]. There, South Wales Switchgear were employed to carry out an overhaul at the factory of UMB Chrysler (Scotland) Ltd. During the overhaul, Smith, an electrical fitter employed by Switchgear, was seriously injured. Smith having recovered substantial damages from the factory owners (for their negligence and breach of statutory duty in failing to take reasonable care for the safety of people working at the site), Chrysler sought to claim from Switchgear under an indemnity clause in the contract. According to this clause, Switchgear undertook to keep Chrysler indemnified against, inter alia:

> Any liability, loss, claim or proceedings whatsoever under statute or common law (i) in respect of personal injury to, or death of, any person whomsoever, (ii) in respect of any injury or damage whatsoever to any property, real or personal, arising out of or in the course of or caused by the execution of this order.

Notwithstanding this broad drafting, the House held that the clause did not provide an indemnity against the consequences of Chrysler's own negligence. In so holding, the House relied on the *Canada Steamship* rules, taking a hard look (particularly in Lord Keith's case) at the closing qualifying words in the provision, and generally being disinclined to accept the interpretation of the clause presented by Chrysler. This disinclination shaped Lord Fraser's response at each stage of the argument.

First, it was argued on behalf of Chrysler that the words '[a]ny liability, loss, claim or proceedings whatsoever' amounted to an express reference to liability for negligence. Lord Fraser disagreed:

> I do not see how a clause can 'expressly' exempt or indemnify the proferens against his negligence unless it contains the word 'negligence' or some synonym for it. ... The word 'whatsoever' ... is no more than a word of emphasis and it cannot be read as equivalent to an express reference to negligence.[9]

This took Lord Fraser on to the second of the *Canada Steamship* rules. His Lordship conceded that, if the clause was read in isolation, it was wide enough to cover negligence. However, the clause, he said, had to be read in context. Viewed in context, the question was not so much whether the clause covered negligence but *whose* negligence it might cover. Whilst it would be perfectly natural for Chrysler to take an indemnity from Switchgear to cover claims arising from the negligence of Switchgear's employees, it was quite another matter for the indemnity to cover claims arising from Chrysler's own negligence. This, Lord Fraser ruled, raised more than a doubt about the scope of the clause; it led to 'a positive conclusion adverse to [Chrysler][10].' Strictly speaking, it was unnecessary for Lord Fraser to resort to the third of the *Canada Steamship* rules. However, his Lordship indicated that, if he had applied the third rule, he would have found other heads of liability to which the clause might apply (including liability arising from the negligence of Switchgear's own employees)[11].

In the light of *Smith v South Wales Switchgear Ltd*, it is tempting to conclude that rules of construction, such as the *Canada Steamship* rules, reflect an underlying general judgment of reasonableness in their formulation; and that, in their application, the rules reflect further, more specific, judgments of reasonableness based on the features of the particular case[12].

Still dealing with first-stage matters, evidence of the parties' intentions can be gleaned not only from the express language of the contract but also from any implied terms that can be unproblematically attributed to the parties. For example, where statutory provision is made for implied terms subject to express contrary intention, and the parties have signalled no such contrary intention, then the implied terms in question can be taken to represent the intention of the contractors. Similarly, where the common law provides for standard implied terms in certain types of contract, subject to express contrary intention, and the parties have not indicated otherwise, such terms can be taken to represent the parties' intentions[13]. Beyond these categories, so-called terms implied in fact may also be read in unproblematically where it is clear that the parties so intended— indeed, the well-known 'officious bystander' test[14] is formulated precisely to ensure that the implication is in line with what the parties must have intended. As with the rules of construction, though, considerations of reasonableness might already have shaped these background implications. For example, the statutory implied terms and the common law category terms might be understood as resting on judgments of what is reasonable in contracts of common occurrence. As Lord Cross put it in *Liverpool City Council v Irwin*[15]:

> When it implies a term in a contract the court is sometimes laying down a general rule that in all contracts of a certain type—sale of goods, master and servant, landlord and tenant and so on—some provision is to be implied unless the parties have expressly excluded it. In deciding whether or not to lay down such a prima facie rule the court will naturally ask itself whether in the general run of such cases the term in question would be one which it would be reasonable to insert.

Even in the case of terms implied in fact, where a bitter doctrinal battle has been waged between the advocates of intention and the advocates of reasonableness[16], we can soon find orthodox intention-based tests smuggling in judgments of reasonableness.

Consider, for example, the 'business efficacy' approach to implied terms taken in *The Moorcock*[17], a case widely regarded as evincing an intention-based jurisprudence. The primacy of intention is plain in most of Bowen LJ's seminal judgment:

> In business transactions such as this, what the law desires to effect by the implication is to give such business efficacy to the transaction as must have been intended at all events by both parties who are business men ...[18]

Bowen LJ also emphasised that implication must respect the principle of freedom of contract:

> This is a business transaction as to which at any moment the parties may make any bargain they please, and either side may by the contract throw upon the other the burden of the unseen and existing danger.[19]

Thus, on the facts of *The Moorcock*, it would have been open to the wharfingers to have expressly stipulated that the risk of grounding at the wharf lay entirely with the shipowners, even though it was the wharfingers who were in the better position to assess such a risk. In the absence of express agreement as to this risk, Bowen LJ continued (and here we have the one fleeting reference to reasonableness in his judgment):

> The question is what inference is to be drawn where the parties are dealing with each other on the assumption that the negotiations are to have some fruit, and where they say nothing about the burden of this kind of unseen peril, leaving the law to raise such inferences as are reasonable from the very nature of the transaction.[20]

By contrast, Lord Esher MR, posing the same question in the same case, asked:

> What, then, is the reasonable implication in such a contract? In my opinion honest business could not be carried on between such a person as the respondent and such people as the appellants, unless the latter had impliedly undertaken some duty towards the respondent with regard to the bottom of the river at this place.[21]

Fusing these dicta, the line between reasonableness and intention can soon become blurred, the test of business efficacy (or, equally, the test of the officious bystander) being earthed in the intentions of honest or reasonable contractors, or implication being carried out on the basis of what is reasonable given the nature of the transaction. So, for example, in *Mosvolds Rederi A/S v Food Corpn of India*[22], Steyn J (as he then was) linked the officious bystander test to the views of 'reasonable men versed in the shipping business, and faced in the real commercial world[23]' with the question of whether a term could be implied into a charterparty to avoid vessels having to make a fruitless deviation of some 80 to 100 miles in order to give notice of readiness at the particular point outside Calcutta provided for in the contract. Relative to such a test, Steyn J upheld the term implied by the arbitrator as one 'so obvious that reasonable men, circumstanced as the parties were, would without doubt have assented to'[24]. Significantly, however, Steyn J distinguished this approach from the reasonable implication test rejected in *Liverpool City Council v Irwin*[25]—in other words, from a test based purely on reasonableness in which intention has dropped away. The distinction between reasonableness related to the parties' situation and reasonableness in a free-standing sense leads on to the second question about the nature of reasonableness as a supplementary principle.

1   See eg *Wallis, Son and Wells v Pratt and Haynes* [1911] AC 394 (exclusion of liability for breach of warranty does not cover liability for breach of condition); *Andrews Bros (Bournemouth) Ltd v Singer* [1934] 1KB 17 (exclusion of liability for breach of implied terms does not cover liability for breach of express terms).

And, cf Unfair Terms in Consumer Contracts Regulations 1994, SI 1994/ 3159, reg 6 under which a seller or supplier's written terms are to be expressed in plain, intelligible language, failing which 'the interpretation most favourable to the consumer shall prevail'.

2 [1952] AC 192.

3 [1952] AC 192 at 208.

4 Cf *Rutter v Palmer* [1922] 2KB 87; *Alderslade v Hendon Laundry Ltd* [1945] KB 189; and the treatment of dicta in those two cases in *Hollier v Rambler Motors (AMC) Ltd* [1972] 1 All ER 399.

5 See para 4.6 below.

6 In principle, and in practice, some judges might consider commercial indemnities, even shifting the risk of one's own negligence, perfectly reasonable. See eg Lord Denning's favourable assessment of the indemnity clause in *Gillespie Bros v Roy Bowles Transport Ltd* [1973] QB 400; and *Thompson v T Lohan (Plant Hire)* [1987] 2 All ER 631.

7 [1952] AC 192, 211. In relation to the exemption clause relied on by the Crown, Lord Morton (at 210) speculated that the company probably would not have accepted such a term if the purport of the exclusion had been fully spelt out.

8 [1978] 1 WLR 165.

9 [1978] 1 WLR 165 at p 173. Cf the majority interpretation of the word 'condition' in the visiting clause in *L Schuler AG v Wickman Machine Tool Sales Ltd* [1974] AC 235.

10 [1978] 1 WLR 165 at 174.

11 See, too, Viscount Dilhorne, [1978] 1 WLR 165 at 169. Generally, cf *EE Caledonia Ltd v Orbit Valve plc* [1995] 1 All ER 174, where the Court of Appeal applied the reasoning of *Canada Steamship* and *Smith v South Wales Switchgear* to hold that the parties had contracted on the basis of a reciprocal indemnity clause, but with each party assuming the risk of its own negligence. The indemnity clause did not explicitly refer to negligence. However, Steyn LJ (as he then was) suggested (at 185) that this reading conformed with the reasonable expectations of the parties.

12 This does not amount to saying, however, that all attempts to avoid liability for negligence will fail. Far from it. Even under the *Canada Steamship* rules, it must be emphasised that the courts accept that liability for negligence is excluded, limited, or transferred where the contract expressly so provides (see eg the actual decision in *Gillespie Bros v Roy Bowles Transport Ltd* [1973] QB 400). Moreover, in construction cases, as in cases of carriage of goods by sea, several of the leading decisions allowing third parties (lack of privity notwithstanding) to rely on protective head contract terms have the effect of excluding or restricting the third party's liability for negligence (see eg *Norwich City Council v Harvey* [1989] 1 All ER 1180 and *New Zealand Shipping Co Ltd v AM Satterthwaite and Co Ltd, The Eurymedon* [1975] AC 154).

13 See eg *Hancock v Brazier* [1966] 1 WLR 1317.

14 See *Shirlaw v Southern Foundries (1926) Ltd* [1939] 2KB 206, 227.

15 [1977] AC 239, 257. See, too, Lord Denning MR's judgment in *Shell UK Ltd v Lostock Garage Ltd* [1977] 1 All ER 481; and cf Rakoff 'The Implied Terms of Contracts: Of "Default Rules" and "Situation-Sense"' in Beatson and Friedmann (eds) *Good Faith and Fault in Contract Law* (1995) 191.

16 See eg *Trollope and Colls Ltd v North West Metropolitan Regional Hospital Board* [1973] 2 All ER 260—culminating in the exchange between Lord Denning MR (for reasonableness) and Lord Wilberforce (for intention) in *Liverpool City Council v Irwin* [1977] AC 239; but, then, cf *Scally v Southern Health and Social Services Board* [1992] 1AC 294.

17 (1889) 14PD 64.

18 (1889) 14PD 64 at 68.
19 (1889) 14PD 64 at 70.
20 (1889) 14PD 64 at 70.
21 (1889) 14PD 64 at 67.
22 [1986] 2 Lloyd's Rep 68.
23 [1986] 2 Lloyd's Rep 68 at 71.
24 [1986] 2 Lloyd's Rep 68. But, for reservations about the practicability of the
    reasonable business standards approach to implied terms, see Lord Hoffmann
    'Anthropomorphic Justice: The Reasonable Man and his Friends' (1995) 29
    The Law Teacher 127, 139: 'The notion that either the Greek shipowner or
    the Indian charterer would have said "of course" to the implication of any
    term against their own interests ... puts an intolerable strain on the judicial
    imagination.'
25 [1977] AC 239.

4.6 If reasonableness operates as a supplementary principle, what is
the reference point for this standard? To paraphrase Lord Wilberforce's
sceptical remarks in *L Schuler AG v Wickman Machine Tool Sales Ltd*[1],
who is the ubiquitous reasonable man? And, if the reasonable man is
a business man, does he adopt the standards of English or German
business people? In principle, there are two ways in which such a
supplementary standard might be regarded.

One approach, reflected in Buckley LJ's remarks in *Gillespie*[2], as
well as in Steyn J's reasoning in *Mosvolds Rederi A/S v Food Corporation
of India*, has the following three features: (i) that the court should
proceed on the basis that the contracting parties are reasonable people;
(ii) that reasonable contractors are more likely to have intended that
disputes concerning their agreement should have reasonable rather
than unreasonable results; and (iii) that the standards of reasonableness
applied by the court are to be the standards of reasonableness accepted
by the contractors themselves.

The other approach is that, the intentions of the contractors having
run out, judicial standards of reasonableness should take over as the
basis for decision. So, for example, where the doctrine of frustration
is based on what the parties, as fair and reasonable contractors, would
have agreed upon had they made express provision for the contingency,
the law is getting very close to operating with a free-standing doctrine
of reasonableness. Indeed, as Lord Radcliffe remarked in *Davis
Contractors Ltd v Fareham UDC*[3], once frustration is so understood,
there is some considerable distance between contract doctrine and the
parties' intentions, such that:

> By this time it might seem that the parties themselves have become so
> far disembodied spirits that their actual persons should be allowed to
> rest in peace. In their place there rises the figure of the fair and
> reasonable man. And the spokesman of the fair and reasonable man,
> who represents after all no more than the anthropomorphic
> conception of justice, is and must be the court itself.[4]

In other words, this latter view presupposes a clean break between the understanding of the contracting parties (once their intentions are exhausted) and the fall-back principle of reasonableness.

Although neither approach places reasonableness in competition with explicit contractual intention, the difference between reasonableness relative to the contracting parties' own lights (as in the former approach) and reasonableness relative to the judges' own lights (as in the latter approach) is of capital importance. Of course, all parties (contractors and judges) might share the same standards of reasonableness; but, in principle, the latter approach privileges judicial standards where they conflict with the standards recognised by the contracting parties. As we turn to consider the function of reasonableness as a limiting principle, the significance of the distinction between the two approaches to reasonableness needs to be emphasised. Quite simply, where a court is guided by the express language of the agreement (as evidence of the parties' intentions) in conjunction with the contracting parties' own standards of reasonableness, this can be understood as a concerted attempt to give effect to the parties' reasonable expectations. In other words, where the court follows such an approach, there is no tension between intention and reasonableness—in both its aspects, the inquiry is dedicated to keeping faith with the parties' own understanding of their obligations. However, where judges rely on their own standards of reasonableness, the parties are no longer in control of their rights and obligations. Accordingly, when we conceive of reasonableness as a limiting, rather than merely as a supplementary, principle, it must be this second approach that is presupposed.

1   [1974] AC 235, 263; see para 1.7.
2   See para 4.3.
3   [1956] AC 696.
4   [1956] AC 696 at 728. Cf Lord Hoffmann 'Anthropomorphic Justice: The Reasonable Man and his Friends' (1995) 29 The Law Teacher 127, 128.

Reasonableness as a limiting principle

4.7 Reasonableness seems to be everywhere in the modern law of contract. The rules of formation are in various ways qualified by the principle of reasonableness—for example, if terms are to be incorporated by notice, the notice given must be reasonable[1]; the classical posting rules will hold good only so long as they do not produce unreasonable results[2]; reliance in and around the formation of a contract will be protected where it is reasonable[3]; the objective test presupposes some standpoint involving reasonableness, and so on.

Where a term is grey-listed under the Unfair Contract Terms Act 1977, it will be valid only if, as s11(1) provides, it was 'a fair and reasonable one to be included having regard to the circumstances which were, or ought reasonably to have been, known to or in the contemplation of the parties when the contract was made'. Similarly, covenants in restraint of trade are enforceable only insofar as they satisfy the *Nordenfelt* tests of reasonableness[4]. Under the doctrine of promissory estoppel, binding adjustments to contracts may not require detrimental reliance by the promisee, but they certainly require reasonable reliance[5]. A party pleading economic duress must show that there was no reasonable alternative other than to accede to the demands made, and steps of avoidance must be taken within a reasonable time[6]. As we have seen, recourse to reasonable men abounds in disputes involving implied terms and frustration. Even (some might say, especially) in relation to the exercise of remedies, the innocent party's rights are qualified by considerations of reasonableness—for example, reasonable steps in mitigation are required, and under Sale and Supply of Goods Act 1994, s4 a commercial buyer's right to withdraw for breach of a statutory implied term is lost if 'the breach is so slight that it would be unreasonable ... to reject'.

1   Originally, *Parker v South Eastern Rly Co* (1877) 2 CPD 416, as refined in *Thornton v Shoe Lane Parking Ltd* [1971] 2QB 163, and *Interfoto Picture Library Ltd v Stiletto Visual Programmes Ltd* [1989] QB 433. See, too, *AEG (UK) Ltd v Logic Resource Ltd* [1996] CLC 265; and Bradgate 'Unreasonable Standard Terms' (1997) 60 MLR 582.
2   See eg *Holwell Securities Ltd v Hughes* [1974] 1 All ER 161.
3   See eg *Errington v Errington and Woods* [1952] 1KB 290; *Blackpool and Fylde Aero Club Ltd v Blackpool Borough Council* [1990] 3 All ER 25; and the use of collateral contracts to protect reasonable reliance on pre-contractual representations. Generally, on the protection of pre-contractual reliance, see Adams and Brownsword *Key Issues in Contract* (1995) 115–121.
4   See *Nordenfelt v Maxim Nordenfelt* [1894] AC 535.
5   Seminally, see *Central London Property Trust Ltd v High Trees House Ltd* [1947] KB 130.
6   See *North Ocean Shipping Co Ltd v Hyundai Construction Co Ltd, The Atlantic Baron* [1979] QB 705.

4.8   The strength of the modern preoccupation with reasonableness can be gauged by considering the much-debated case of *Ruxley Electronics and Construction Ltd v Forsyth*[1]. In that case, the company were in breach of contract by building a swimming pool to a depth that did not conform to the agreed specification. Mr Forsyth was entitled to damages. However, the question was whether he should be awarded the cost of cure (some £21,560) or the diminution of value (nothing in this case, because the shortfall in the depth of the pool did not decrease its value) or some other measure. Controversially, the Court of Appeal awarded the cost of cure, only for the House of Lords to restore the trial judge's award of £2,500 (ostensibly for loss of amenity). One of the remarkable features of the case, however, is that whether we look at the opinions that prevailed in the Court of Appeal or at those that prevailed in the House of Lords, the reasonableness (or unreasonableness) of Mr Forsyth pocketing cost of cure damages is a dominant consideration. In defence of a cost of cure award, Staughton LJ said:

> In my judgment the key lies in the proposition ... that reasonableness is a matter of mitigation. It is unreasonable of a plaintiff to claim an expensive remedy if there is some cheaper alternative which would make good his loss. Thus he cannot claim the cost of reinstatement if the difference in value would make good his loss by enabling him to purchase the building or chattel that he requires elsewhere. But if there is no alternative course which will provide what he requires, or none which will cost less, he is entitled to the cost of repair or reinstatement even if that is very expensive.[2]

Since there was no alternative way by which Mr Forsyth could make good his loss, the majority view in the Court of Appeal was that it was not unreasonable for the cost of cure to be awarded. Dillon LJ (dissenting), however, took a rather different view:

> It is of course true that reasonableness lies at the heart of the doctrine of mitigation of damages. But that is not, in my judgment, the only impact of the concept of reasonableness on the law of damages.[3]

According to Dillon LJ, if there had been a significant difference in value, albeit less than the cost of cure, 'the obvious course would have been to award Mr Forsyth the loss of value[4]'. Dillon LJ continued:

> The basis of that would have been reasonableness. He has no absolute right to be awarded the cost of reinstatement. I see no reason, therefore, why if there has been no loss in value, he should automatically become entitled to the cost of reinstatement, however, high. That would be a wholly unreasonable conclusion in law.[5]

The House of Lords shared Dillon LJ's view. As Lord Lloyd read the authorities, they showed:

> the court emphasising the central importance of reasonableness in selecting the appropriate measure of damages. If reinstatement is not the reasonable way of dealing with the situation, then diminution in value, if any, is the true measure of the plaintiff's loss ...
> [Thus] Dillon LJ was right when he held, that mitigation is not the only area in which the concept of reasonableness has an impact on the law of damages.
> If the court takes the view that it would be unreasonable for the plaintiff to insist on reinstatement, as where, for example, the expense of the

work involved would be out of all proportion to the benefit to be obtained, then the plaintiff will be confined to the difference in value.[6]

So, the cost of reinstatement award was wholly unreasonable. The award of difference of value might have been reasonable in some cases; but, in this case, the trial judge clearly felt that this under-compensated Mr Forsyth. There was a suggestion in the House of Lords that the trial judge's award of £2,500 was generous, Mr Forsyth being 'lucky to have obtained so large an award for his disappointed expectations'[7]. However, there was no real dispute about the quantum of the trial judge's award before the House and, even if it had been an issue, the House would probably have allowed it to stand as not wholly unreasonable.

1   [1994] 3 All ER 801, CA; revsd [1995] 3 All ER 268, HL.
2   [1994] 3 All ER 801, 810.
3   [1994] 3 All ER 801 at 813.
4   [1994] 3 All ER 801 at 813.
5   [1994] 3 All ER 801 at 813–814.
6   [1995] 3 All ER 268, 284–285.
7   [1995] 3 All ER 268 at 289.

4.9   Reasonableness, it seems, is here, there, and everywhere. As we have seen, however, we need to discriminate between situations where reasonableness is employed in order to give effect to the parties' expectations (where reasonableness is judged relative to the parties' own lights) and those cases where a judicial reasonableness discretion takes over. To what extent does the modern obsession with reasonableness reflect an attempt to keep faith with the parties' expectations rather than the courts legislating their own standards of reasonableness?

If we start with cases such as *Ruxley Electronics* and *Schuler v Wickman*[1], we might find that more than one interpretation is plausible. It might be argued that the courts' inquiries into reasonableness were simply a way of speculating whether (in *Ruxley Electronics*) the parties contracted on the footing that cost of cure damages would be awarded even if hugely expensive, or whether (in *Schuler v Wickman*) they assumed that Schuler would be entitled to terminate for a single breach of the visiting obligation. Equally, though, we might read such inquiries as evincing the courts' concern to set out their own idea of a reasonable remedial regime irrespective of the parties' own standards and expectations. To put this another way, we can detect in both *Ruxley Electronics* and *Schuler v Wickman* the idea that the innocent party's remedies should not be disproportionate to the breach (or unreasonably expensive for the contract breaker). However, this concern with maintaining some degree of proportionality between breach and remedy could be read as the courts second-guessing the parties' understanding of their rights and obligations, or as the courts imposing their own canons of reasonableness on the parties.

Are there not, though, some clear cases, where there is little room for argument about the role that reasonableness is playing? No doubt, there are such cases. For example, the reasonable notice requirement for the incorporation of terms seems to be designed to ensure that contractual provisions are not enforced unless they reflect the parties' own understanding. Similarly, where Unfair Contract Terms Act 1977, s3(2)(b)(i) grey-lists a term under which a party claims to be entitled 'to render a contractual performance substantially different from that which was reasonably expected of him', the intention seems to be to enforce the contract as it would have been understood by the party who 'deals as consumer or on the other's written standard terms of business'[2]. Again, where the test for an implied term is of the kind proposed by Steyn J in *Mosvolds Rederi A/S v Food Corpn of India*[3], the perspective from which the criterion of reasonableness is applied to the dispute is that of the contracting parties themselves[4]. By contrast, however, where the courts declare that, say, a covenant in restraint of trade is unenforceable (because unreasonable) or where legislation decrees that particular kinds of exclusion clauses are void or that, notwithstanding express provision in the contract, a buyer is not allowed to reject goods where the breach is trivial, is this not a clear case of the law imposing its own standards of reasonableness on the parties? To the extent that it is such an imposition, and to the extent that it cannot be justified as protecting the interests of third parties, or as indirectly supporting the autonomy of the contractors[5], the legitimacy of the law is brought into question. In the case of *legislative* imposition, there is perhaps a short answer: the legislation reflects a collective community judgment that certain transactional practices should not be supported because they are thought to be unreasonable. In the case of judicial imposition, however, the task is more challenging. Unless judges are philosopher kings, why should their judgments of reasonableness be superior to the judgments of the contracting parties?

As we move on to our next topic, good faith, where we will review the arguments for and against the adoption of a general principle of good faith in contracts, we will see more clearly a fundamental question that we can detect already in the present reflections on reasonableness. Namely, if the law is to employ concepts such as reasonableness, fair dealing, good faith, and the like, and if judicial notions of reasonableness have no special warrant, how are these ideas to be grounded[6]?

1   See para 1.23.
2   Unfair Contract Terms Act, 1977, s 3.
3   [1986] 2 Lloyd's Rep 68.
4   Cf Article 1.108 of the Lando Commission's Principles of European Contract Law, according to which 'reasonableness is to be judged by what persons acting in good faith and in the same situation as the parties would consider to be reasonable. In particular, in assessing what is reasonable the nature and purpose of the contract, the circumstances of the case, and the usages and practices of the trades or professions involved should be taken into account': see Lando and Beale (eds) *The Principles of European Contract Law: Part I* (1995). The annotations make it clear that the intention is to tie the idea of reasonableness (which is employed pervasively in the Principles) to the context in which the parties contracted, see Lando and Beale at pp 62–63. Similarly, see Nassar *Sanctity of Contract Revisited* (1995) passim but eg 239–240.
5   Cf para 2.14, for analysis of the real import of the Sch 2 guidelines on the reasonableness test in the Unfair Contract Terms Act 1977.
6   See, too, note 4 for the way in which the Lando Commission includes the idea of good faith within its concept of reasonableness.

CHAPTER 5

Good Faith

A general principle of good faith

5.1 Article 1.106 of the Lando Commission's Principles of European Contract Law, provides in the following terms for a general principle of good faith and fair dealing:

(i) In exercising his rights and performing his duties each party must act in accordance with good faith and fair dealing.

(ii) The parties may not exclude or limit this duty[1].

In so providing, the Commission reflects the doctrinal position of many European legal systems. For example, section 242 of the German BGB (Civil Code) provides that contracts must be performed in the manner required by good faith and fair dealing, taking into consideration the general practice in commerce; art 1134 of the French Civil Code likewise provides that contracts must be performed in good faith; and the Italian Civil Code refers to good faith and fair dealing in negotiation (art 1337), interpretation (art 1366), and performance (art 1375)[2]. Good faith in the performance and enforcement of contracts is a recognised principle, too, in many other legal systems around the world, including major common law systems such as that of the United States[3].

---

1 See Lando and Beale (eds) *The Principles of European Contract Law: Part I* (1995). The Commission takes 'good faith' to mean 'honesty and fairness in mind, which are subjective concepts', and 'fair dealing' to mean 'observance of fairness in fact which is an objective test' (*The Principles of European Contract Law: Part I* at p 55). As an illustration of fair dealing, the Commission cites the case of a one-year distributorship contract, renewed each year for over 40 years, and then terminated by one party by giving one month's notice as stipulated by the contract. Given the length of the relationship between the

parties, such short notice (even though in accordance with the contract) violates the principle of fair dealing (see *The Principles of European Contract Law: Part I* at p54).

See, too, art 1.7 of the UNIDROIT General Principles for International Commercial Contracts, according to which both parties should 'act in accordance with good faith and fair dealing in international trade'. See further chapter 7 below.

2   See Lando and Beale, *The Principles of European Contract Law: Part I*, for an extremely helpful survey, pp 56–58.

3   See Uniform Commercial Code s 1–203 and *Restatement (Second) of Contracts* (1981) s 205.

5.2 Whilst English contract lawyers have long been familiar with the concept of (subjective) good faith in the sense of honesty in fact or a clear conscience—an idea to be found, for instance, in the context of negotiable instruments and the sale of property—until quite recently, the idea of a general doctrine of good faith, in the sense of an overriding (and objective) requirement of fair dealing, was not part of the lexicon of English contract law. Or, at any rate, it was not part of the lexicon in the twentieth century[1]. With the exception of Raphael Powell's inaugural lecture in 1956[2], good faith in contract was not a topic addressed by academics or textbook writers; nor was a violation of the principle of good faith a matter openly pleaded or addressed in litigation, although references to bad faith occasionally appeared explicitly or implicitly in judicial opinions[3]. Of course, in a handful of special contexts, most notably that of insurance contracts, the governing principle was that of uberrima fides—but these special contexts were by definition the exception rather than the rule[4].

Starting with the judgment of Sir Thomas Bingham in *Interfoto Picture Library Ltd v Stiletto Visual Programmes Ltd*[5], however, the picture has changed quite dramatically. In the *Interfoto* case, Sir Thomas (in a much-quoted passage) said:

> In many civil law systems, and perhaps in most legal systems outside the common law world, the law of obligations recognises and enforces an overriding principle that in making and carrying out contracts parties should act in good faith. This does not simply mean that they should not deceive each other ... ; its effect is perhaps most aptly conveyed by such metaphorical colloquialisms as 'playing fair,' 'coming clean' or 'putting one's cards face upwards on the table.' It is in essence a principle of fair and open dealing ...
>
> English law has, characteristically, committed itself to no such overriding principle but has developed piecemeal solutions in response to demonstrated problems of unfairness.[6]

With further impetus from the EC Directives on Commercial Agents[7] and (especially) on Unfair Terms in Consumer Contracts[8], and with a considerable body of writing on the topic[9], the concept of good faith is no longer an unfamiliar idea. Nevertheless, it would be wrong to assume that English lawyers now agree that the adoption of a general doctrine of good faith would be sensible. To the contrary, there is considerable resistance to any such idea; and, as we will see, even those who are apparently neutral will (at best) see no point in adopting the doctrine.

1 Cf Harrison, *Good Faith in Sales* (1997). Harrison contends that in the case law of the eighteenth and earlier nineteenth centuries, good faith was identified with 'a reasonably consistent set of fair dealing principles' (p 4); but that there was a reaction against good faith 'roughly from the 1870's onwards' (p 7).

2 Powell 'Good Faith in Contracts' (1956) 9 CLP 16. On which, see Brownsword '"Good Faith in Contracts" Revisited' (1996) 49 CLP 111.

3 An interesting case in point is the decision of the Court of Appeal in *Bournemouth and Boscombe Athletic Football Club v Manchester United Football Club* (1980) Times, 22 May. For analysis, see Adams and Brownsword *Key Issues in Contract* (1995) 208–211. Cf the Right Hon Lord Justice Staughton, 'Good Faith and Fairness in Commercial Contract Law' (1994) 7 JCL 193.

4 It is also widely accepted that, in relation to insurance contracts, whatever Lord Mansfield's original intentions in *Carter v Boehm* (1766) 3 Burr 1905, the principle of uberrima fides has come to operate in a one-sided fashion in favour of the insurer. See, Law Commission, *Insurance Law: Non-Disclosure and Breach of Warranty* (Law Com No 104) (1980). For a clear illustration of the way in which the law tolerates blatant departures from fair dealing by insurers, see *Sprung v Royal Insurance (UK) Ltd* [1997] CLC 70.

5 [1989] QB 433; see, too, the judgment of Steyn J (as he then was) in *Banque Financière de la Cité SA v Westgate Insurance Co Ltd* [1987] 2 All ER 923; on appeal, see [1989] 2 All ER 952, CA; affd [1990] 2 All ER 947, HL.

6 [1989] QB 433, 439.

7 Directive 86/653/EEC, implemented by the Commercial Agents (Council Directive) Regulations 1993, SI 1993/3053, Regulations 3(1) and 4(1) lay down reciprocal duties on principal and agent to 'act dutifully and in good faith' in relation to one another's interests.

8 Directive 93/13/EEC, implemented by the Unfair Terms in Consumer Contracts Regulations 1994, SI 1994/3159. Article 3(1) of the Directive, implemented by reg 4(1), provides that a term is unfair if 'contrary to the requirement of good faith, it causes a significant imbalance in the parties' rights and obligations arising under the contract, to the detriment of the consumer'. For analysis of art 3, see Brownsword, Howells and Wilhelmsson 'Between Market and Welfare: Some Reflections on Article 3 of the EC Directive on Unfair Terms in Consumer Contracts' in Willett (ed) *Aspects of Fairness in Contract* (1996) 25; and for analysis of the Regulations, see Brownsword and Howells 'The Implementation of the EC Directive on Unfair Terms in Consumer Contracts—Some Unresolved Questions' (1995) JBL 243.

9 For initial indications of an emerging interest in good faith, see O'Connor *Good Faith in English Law* (1991) Ch 3; The Hon Johan Steyn 'The Role of Good Faith and Fair Dealing in Contract Law: A Hair-Shirt Philosophy?' [1991] Denning LJ 131; and Goode, 'The Concept of 'Good Faith' in English Law' (Centro di Studi e Richerche di Diritto Comparato e Straniero, Saggi, Conferenze e Seminari 2, Rome 1992). For clear confirmation of this interest, see eg the several papers arising from the Fourth Annual Conference of the *Journal of Contract Law* on 'Good Faith and Fairness in Commercial Contract Law' (1993), published in (1994) 7 JCL and (1995) 8 JCL; Collins, *The Law*

of Contract 3rd edn (1997) passim; Beatson and Friedmann (eds) *Good Faith and Fault in Contract Law* (1995); Adams and Brownsword *Key Issues in Contract* (1995), esp Ch 7; Harrison, *Good Faith in Sales* (1997); and Brownsword, Hird and Howells (eds) *Good Faith in Contract: Concept and Context* (1999).

The sceptical view

5.3   The arguments against adopting a general principle of good faith are well-rehearsed. At least five negative themes are recurrent[1].

1   Cf eg Brownsword 'Positive, Negative, Neutral: the Reception of Good Faith in English Contract Law' in Brownsword, Hird and Howells (eds) *Good Faith in Contract: Concept and Context* (1999) 13, where the five themes in the text are considered. In Harrison *Good Faith in Sales* (1997) 685–687, four objections are considered: (i) that good faith is a European invention, now glossed with EU bureaucratic thinking; (ii) that regulation of fair dealing is for Parliament rather than the courts; (iii) that good faith would involve the death of contract as we know it; and (iv) that good faith would make it difficult for commercial people to know where they stand.

5.4   First, it is objected that a doctrine of good faith, by requiring the parties to take into account the legitimate interests or expectations of one another, cuts against the essentially individualist ethic of English contract law[1]. As Lord Ackner asserted in *Walford v Miles*[2], the adoption of a requirement of good faith would be incompatible with the adversarial ethic underpinning English contract law. Thus:

> [T]he concept of a duty to carry on negotiations in good faith is inherently repugnant to the adversarial position of the parties when involved in negotiations. Each party to the negotiations is entitled to pursue his (or her) own interest, so long as he avoids making misrepresentations ... A duty to negotiate in good faith is as unworkable in practice as it is inherently inconsistent with the position of a negotiating party.[3]

If contract is narrowly concerned with self-interested dealing, then a doctrine of good faith—particularly if it regulates the negotiation of contracts—is a hostage to fortune, encouraging judicial conscience to ameliorate the outcomes of hard-headed commercial dealing[4].

1   Cf para 1.22.
2   [1992] 2 AC 128.
3   [1992] 2 AC 128 at 138. For similar assertion of the adversarial view, see eg, Slade LJ in *Banque Financière de la Cité SA v Westgate Insurance Co Ltd* [1989] 2 All ER 952, 1013; and May LJ in *Bank of Nova Scotia v Hellenic Mutual War Risks Association (Bermuda) Ltd, The Good Luck* [1989] 3 All ER 628, 667.
4   Similar reservations have been expressed in both Australian and Canadian courts. See *Austotel Property Ltd v Franklins Selfservice Pty Ltd* (1989) 16 NSWLR

582, 585 (Kirby P); and the dissenting opinion of Wallace JA in *Re Empress Towers Ltd and Bank of Nova Scotia* (1991) 73 DLR (4th) 400, 409–410.

5.5 Secondly, echoing a point commonly encountered in sceptical North American commentaries, it is said that good faith is a loose cannon in commercial contracts[1]. Whilst everyone agrees that a doctrine of good faith represents some set of restrictions on the pursuit of self-interest, the objection is that it is not clear how far these restrictions go. In other words, good faith presupposes a set of moral standards against which contractors are to be judged, but it is not clear whose (or which) morality this is. Without a clear moral reference point, there is endless uncertainty about a number of critical questions—for example, about whether good faith requires only a clear conscience (subjective good faith) or whether it imports a standard of fair dealing independent of personal conscience (objective good faith)[2]; whether good faith applies to all phases of contracting, including pre-contractual conduct; whether good faith regulates only conduct (namely, how the parties conduct themselves during the formation of the contract and, subsequently, how they purport to rely on the contractual terms for performance, termination, and enforcement) or also the content (substance) of contracts (in other words, whether good faith regulates matters of procedure and process or also matters of contractual substance)[3]; whether a requirement of good faith adds anything to the regulation of bad faith (that is, whether good faith simply comprises so many instances of bad faith)[4]; whether good faith imposes both negative and positive requirements (covering, say, non-exploitation, non-opportunism, non-shirking as well as positive co-operation, support, and assistance); and so on.

1 See e g Bridge 'Does Anglo-Canadian Contract Law Need a Doctrine of Good Faith?' (1984) 9 Canadian JBL 385; Gillette 'Limitations on the Obligation of Good Faith' (1981) Duke LJ 619; Snyderman 'What's So Good About Good Faith? The Good Faith Performance Obligation in Commercial Lending' (1988) 55 UChiLR 1335.

2 Seminally, cf Farnsworth 'Good Faith Performance and Commercial Reasonableness Under the Uniform Commercial Code' (1962–3) 30 UChiLR 666; and for reflections on the distinction between a subjective and an objective standard of good faith, see 'The Concept of Good Faith in American Law' (Centro di Studi e Richerche di Dritto Comparato e Straniere, Saggi, Conferenze eSeminari 3, Rome, April 1993).

3 Cf eg South African Law Commission, *Unreasonable Stipulations in Contracts and the Rectification of Contracts* (Working Paper 54, Project 47, 1994), in which the concept of good faith is viewed as a doctrinal resource regulating unfair contract terms (although, subsequently, in Discussion Paper 65 (1996) the Commission substituted the standard of unconscionability for that of good faith). See Hutchison 'Good Faith in the South African Law of Contract' in Brownsword, Hird and Howells (eds) *Good Faith in Contract: Concept and Context* (1999) 213.

4   As argued by Summers '"Good Faith" in General Contract Law and the Sales Provisions of the Uniform Commercial Code' (1968) 54 VirLR 195.

5.6   Closely related to the second concern (which, essentially, is about an undesirable lack of calculability), there is a third concern, namely that a doctrine of good faith would call for difficult inquiries into contractors' states of mind. Often the literature on good faith emphasises that the question of whether a contractor has acted in good faith hinges on the contractor's reasons for action[1]. This is not to be confused with matters of subjective honesty, but it does involve speculating about a contractor's reasons. For example, in a case such as *Walford v Miles* (and, similarly, the more recent *Regalian Properties* case[2]), how might a court decide whether a party has broken off negotiations because it suits their economic interests to do so or because they simply could not close the bargaining distance between themselves and the other party? Motives are sometimes mixed, such that unravelling a party's real reasons would involve a whole host of problems[3].

1   See e g Burton 'Breach of Contract and the Common Law Duty to Perform in Good Faith' (1980–81) 94 Harv LR 369.
2   *Regalian Properties plc v London Dockland Development Corpn* [1995] 1 All ER 1005; but cf *Sabemo Property Ltd v North Sydney Municipal Council* [1977] 2 NSWLR 880.
3   Cf Waddams 'Good Faith, Unconscionability and Reasonable Expectations' (1995) 9 JCL 55, esp at 63–64. In addition to raising a query about the workability of a good faith-driven inquiry into motives, Waddams sees a potential perversity in such an approach. Thus, Waddams suggests that a party seeking to terminate for late payment 'would presumably be advised to think very hard, while writing the crucial letter [of termination], about the evils of unpunctuality, and to think not at all about the balance sheet disclosing the unprofitable nature of the contract' (at 63).

5.7   Fourthly, if good faith regulates matters of substance in a broad sense (including the remedial regime) (which it seems to do once we view it as a kind of implied term for co-operation)[1], then this impinges on the autonomy of the contracting parties. Accordingly, even if the sceptics allow (if only for the sake of argument) that good faith may legitimately regulate the process of contracting, to ensure that agreement is genuine, they will argue that, once good faith trespasses on substance, it restricts the autonomy of the parties and it is inconsistent with the fundamental philosophy of freedom of contract, with the idea that contract law should set a calculable framework for self-regulation by the parties[2]. If we combine the thought that good faith imports an uncertain discretion with the thought that good faith challenges the autonomy of contracting parties, we have powerful reasons to be sceptical about the wisdom of adopting such a doctrine.

Thus, in the recent Privy Council decision in *Union Eagle Ltd v Golden Achievement Ltd*[3], we see these ideas combining to resist the 'beguiling heresy' that the court has an unfettered discretion to relieve against the express terms of a contract where enforcement would be 'unconscionable' (for present purposes, instead of 'unconscionable', read 'contrary to good faith')[4]. In the *Union Eagle* case, the contract was for the purchase of a flat on Hong Kong Island. In accordance with the contract, the purchaser paid a 10% deposit to the vendor's solicitors as stakeholders, and completion was to take place on or before 5.00 pm on 30 September 1991. Clause 12 of the contract provided that, if the purchaser failed to comply with any of the terms of the agreement, then the deposit was to be forfeited and the vendor had the option of rescinding the agreement. The purchaser was ten minutes late in completing on the due date, whereupon the vendor declared that the deposit was forfeited and the contract rescinded. A number of points were taken by the purchaser but the main question was whether the court should invoke its equitable jurisdiction to relieve against this allegedly unconscionable outcome. Lord Hoffmann, speaking for the court, explained why the strict terms of the contract should be adhered to:

> The principle that equity will restrain the enforcement of legal rights when it would be unconscionable to insist upon them has an attractive breadth. But the reasons why the courts have rejected such generalisations are founded not merely upon authority ... but also upon practical considerations of business. These are, in summary, that in many forms of transaction it is of great importance that if something happens for which the contract has made express provision, the parties should know with certainty that the terms of the contract will be enforced. The existence of an undefined discretion to refuse to enforce the contract on the ground that this would be 'unconscionable' is sufficient to create uncertainty. Even if it is most unlikely that a discretion to grant relief will be exercised, its mere existence enables litigation to be employed as a negotiating tactic. The realities of commercial life are that this may cause injustice which cannot be fully compensated by the ultimate decision in the case.[5]

Having expressed these general considerations, Lord Hoffmann then qualified his remarks by conceding that 'the same need for certainty is not present in all transactions and the difficult cases have involved attempts to define the jurisdiction in a way which will enable justice to be done in appropriate cases without destabilising normal commercial relationships'[6]. On this basis, an exception is made to grant relief against forfeiture in the event of late payment under a mortgage agreement, the reasoning being that the right of forfeiture is effectively a security for payment. However, the vendor's right to rescind, where time of completion is expressed to be of the essence, is a different matter.

> [The purpose of the right to rescind] is, upon breach of an essential term, to restore to the vendor his freedom to deal with his land as he pleases. In a rising market, such a right may be valuable but volatile. Their Lordships think that in such circumstances a vendor should be able to know with reasonable certainty whether he may resell the land or not.[7]

On the particular facts of *Union Eagle*, there were no complicating features, such as the purchaser incurring an excessive penalty for a trivial breach, or of the vendor being unjustly enriched, or of the vendor having misled the purchaser[8]. The simple fact was that the purchaser was late in completing; to build an argument on the basis that the purchaser was only 'slightly late' would be to encourage litigation about 'how late is too late[9]'; and, as the plight of the vendor in the present case illustrated all too clearly, litigation can sterilise the property leaving the owner uncertain for a period of years whether or not he is entitled to resell. Accordingly, the Privy Council determined that, in cases of this kind, far from indulging the purchaser's trivial breach, it was appropriate to restate quite firmly that equity would not intervene.

1   Seminally, see Farnsworth 'Good Faith Performance and Commercial Reasonableness Under the Uniform Commercial Code' (1962–3) 30 UniChicLR 666; and see, too, Burrows 'Contractual Co-operation and the Implied Term' (1968) 31 MLR 390.
2   Generally, see chapter 2.
3   [1997] 2 All ER 215.
4   For support for the 'beguiling heresy', see *Shiloh Spinners Ltd v Harding* [1973] AC 691, 726 (Lord Simon); for its rejection, see *Scandinavian Trading Tanker Co AB v Flota Petrolera Ecuatoriana, The Scaptrade* [1983] 2AC 694, 700. For reflections on the tendency to reject, see Atiyah, *Essays on Contract* (1988) 370–372.
5   [1997] 2 All ER 215, 218–219.
6   [1997] 2 All ER 215 at 219.
7   [1997] 2 All ER 215 at 220.
8   Complications of this kind troubled the Australian courts in *Legione v Hateley* (1983) 152 CLR 406 and *Stern v McArthur* (1988) 165 CLR 489. It appears that the purchasers in Union Eagle were not asking for repayment of the deposit. Possibly, this was for tactical reasons; or, query, was it because local law did not empower the courts to order repayment (cf Law of Property Act 1925, s49(2))?
9   [1997] 2 All ER 215, 222.

5.8   The final thread in the sceptical negative view is that a general doctrine of good faith goes wrong in failing to recognise that contracting contexts are not all alike. If contract law is to be sensitive to context, it cannot be right to apply a doctrine of good faith irrespective of context. As Michael Bridge has said:

It is a fair reproach to English contract law that it unthinkingly treats the rules and principles of commodity sales, time and voyage charterparties and so on as though they could be applied without modification in very different contractual settings. Good faith theorists should avoid making the same sort of mistake. In my view, what is needed is an informed treatment of different areas of commercial contract and market activity.[1]

Bridge goes on to argue that it would be wholly inappropriate to introduce a doctrine of good faith into the commodities markets, where dealing is intrinsically competitive and where opportunistic behaviour is to be expected. This is not to say that, even in the commodities markets, good faith is totally rejected. However, insofar as notions of good faith are accepted, they are taken up in the standard terms of the trade and this, Bridge argues, is the way that the market best deals with new questions of fair dealing.

1   Bridge 'Good Faith in Commercial Contracts' in Brownsword, Hird and Howells (eds) *Good Faith in Contract: Concept and Context* (1999) 139, 147.

5.9 To sum up, the case against the adoption of a general principle of good faith is that English contract law is premised on adversarial self-interested dealing (rather than other-regarding good faith dealing); that good faith is a vague idea, threatening to import an uncertain discretion into English law; that the implementation of a good faith doctrine would call for difficult inquiries into contracting parties' reasons in particular cases; that good faith represents a challenge to the autonomy of contracting parties; and, that a general doctrine cannot be appropriate when contracting contexts vary so much—in particular, harking back to the first objection, a general doctrine of good faith would make little sense in those contracting contexts in which the participants regulate their dealings in a way that openly tolerates opportunism.

Neutrality and scepticism

5.10 In the *Interfoto* case, Sir Thomas Bingham, having noted that many legal systems employ a doctrine of good faith to regulate fair dealing in contract, observed that English law has arrived at much the same position by developing 'piecemeal solutions in response to demonstrated problems of unfairness'[1]. Such remarks might be read as encouraging a pragmatic neutrality towards good faith[2]. According to this view, whilst there is nothing intrinsically objectionable about a good faith doctrine, English law has its own doctrinal tools for achieving the results that are achieved via a good faith doctrine in other jurisdictions[3]. Moreover, Sir Thomas's relatively sanguine assessment seems to be vindicated by both the approach and the outcome of *Interfoto* where, in the context of a commercial contract, the English doctrine of 'reasonable notice' was manipulated to disallow a standard term that had not been adequately disclosed—English piecemeal solutions, in other words, are no less effective than single principle good faith solutions.

1   [1989] QB 433 at 439.
2   Cf Brownsword 'Two Concepts of Good Faith' (1994) 7 JCL 197.
3   The English doctrine of frustration is a standard example in this context. Cf Ebka and Steinhauer 'The Doctrine of Good Faith in German Contract Law', in Beatson and Friedmann (eds) *Good Faith and Fault in Contract Law* (1995) 171, and Lorenz 'Contract Modification as a Result of Change of Circumstances' Beatson and Friedmann, 357. For evidence of convergent solutions, arrived at by a variety of doctrinal routes, see Whittaker and Zimmermann 'Good Faith in European Contract Law' paper presented at SPTL Conference, University of Warwick, September 1997.

5.11   The paradigm of neutrality holds: (i) that there is a strict equivalence between a general doctrine of good faith and the piecemeal provisions of English law that regulate fair dealing (we can call this 'the equivalence thesis'); and (ii) that it makes no difference whether English law operates with a general doctrine or with piecemeal provisions (we can call this 'the indifference thesis'). Once we differentiate between the equivalence and the indifference theses, and once we distinguish between holding these theses in the abstract as against in the context of an ongoing legal system, it becomes apparent that the neutral view has a strong bias to slide towards the negative view.

One way in which this bias will reveal itself is if we imagine a neutral, who accepts both the equivalence and the indifference theses *in the abstract*, but who is now asked whether it would be sensible to replace the English piecemeal approach with a general doctrine of good faith. Clearly, since (ex hypothesi) nothing is to be gained by replacing one approach with the other, the neutral must take a negative view on this practical question (unless, for some bizarre reason, incurring transaction costs is judged to be a good thing).

Suppose, though, the proposal is not to replace the English piecemeal approach with a general doctrine of good faith, but to supplement the former with the latter so that they would exist alongside one another in English law. What would the neutral say to this? Again, the neutral would have good reason to take the negative view. If, as the neutral believes, there is a strict equivalence between the piecemeal approach (involving such specific doctrines as economic duress, promissory estoppel, misrepresentation, mistake, frustration, and the like) and a general doctrine of good faith, it seems a needless duplication to supplement the former with the latter. Worse, the neutral might fear that specific doctrines, with well-defined functions, are liable to become clouded once a general background standard is in play, for lawyers might be uncertain not only about whether they should found themselves on the traditional doctrines or the new general standard[1] but also about where the boundaries of the traditional doctrines now lie[2].

1   Cf Cohen 'Good Faith in Bargaining and Principles of Contract Law' (1989) 9 Tel Aviv University Studies in Law 249 and 'The Effect of the Duty of Good Faith on a Previously Common Law System: The Experience of Israeli Law' in Brownsword, Hird and Howells (eds) *Good Faith in Contract: Concept and Context* (1999) 189.

2   Similar difficulties might be experienced in a legal system where a broad doctrine of unconscionability pre-dates the adoption of a doctrine of good faith. See, eg the extended analysis of good faith in Gummow J's judgment in *Service Station Association v Berg Bennett* (1993) 117 ALR 393, 401–407. In this case, the applicants pleaded inter alia that that it was an implied term of the parties' agreement that 'the respondent was obliged to act in good faith toward the applicant'. Gummow J rejected this ground of the application, being unwilling to take what was seen as 'a major step' (407), requiring 'a leap of faith' (406), when this was not required by authority. Significantly, though, the applicants' pleadings relied, too, on Trade Practices Act 1974, s 52A which deals with unconscionable conduct. For some reflections on the relationship between good faith and unconscionability where the doctrines are assumed *not* to be equivalent, see Waddams 'Good Faith, Unconscionability and Reasonable Expectations' (1995) 9 JCL 55, esp at 60–61.

5.12   Thus far, we have assumed, so to speak, a fully committed neutral (holding both the equivalence and the indifference theses in the abstract). Consider, now, the case of a half-committed neutral. Perhaps the clearest example of such a view is that of the neutral who holds to the equivalence thesis but who rejects the indifference thesis by contending that specific rules are to be preferred to general exhortations to act in good faith[1]. On this view, the piecemeal provisions of English law, provided that they are sufficiently clear and precise, are to be preferred to an open-ended good faith provision (even if the outcomes, when litigated, would be identical). Whether we ask such a neutral about the wisdom of adopting a general principle of good faith either in the abstract or in the context of a going legal system, a negative view will be taken[2].

1   Cf Waddams 'Pre-Contractual Duties of Disclosure' in Cane and Stapleton (eds) *Essays for Patrick Atiyah* (1991) 237 at 253–4. Waddams suggests that, whilst there are, at first sight, attractions in embracing broad concepts such as good faith and fair dealing, this does not always produce expected results. Experience indicates that:

      What is needed is a set of rules sufficiently in conformity with the community sense of morality not to produce results perceived as outrageous, while at the same time preserving sufficient content to be workable and reasonably inexpensive of regular application, and maintaining a fair degree of security of property transfers.

In the light of this, Waddams concludes that, rather than espousing a general good faith doctrine, a 'more effective way of producing honest behaviour is likely to be the adoption of specific rules that, in particular contexts, make honesty the best policy.' Taking this view, English pragmatism would seem a sound approach. But cf Wilhelmsson 'Good Faith and the Duty of Disclosure in Commercial Contracting—The Nordic Experience' in Brownsword, Hird and Howells (eds) *Good Faith in Contract: Concept and Context* (1999) 165.

2   If the half-committed neutral favours tailored rules rather than general principles, such a neutral also favours the use of familiar rather than unfamiliar language (even if the languages are equivalent). We can detect such reasoning in the way in which the general test of unfairness in the EC Directive on Unfair Terms in Consumer Contracts was first negotiated at EU level and then 'translated' into English law. See further Tenreiro 'The Community Directive on Unfair Terms and National Legal Systems' (1995) 3 *European Review of Private Law* 273; and Brownsword, Howells and Wilhelmsson, 'Between Market and Welfare: Some Reflections on Article 3 of the EC Directive on Unfair Terms in Consumer Contracts' in Willett (ed) *Aspects of Fairness in Contract* (1996) 25, 47–48.

5.13   In principle, then, the ostensibly neutral view covers a number of possible positions. In practice, however, where the adoption of good faith is being considered in the context of a legal system that already has a variety of resources for dealing with unfairness in contract, neutrality will lean towards the negative view. It follows that English neutrals, even those who fully accept the equivalence and indifference theses, will tend to oppose the incorporation of a general doctrine of good faith.

Against scepticism

5.14   In his seminal paper, Raphael Powell argued that the adoption of a good faith doctrine would be beneficial in that it would enable the English courts to avoid having 'to resort to contortions or subterfuges in order to give effect to their sense of the justice of the case'[1]. Moreover, citing the notorious decision in *L'Estrange v Graucob Ltd*[2] and implicitly rejecting a neutral view, Powell argued that a good faith doctrine would sometimes be a more powerful and effective resource than the favoured English tools for dealing with perceived unfairness. Although such a positive view is probably shared by no more than a minority of English contract lawyers[3], at least four arguments can be offered in its support as follows.

1   Powell 'Good Faith in Contracts' (1956) 9 CLP 16, 26.
2   [1934] 2KB 394.

3   But cf The Hon Johan Steyn 'The Role of Good Faith and Fair Dealing in
     Contract Law: A Hair-Shirt Philosophy?' [1991] Denning LJ 131; Collins
     'Good Faith in European Contract Law' (1994) OJLS 229, and *The Law of
     Contract* (3rd edn, 1997) passim; Adams and Brownsword *Key Issues in Contract*
     (1995), ch 7; and Brownsword "Good Faith in Contracts' Revisited' (1996)
     49 CLP 111.

5.15   First, to the extent that English law already tries to regulate
bad faith dealing, it may be argued that it would be more rational to
address the problem directly (rather than indirectly) and openly (rather
than covertly) by adopting a general principle of good faith. This is
Powell's first line of argument and it is a familiar theme in the North
American literature advocating adoption of good faith. Robert
Summers, for example, maintains that

> [without a principle of good faith, a judge] might, in a particular case,
> be unable to do justice at all, or he might be able to do it only at the
> cost of fictionalizing existing legal concepts and rules, thereby snarling
> up the law for future cases. In begetting snarl, fiction may introduce
> inequity, unclarity or unpredictability. In addition, fiction can divert
> analytical focus or even cast aspersions on an innocent party.[1]

Powell's example of 'snarl' (as Summers calls it) in the law happens
to be in the field of implied terms[2]. However, it could equally well
have been in some other area of contract law—abusive (or
opportunistic) termination, for example, is another fertile area[3].
Whatever the example, the point is the same: that the law should be
transparent and that a doctrine of good faith assists the law to achieve
this ideal.

1   Summers '"Good Faith" in General Contract Law and the Sales Provisions
     of the Uniform Commercial Code' (1968) 54 Vir LR 195, 198–199. To similar
     effect, see eg, Knapp 'Enforcing the Contract to Bargain' (1969) 44 NYULR,
     673, 727; Summers 'The General Duty of Good Faith—Its Recognition and
     Conceptualization' (1982) 67 Corn LR 810, 812; and (in Australia) Priestley
     in *Renard Constructions (ME) Pty Ltd v Minister for Public Works* (1992) 26
     NSWLR 234, 266.
2   The case in point is *Ingham v Emes* [1955] 2 All ER 740. For discussion, see
     Brownsword, '"Good Faith in Contracts" Revisited' (1996) 49 CLP 111, 116–
     117.
3   Cf Brownsword 'Retrieving Reasons, Retrieving Rationality? A New Look at
     the Right to Withdraw for Breach of Contract' (1992) 5 JCL 83.

5.16   Secondly, in the absence of a doctrine of good faith, it may be
argued—as Powell contended in relation to English law, and as
Summers says (above) with reference to US law—that the law of
contract is ill-equipped to achieve fair results, on occasion leaving
judges 'unable to do justice at all'. This particular argument in favour
of good faith can be developed in several ways. For example, if we

imagine good faith as an umbrella principle[1], covering, unifying, and filling the gaps between a range of specific doctrines designed to secure fair dealing, then in hard cases (of the kind that supposedly make bad law) judges could appeal to the umbrella principle to justify a one-off decision, or to adumbrate some new principle of fairness, or to extend the range of an already recognised principle (for example, extending the range of equitable estoppel into pre-contractual dealings, or extending the principle of duress to some forms of economic pressure, and so on). So equipped, judges in the *appeal courts*, would have no need *covertly* to stretch and manipulate existing resources; and they would have no excuse for handing down patently unfair decisions—with good faith in play, *L'Estrange v Graucob* becomes *Tilden Rent-A-Car v Clendenning*[2]. Moreover, in the *trial courts*, judges who might otherwise bow to the pressure of precedent, would have the opportunity to avoid declaring that hard cases simply yield hard decisions. With good faith openly adopted as a foundational doctrine, there would be no need for *sub rosa* adjudication; and both trial judges and appeal courts would have the legal support that they require.

1   Cf Hutchison 'Good Faith in South African Contract Law', in Brownsword, Hird and Howells (eds) *Good Faith in Contract: Concept and Context* (Aldershot, Ashgate, 1999) 213.
2   (1978) 83 DLR (3d) 400, 18OR (2d) 601.

5.17   Thirdly, turning on its head one of the negative arguments against a general principle of good faith, it might be argued that, with such a principle, the courts are better equipped to respond to the varying expectations encountered in the many different contracting contexts—and, in particular, it might be argued that the courts are better able to detect co-operative dealing where it is taking place[1]. Thus, the argument runs, if English contract law adopted a doctrine of good faith, it would pose questions of contractual interpretation and implication in a context, not only of background standards of fair dealing, but more immediately of the concrete expectations of the parties. Such concrete expectations would be based as much on the way that the parties related to one another (whether they dealt with one another in an adversarial or non-adversarial manner) as on the express provisions of the agreement. As a result, English law would recover the ability to give effect to the spirit of the deal in a way that prioritised the parties' own expectations.

   To appreciate the significance of this argument, consider the judgment of the Court of Appeal in the *BSkyB* case[2]. The dispute in this case arose out of a number of agreements made in 1989 and 1990 between British Satellite Broadcasting (BSB) and Philips at the time that BSB and Sky were locked in competition to control the satellite television market in the UK. By late 1990, BSB had lost the battle and had merged with Sky. One of the results of this merger was that Philips, who had contracted with BSB to develop and manufacture receivers for the BSB system, were left with unsold stock, surplus manufacturing capacity, and no continuing opportunity to sell the receivers. Philips tried to recoup their losses by arguing that BSB were in breach of various implied terms of their agreements, but particularly an implied term to the effect that BSB 'would not commit any act which would tend to impede or render impossible the marketing of the Receivers and/or to render the Receivers useless or unmarketable'. Although Philips persuaded the trial judge that such an implied term was part of the agreement, they failed before the Court of Appeal. According to Sir Thomas Bingham MR[3]:

> Had the parties addressed their minds at the outset to the eventuality that the operation turned out to be a major commercial flop, it is by no means clear how they would have agreed that the risk should be allocated or, if they had agreed that Philips should be protected, what form they would have agreed that that protection should take. It seems likely that there would have been tough negotiation, with Philips seeking maximum protection and BSB conceding the minimum.

Sir Thomas, however, was not wholly unsympathetic to Philips's position for he indicated that, if it had been material, he would have been prepared to 'imply a term that BSB should act with good faith in the performance of [the] contract'[4].

In the *BSkyB* case, we find the court willing to speak the language of good faith performance, and yet apparently respecting the orthodox view that only such terms as can be confidently attributed to the parties' unstated intentions are to be implied. Underlying this orthodoxy is an adversarial model of each contracting party seeking to maximise its utility, as in Sir Thomas's picture of tough negotiation, with one side seeking the maximum protection against risk and the other side conceding the minimum. If the adoption of a doctrine of good faith simply adds a rhetorical gloss to this orthodox view, it involves no substantive change to the law.

We need to look more carefully, however, at Sir Thomas's model of the negotiating situation. The classical version of this model is one of tough self-interested bargaining in the context of a discrete contract—it is a model of self-interested dealers converging on a market-place, making their one-off exchanges, and going their separate ways[5]. However, although we can assume that BSB and Philips would meet as self-interested dealers, the classical picture is hardly appropriate. For one thing, the transaction between BSB and Philips was more in the nature of a joint venture than a spot contract and, equally importantly, we must assume that each party would pursue its self-interest in a reasonably enlightened way. With these revisions to the classical picture, we can see that the parties' 'tough negotiation, with Philips seeking maximum protection and BSB conceding the minimum' is potentially constrained in at least three respects. First, prudent would-be contractors must calculate the disutility of failed negotiations (ie no contract) and give ground up to the point where the disutility of concession is less than the disutility of being excluded from the deal. Secondly, where the contractors are involved in long-term dealing, intelligent negotiation will involve smaller (expected) short-term utilities being subordinated to greater (expected) long-term utilities. Thirdly, and linked to the second point, the symbolic utility of a co-operative gesture is one element that must enter into an enlightened contractor's calculations[6]. Of course, the background picture remains one of minimal concession and, even if we assume constraints against the blinkered pursuit of short-term self-interest, this does not demonstrate that, if the question of the venture failing had been raised during negotiations, BSB would have agreed to underwrite some of the risk to which Philips would be exposed. However, once we have transposed the issue from the classical context of the discrete (spot) contract and short-term adversarial dealing to the context of longer term dealing with a willingness to invest in the future, it is a great deal more plausible to imply terms that involve some act of co-operation or sharing of risk—and, what is more, to do this on the basis that such implications are necessary if we are to be faithful to the parties' unexpressed intentions and expectations. In other words, if a good faith doctrine is adopted there is a substantive change to the law; but it is not so much a rewriting of general principle as a recognition that adversarial dealing is not the only game in town and, concomitantly, a modification to our appreciation of the possible range of transactional settings within which doctrine is to be applied.

This third argument in favour of good faith might be put more directly in terms of the protection of reasonable expectation. Indeed, Lord Steyn has recently couched the argument in precisely this way, taking as his starting point the idea that the principal task for the modern law of contract is to protect the contractors' reasonable expectations[7]. Having outlined the revisionist nature of such a general principle in relation to questions of formation, privity, and the like, Lord Steyn turns to criticise the narrow approach in *Walford v Miles*, claiming that a good faith principle is perfectly practical and workable. However, he continues:

> I have no heroic suggestion for the introduction of a general duty of good faith in our contract law. It is not necessary. As long as our courts always respect the reasonable expectations of parties our contract

law can satisfactorily be left to develop in accordance with its own pragmatic traditions. And where in specific contexts duties of good faith are imposed on parties our legal system can readily accommodate such a well tried notion. After all, there is not a world of difference between the objective requirement of good faith and the reasonable expectations of parties.[8]

Although this might be mistaken for the neutral view, it is in fact a quite different position. Lord Steyn's (implicit) premise is that there is no equivalence between the traditional piecemeal approach of English law and a general requirement of good faith. Having rejected the equivalence thesis, his argument is that we should adopt what is in effect a general duty of good faith but that this can be cast in the more familiar form of a general principle that the reasonable expectations of the parties should be respected (and, to this extent, we can be indifferent about our doctrinal terminology). In other words, an overriding principle of reasonable expectation serves the same purpose as a general principle of good faith. The language might be different but the idea is the same[9].

1   Cf Brownsword 'Contract Law, Co-operation, and Good Faith: the Movement from Static to Dynamic Market-Individualism' in Deakin and Michie (eds) *Contracts, Co-operation and Competition: Inter-Disciplinary Perspectives*, (1997) 255; and, generally, see the critique of the inflexible doctrines of classical contract law in Nassar, *Sanctity of Contracts Revisited* (1995).

2   *Philips Electronique Grand Public SA v British Sky Broadcasting Ltd; Philips International BV v British Satellite Broadcasting Ltd* (unreported, 19 October 1994) (Lexis Transcript).

3   *Philips Electronique Grand Public SA v British Sky Broadcasting Ltd* [1995] EMLR 472; *Philips International BV v British Satellite Broadcasting Ltd* (unreported, 19 October 1994) (Lexis Transcript).

4   *Philips Electronique Grand Public SA v British Sky Broadcasting Ltd* [1995] EMLR 472; *Philips International BV v British Satellite Broadcasting Ltd* (unreported, 19 October 1994) (Lexis Transcript).

5   Seminally, see Macneil, 'The Many Futures of Contract' (1974) 47 Southern California LR 691.

6   Cf Nozick, *The Nature of Rationality* (1993) esp Ch 1.

7   Steyn 'Contract Law: Fulfilling the Reasonable Expectations of Honest Men' (1997) 113 LQR 433.

8   Steyn 'Contract Law: Fulfilling the Reasonable Expectations of Honest Men' (1997) 113 LQR 433 at 439.

9   But cf Waddams 'Good Faith, Unconscionability and Reasonable Expectations' (1995) 9 JCL 55, 58–59 for the view that, although '[g]ood faith, unconscionability and reasonable expectations are concepts that sound somewhat similar ... good faith is related in very different ways to each of the other two concepts mentioned.' Put simply, Waddams' critique of good faith involves (i) contrasting subjective good faith with objective reasonable expectation (such that good faith sometimes seems to detract from fairness) and (ii) comparing objective good faith with objective reasonable expectation (such that good faith seems to add nothing to existing standards of fairness). Thus, speaking of the *Interfoto* case, Waddams says: 'If the court recognises

that reasonable notice of the clause must be given, and that the clause must be fair and reasonable, a principle of good faith is not needed, and to rest the result on good faith might suggest the additional need for the defendant to establish misconduct or bad motive on the plaintiff's part' (at 61).

5.18   Finally, it is arguable that the beneficial effects of a good faith doctrine go beyond (reactive) dispute-settlement, for a good faith contractual environment has the potential to give contracting parties greater security and, thus, greater flexibility about the ways in which they are prepared to do business. In a society without any kind of contract law dealing will tend to be very defensive—present (and simultaneous) exchange will be the order of the day, credit being extended only to those who are already known and trusted. Whilst English law goes some way towards meeting the concerns of defensive contractors and, to some extent, liberates practice, it falls short of what is required if the potential synergies of co-operation are to be fully exploited. Consider, again, the nature of the contract in the *BSkyB* case. From the point of view of BSB, it was imperative that the receivers associated with its system were readily available to would-be subscribers—otherwise, if there was a delay in obtaining the equipment, some potential customers might be lost to the rival satellite system. From Philips's point of view, however, to make such an asset-specific investment was a highly risky venture—the risk being that they would be left holding stock for which there was no market[1]. For whatever reason, Philips decided to proceed with the deal; and we can only speculate about their assessment of the risk. However, a priori, we can be less speculative about the impact of the contractual environment in a situation of this kind: for, other things being equal, Philips surely would be more willing to enter into a contract for the manufacture of BSB receiving equipment (in advance of customer orders for the equipment) where the law had a doctrine of good faith in contract than where it had no such doctrine (in name or in substance).

Now, the general difficulty facing parties who contract for future performance is that they cannot be sure (i) how market conditions will change (in particular, whether market prices will rise or fall) and (ii) how the other party will act. In relation to the latter difficulty, the most defensive assumption is to proceed on the basis that the other side will act in whatever way seems to advance its own immediate interests (that is, as a so-called 'straightforward maximiser')[2]. Such a defensive assumption, however, sometimes obstructs our ability to optimise our own interests. Thus, in the standard example of the Prisoner's Dilemma[3], A assumes that B will act as a straightforward maximiser (and vice versa), as a result of which A and B each avoid the worst possible outcome but fail to achieve the best available outcome. Had A assumed that B would act co-operatively (and vice versa), A and B could have relied on one another so as to produce the best available (joint) outcome. Why, then, does A not make such an assumption? Quite simply, A will not make such an assumption unless he is confident that B is to be trusted or, failing this, A has security against the risk that will eventuate should B prove to be an opportunist.

The present argument for good faith is that the same considerations apply in contract. The more that contract doctrine provides a security against the risks of opportunism and exploitation to which co-operative dealing exposes a contractor, the more willing (other things being equal) contractors will be to deal in a way that optimises their interests (even though they are thereby exposed to risk). Thus, as good faith finds a place in the law, and as the contractual environment becomes more congenial to trust and risk-taking, it is possible that these reciprocal influences will work together to promote ever more co-operative thinking in both legal doctrine and contracting practice.

1   Cf the general analysis in Deakin, Lane, and Wilkinson '"Trust" or Law? Towards an Integrated Theory of Contractual Relations Between Firms' (1994) 21 Journal of Law and Society 329, 332.
2   See Gauthier *Morals by Agreement* (1986).
3   See eg Gauthier *Morals by Agreement* (1986) 79–82; Nozick The Nature of Rationality (1993) 50–59.

5.19   In sum, there are four strands in the positive view of good faith. A good faith doctrine allows problems of bad faith to be addressed in a clean and direct fashion; it enables judges at all levels to deal in a coherent and an effective manner with cases of unfair dealing; it can bring the law much more closely into alignment with the protection of reasonable expectations (which, it must be recognised, vary from one contracting situation to another); and it can contribute to a culture of trust and co-operation that enhances the autonomy of contractors and that, on a larger scale, is an important feature of successful economies[1].

1   See eg Arrighetti, Bachmann, and Deakin, 'Contract Law, Social Norms and Inter-Firm Cooperation' (1997) 21 Cambridge Journal of Economics 171; and Burchell and Wilkinson 'Trust, Business Relationships and the Contractual Environment' (1997) 21 Cambridge Journal of Economics 217.

Three models of good faith

5.20   What are we to make of the arguments for and against adopting a general doctrine of good faith? This rather depends on which model of good faith we have in mind; for, essentially, there are three such models, each of which needs to be made explicit before either the negative or the positive arguments can be evaluated. The first model, 'a good faith requirement' as we can call it[1], simply acts on the standards of fair dealing that are already recognised in a particular contracting context. These standards may or may not yet have crystallised into express terms commonly used, but they nevertheless represent the informal expectations of those who deal in the particular market[2]. The second model, 'a good faith regime' as we may term it[3], acts on the standards of fair dealing that are dictated by a critical morality of co-operation. Unlike the first model of good faith, this second model does not track recognised standards (although it may sometimes coincide with them) but, instead, tries to make the market in the sense of prescribing the co-operative ground rules. The third model of good faith is what Michael Bridge evocatively calls 'visceral justice'[4]. Here, judges react impressionistically to the merits of a situation and dispose of cases accordingly—all in the name of good faith. Unlike either the first or the second models of good faith, this third model is judicial licence.

1   See Brownsword '"Good Faith in Contracts" Revisited' (1996) 49 CLP 111.
2   Cf section 205 of the *Restatement (2d) of Contracts*, which provides for a requirement of good faith in the performance and enforcement of contracts. The linking of the good faith requirement to commercial expectations is made clear by the Official Comment to the Restatement. Thus:
    The phrase 'good faith' is used in a variety of contexts and its meaning varies somewhat with the context. Good faith performance or enforcement of a contract emphasizes faithfulness to an agreed common purpose and consistency with the justified expectations of the other party; it excludes a variety of types of conduct characterized as involving 'bad faith' because they violate community standards of decency, fairness or reasonableness.
    See, too, Nassar *Sanctity of Contracts Revisited* (1995) eg at pp 167–168, and 239–242.
3   Cf '"Good Faith in Contracts" Revisited' (1996) 49 CLP 111; and Cohen 'Pre-Contractual Duties: Two Freedoms and the Contract to Negotiate' in Beatson and Friedmann (eds) *Good Faith and Fault in Contract Law* (1995) 25.
4   Bridge 'Good Faith in Commercial Contracts' in Brownsword, Hird, and Howells (eds) *Good Faith in Contract: Concept and Context* (1999) 139, at 140.

5.21   On the face of it, judicial licence has little to recommend it; thus, the third model of good faith does not merit serious consideration. It follows that the only plausible choices are between the status quo and the first or second models of good faith[1]. In this light we can reconsider the sceptical arguments, not with a view to cashing the positive case, but simply to observe where such arguments register against the adoption of a good faith requirement or a good faith regime.

1 For a penetrating discussion of the way in which different models of good faith ('normative good faith' and 'contextual good faith') might be *selectively* incorporated into the law, see Wightman 'Good Faith and Pluralism in the Law of Contract' in Brownsword, Hird and Howells (eds) *Good Faith in Contract: Concept and Context* (1999) 41.

5.22 To adopt a *good faith requirement* would be to make a relatively modest adjustment to the status quo. When, in a particular contracting context, the participants have a shared understanding of where the line is drawn between fair and unfair dealing—and, concomitantly, shared expectations about the conduct of fellow contractors—then the law simply adopts this shared view of fair dealing[1]. On occasion, this might involve moving ahead of the standard form terms currently in circulation, but it would scarcely be vanguard law-making. Rather, a court operating with a good faith requirement would aspire simply to follow the shared sense of good faith in the particular contractual setting. Certainly, there would be no question, on this view, of good faith being employed to override clear expectations (such as those perhaps to be found in the Hong Kong property market that provided the background in the *Union Eagle* case); nor would good faith be employed to thicken up the relatively thin sense of fair dealing that one would expect to find in highly competitive contracting contexts[2].

What, though, would a good faith requirement signify (a) where a particular transaction does not readily fit within an identifiable context or (b) where there is an identifiable context, but there is no shared understanding of fair dealing? In cases of this kind, the law must do its best to construct the backcloth of expectation against which the parties dealt; for it cannot be emphasised too strongly that a good faith requirement is dedicated to articulating and respecting the parties' expectations. Where that backcloth involves a serious conflict of opinion about the requirements of fair dealing, the law must follow the 'better' view[3]. Where there is a dominant view, there might well be a presumption in favour of protecting expectations that are reasonable relative to that view; where there is no such view, the law cannot avoid making an invidious choice and tie-breaking rules need to be agreed. This, however, hardly justifies condemning a good faith requirement out of hand.

1 Here, so to speak, we have the elements of a 'contractual community'. Cf Wightman in 'Good Faith and Pluralism in the Law of Contract' in Brownsword, Hird and Howells (eds) *Good Faith in Contract: Concept and Context* (1999) 41 at 43–44, where three requirements are suggested for a contractual community: (i) regular dealing; (ii) an absence of 'gross disparities of power between different contractual interests'; and (iii) relational contracting to the extent that there is a body of experience 'not just of making and performing the contracts, but also of handling problems when the contract goes wrong'.

2   Article 1.106(2) of the Lando Commission's Principles of European Contract Law: Part I provides that the duty to act in accordance with good faith and fair dealing (in art 106.1(1)) may not be excluded or limited. Given that the intention of the Commission seems to be to prescribe a good faith requirement, how far does this constrain the parties? If the parties can draw the line between fair and unfair dealing as they wish, good faith is entirely self-regulating—the only restriction is that the parties cannot stipulate that they are not bound by their own standards of fair dealing (whatever those standards are). If, however, the standards of the relevant business community apply, then although the non-excludable duty remains context-sensitive—so that, in some contexts, only a relatively thin regime of fair dealing might be recognised—there might now be a constraint on the parties' freedom to set lower standards of good faith. This depends upon whether the relevant standards of fair dealing allow for the parties to set their own (lower) standards. If they do, the parties remain free to self-regulate (in accordance with the non-excludable background regime); if they do not, the parties are constrained.

3   Cf Wilhelmsson 'Good Faith and the Duty of Disclosure in Commercial Contracting—the Nordic Experience' in Brownsword, Hird, and Howells (eds) *Good Faith in Contract: Concept and Context* (1999) 165, for the distinction between a private autonomy model of good faith and the Nordic moral model of good faith. The former relates closely to a good faith requirement; the latter is closer to a good faith regime. In the former model, the 'better' view (as explained in the text hereto) reflects what is accepted and recognised in business practice. In the latter, however, at least in the Nordic model, good faith operates as a pressure to improve standards of fair dealing and, insofar as it taps into recognised standards, the 'better' view is the better view relative to the decision-maker's critical moral perspective.

5.23   The adoption of a *good faith regime* would be an altogether more ambitious, and controversial, move, inviting two lines of objection. First, if the regime is simply presented as one in which the parties should act with good faith towards one another[1], or should act in a way that evinces loyalty or respect for the legitimate interests of one another, the application of such an idea is likely to be unpredictable—at any rate, this is liable to be so in the absence of a developed background jurisprudence of good faith. Accordingly, if a good faith regime is not to be condemned as too vague and uncertain, it needs to be prescribed in a way that offers contractors clear guidance as to its principal requirements. Secondly, because a good faith regime is not designed to track recognised standards of fair dealing, it invites the objection that it is liable to override the intentions of the contractors. For example, it might be objected that it would be absurd to prescribe a good faith regime for a market as ruthlessly competitive as that in financial derivatives. Insofar as the good faith regime is simply a default position, which contractors can agree to displace (as, say, in commodities and derivatives markets), the objection falls away—and this is largely the response to the problem. However, this assumes that a good faith regime is adopted as a facilitative measure when, to some extent, we might wish to adopt such a regime as a protective measure for the benefit of contractors who might otherwise be exploited. To bite this bullet, we certainly need to say that the good faith regime can only be displaced where there is compelling evidence of mutual agreement; and we might need to go a step further in some contracting contexts, saying that there can be no derogation from good faith[2].

1 E g as in the Commercial Agents (Council Directive) Regulations 1993, SI 1993/3053 (see para 5.2 note 7 above).
2 Again, as e g in the Commercial Agents (Council Directive) Regulations 1993, SI 1993/3053) (see note 1), in which reg 5 provides that the parties may not derogate from the good faith principles in regs 3 and 4. And, cf the analysis in Teubner 'Legal Irritants: Good Faith in British Law or How Unifying Law Ends Up in New Divergences' (1998) 61 MLR 11.

5.24 If it is accepted that good faith as visceral justice is not an option, then where do the sceptical arguments hit home at the real targets? In the case of a *good faith requirement*, it has to be conceded that there might be some uncertainty (where the parties' expectations themselves are unclear, or where the case falls outside any recognised context); and, at various levels, there might be some difficulties of application. For example, there might be problematic inquiries into a party's reasons or motives where the recognised standards of fair dealing make such matters material. The scale of this problem should not be exaggerated, however. If there is a difficulty, it arises only where the setting in which the parties have contracted makes reasons and motives relevant factors—and, with a good faith requirement, such a setting is largely the product of the parties' own custom and practice[1]. As for the (negative) arguments that good faith represents a challenge to the autonomy of the parties and that it does not allow for the heterogeneity of contracting contexts, these objections simply fall wide of the mark. Indeed, the positive view can turn these arguments round to claim that a good faith requirement is designed precisely to respect the autonomy of contractors—good faith, far from being a licence for visceral justice is a necessity if the contractual project is not to be eviscerated[2]—and to do so in a way that is sensitive to the variations found in contracting contexts. In the case of a *good faith regime*, so long as this is simply the default position in contract law, there is no challenge to the parties' autonomy, and there is some allowance for variation from one contracting situation to another. However, under-prescription of such a regime will expose it to the charge of uncertainty; and, if the regime is one from which the parties are not permitted to contract-out, then the negative view strikes home unless the concept of autonomy is given a radical re-interpretation (such that, for instance, autonomous action is understood in a Kantian sense as rational moral action).

Finally, although both a good faith requirement and a good faith regime are less vulnerable to the negative view than that of good faith as visceral justice, does either have any response to the argument that English law should never be guided by anything but an adversarial ethic? The short answer is that this opening gambit on the part of the negative view is less an argument than a declaration of faith. However, if an answer is needed, supporters of good faith can point to the failure of the adversarial view to measure up to the expectations of contractors in non-adversarial contexts, as well as to the body of recent writing that holds that adversarial relations in contract are sometimes inimical to our individual and collective economic well-being[3].

1   To this extent, there is no reason to take issue with Stephen Waddams' remark that few business people would 'be inclined to favour a rule that the right to reject should depend on the actual motives of the buyer, a rule that would involve costly enquiries and create incentives to assemble unreliable and self-serving evidence of good motive': see 'Good Faith, Unconscionability and Reasonable Expectations' (1995) 9 JCL 55, 64.
2   Cf Nassar *Sanctity of Contracts Revisited* (1995) 241–242.
3   Generally, see Deakin and Michie (eds) *Contracts, Co-operation and Competition: Inter-Disciplinary Perspectives*, (1997).

Good faith and reasonableness

5.25   There is an obvious symmetry in debates about the adoption of general principles of good faith and/or reasonableness. Those who advocate that English law (or, indeed, any modern common law system) should adopt such general principles must overcome two fundamental objections: first, that there is no reason why contracting should be subjected to moral constraints—it is simply a matter of parties pursuing their own self-interest; and, secondly, that if moral constraints are to be introduced, this is unworkable until agreement is reached about whose (or which) morality is to serve as the reference point for such doctrines[1]. The first objection is easily dealt with. No one thinks that contract law is, or can be, morally neutral. Even the minimal constraints of the classical law reflect a certain kind of morality[2]; and, even if contract is seen as essentially self-interested dealing, there are all sorts of moral (or public interest) constraints on the kind of agreements that the parties can enforce. The more serious objection, therefore, is the second one, that a moral reference point must be specified.

The second objection is undoubtedly well taken. Good faith, like reasonableness, only makes sense relative to some particular moral reference point. What is that reference point? The principal options are: (i) the standards of fair dealing recognised by the community of which the contractors are most proximately a part (as in a good faith requirement); and (ii) the standards of fair dealing and co-operation that would be prescribed by the best (ie most defensible) moral theory (as in a good faith regime). The former are the standards of a positive accepted morality; the latter are the standards of a critical (not necessarily accepted or recognised) morality. In the absence of philosopher kings, though, the latter option looks difficult to defend (either in terms of the practical legitimacy of judicial decisions or in terms of their theoretical justification)[3].

Accordingly, what we might anticipate in the modern law of contract in England, in which the notion of reasonableness (if not that of good faith) abounds, is a tendency for doctrine to reflect the expectations associated with good practice (in both the field of consumer and commercial contracting)[4]. In other words, we might expect that English law will move towards the adoption of good faith as a requirement (in substance, if not in name). In the next section, we will suggest that such a tendency is already clearly established.

1   Cf the issues identified by Wilhelmsson, para 5.22 note 2 above.
2   Cf eg Collins, *The Law of Contract* (3rd edn, 1997); 'The Sanctimony of Contract' in Rawlings (ed) *Law, Society and Economy* (1997) 63; and Kronman 'Contract Law and Distributive Justice' (1980) 89 Yale LJ 472.
3   Cf Mason 'The Impact of Equitable Doctrine on the Law of Contract' (1998) Anglo-Am LR 1; and see, further, chapter 9.
4   Cf Brownsword 'The Philosophy of Welfarism and its Emergence in the Modern English Law of Contract' in Brownsword, Howells, and Wilhelmsson (eds) *Welfarism in Contract Law* (1994) 21; and 'Static and Dynamic Market Individualism' in Halson (ed) *Exploring the Boundaries of Contract* (1996) 48.

CHAPTER 6

The Tendency of the Modern Law

The ideologies of contract

6.1 Law might be said to be 'ideological' in more than one sense. In a pejorative sense, it might be described (and, by implication, criticised) as 'ideological' where it is perceived to serve a particular political dogma without giving due weight to the requirements of the public interest, or where it is accompanied by rhetoric that masks or misrepresents the nature of the regulation, or the like. Contract law may or may not be thought to be ideological in this sense[1]. In another (non-pejorative) sense, however, all law is ideological, meaning simply that it is guided by a set of ideas about how social and economic life should be organised. To this extent, the law of contract is as much ideological[2] as, say, the regulation of the trade unions[3] or the programmes of privatisation and marketisation in and around the public sector[4].

1   See eg Gabel and Feinman 'Contract Law as Ideology' in Kairys (ed) *The Politics of Law* (1982) 172; and Hadfield 'The Dilemma of Choice: A Feminist Perspective on *The Limits of Freedom of Contract*' (1995) 33 Osgoode Hall LJ 337, esp at 340 (for feminist critique of the traditional rhetoric of contract).
2   The fact that contract doctrine reflects a number of competing values has been remarked upon by many writers. See eg Adams and Brownsword *Understanding Contract Law* (2nd edn, 1994; 1996); Brownsword, Howells and Wilhelmsson (eds) *Welfarism in Contract Law* (1994); Collins *The Law of Contract* (3rd edn, 1997); Hillman *The Richness of Contract Law* (1997); Wightman *Contract: A Critical Commentary* (1996); Kennedy 'Form and Substance in Private Law Adjudication' (1976) 89 Harv LR 1685; and Unger 'The Critical Legal Studies Movement' (1983) 96 Harv LR 563.
3   See eg Fredman 'The New Rights: Labour Law and Ideology in the Thatcher Years' (1992) 12 OJLS 24.
4   See eg Graham and Prosser 'Privatising Nationalised Industries: Constitutional Issues and New Legal Techniques' (1987) 50 MLR 16; and Harden *The Contracting State* (1992). See further chapter 8.

6.2   The leading doctrines of the English law of contract, whether in legislation or case law, reflect two principal ideologies, 'market-individualism' and 'consumer-welfarism'[1]. Putting the contrast very generally, whereas the former ideology insists upon contractors being held to their freely agreed exchanges, the latter seeks to ensure a fair deal for consumer contractors and, more generally, to relieve against harsh or unconscionable bargains. Where we are dealing specifically with the case law of contract, however, we must reckon with a second layer of ideological complexity. All adjudication, in all branches of law, is caught up in a tension between an ideology of 'formalism' (which dictates that the settled law should be applied, the precedents followed, and so on)[2] and an ideology of 'realism' (which, at its most robust, demands that cases should be determined according to their merits, settled law notwithstanding)[3]. In practice, this double layering of ideological tensions generates three strands in judicial reasoning— first, a formalist regard for applying the law, secondly a market-individualist brand of realism with an emphasis on calculability and holding contractors to their bargains, and thirdly a consumer-welfarist brand of realism concerned with protecting consumers against sharp practice and generally relieving against unconscionable deals.

1   See Adams and Brownsword 'The Ideologies of Contract' (1987) 7 LS 207; and *Understanding Contract Law* (2nd edn, 1994; 1996).
2   Cf Steyn 'Does Legal Formalism Hold Sway in England' (1996) 49 CLP 43.
3   For the opening up of this issue in England, see Lord Radcliffe *The Law and its Compass* (1961) and esp Lord Reid 'The Judge as Law Maker' (1972) XII JSPTL (NS) 22; generally, see Adams and Brownsword *Understanding Law* (Harper Collins, 1992; Sweet and Maxwell 1996). In the area most adjacent to contract law, the law of torts, perhaps the classic example of the contrast between formalist and realist approaches is *Donoghue v Stevenson* [1932] AC 562, Lord Atkin's majority opinion symbolising a realist concern for practical justice, the minority opinions symbolising a concern to stay within the settled limits of the authorities. More recently, a similar contrast can be read into the conflicting approaches of Lords Goff and Mustill in *White v Jones* [1995] 2AC 207: see paras 8.23 ff.

6.3   If we treat the modern law of contract as having two principal divisions, one regulating commercial contracts and the other regulating consumer contracts, then it is fairly clear how the ideas of reasonableness, inequality of bargaining, and the like, have shaped the modern law of consumer protection. However, it is perhaps less clear what the modernising tendencies are in relation to commercial contracts. In this section, we will seek to clarify the modernisation of the commercial law of contract by drawing a distinction between two versions of market-individualism, which we can term 'static' and 'dynamic' market-individualism[1]. Although both versions of market-individualism take the process of contracting to be an essentially self-interested activity, with a freely agreed exchange as the paradigm, they rest on rather different bases. Static market-individualism is a fully detached or independent ideology: it has a particular vision of the purpose of contract and how transactions should be regulated; it imposes this view on the contracting community; and, in this sense, it 'constitutes' the market. By contrast, the ideology of dynamic market-individualism is to a considerable extent dependent, reflecting the practice and expectations of the contracting community (particularly the business community). It follows that, as the practice and the views of the contracting community change, the ideology of dynamic market-individualism moves to track these changes. To this extent, therefore, dynamic market-individualism is less than fully constitutive of the market[2].

1 Originally, see Brownsword 'Static and Dynamic Market Individualism' in Halson (ed) *Exploring the Boundaries of Contract* (1996) 48.
2 Cf Collins *The Law of Contract* (3rd edn, 1997) 17–18.

Static and dynamic market-individualism contrasted

6.4 Market-individualism, whether static or dynamic, is an ideology with two aspects, a market and an individualistic aspect. To draw the contrast between static and dynamic market-individualism, we can work first through the market dimension of each version of the ideology and then through their individualistic aspects.

6.5 Static market-individualism sees the principal function of contract law as being to establish a clear set of ground rules within which a market can operate. To this extent, contract law is constitutive of the market. Markets, of course, may operate with all sorts of ground rules, customs and practices[1]. In some markets, a nod and a wink may be sufficient to close a deal; in others, the deal is not closed until the sealing wax has dried on the contractual documents. For the static market-individualist, the distinctive contribution of the English law of contract is to declare the conventions in such a way that all those who deal in the contract-constituted market place know exactly where they stand.

Three of the most important ground rules concern formation (ie at what moment the parties are bound), third-party effects, and remedies for breach. Here, static market-individualism develops its rules around two key concepts, exchange and expectation[2]. First, the (formation) rule is that a contract comes into existence when, and only when, the terms of an exchange have been fully specified and freely agreed upon. Secondly, only those who deal as parties to the exchange can take the benefit of the contract (or be burdened by its terms). And, thirdly, the basic remedial rule is that, where there is a breach, the innocent party's expectation of performance (by the contract-breaker) is to be protected—generally speaking, by damages or an action for the agreed price rather than by a decree of specific performance as such[3].These ground rules have the virtue of drawing bright lines (between situations where a binding contract is in place and where it is not, between those who can sue on a particular contract and those who cannot, and so on). However, the rules do not always generate results that seem entirely reasonable. Examples of such hard cases are legion: for instance, cases where an expected contract does not eventuate and one side incurs significant (anticipatory) reliance costs, cases where an agreed variation of a contract does not qualify as an exchange, cases where an intended third-party beneficiary is unable to enforce a contract, cases where the expectation measure of compensation seems over-generous, and so on. Now, although it can be argued in response to such hard cases that the results are simply in line with the constitutive rules, and that these rules are well-known, this does not assist where significant numbers in both the commercial and the legal communities feel uneasy with these outcomes.

1   See eg Daintith 'Comment on Lewis: Markets, Regulation and Citizenship' in Brownsword (ed) *Law and the Public Interest* (1993) 139.
2   Cf Eisenberg 'The Bargain Principle and its Limits' (1981–82) 95 *HarvLR* 741.
3   Cf para 2.3.

6.6   Dynamic market-individualism responds to these difficulties by favouring a more flexible approach, guided by the practices and expectations of the contracting community (particularly the commercial community)[1]. Accordingly, the paradigms of static market-individualism remain central but they are qualified in significant ways. For example, if the commercial community favours protection in certain situations for pre-contractual reliance, enforcement of agreed variations (even though they might be one-sided), recognition of third-party interests, and the like, then dynamic market-individualism argues that the law should run with the grain of opinion. A textbook statement of such sentiments can be found in Lord Wilberforce's well-known remarks in *The Eurymedon*[2] (where, it will be recalled, the point at issue was whether the stevedore third-parties were entitled to rely on protective provisions in the main carriage contract):

> The whole contract is of a commercial character, involving service on one side, rates of payment on the other, and qualifying stipulations as to both. The relations of all parties to each other are commercial relations entered into for business reasons of ultimate profit. To

describe one set of promises in this context as gratuitous, or *nudum pactum*, seems paradoxical and is *prima facie* implausible. It is only the precise analysis of this complex of relations into the classical offer and acceptance, with identifiable consideration, that seems to present difficulty, but this same difficulty exists in many situations of daily life, eg sales at auction; supermarket purchases; boarding an omnibus; purchasing a train ticket; tenders for the supply of goods; offers of rewards; acceptance by post; warranties of authority by agents; manufacturers' guarantees; gratuitous bailments; bankers' commercial credits. These are all examples which show that English law, having committed itself to a rather technical and schematic doctrine of contract, in application takes a practical approach, often at the cost of forcing the facts to fit uneasily into the marked slots of offer, acceptance and consideration.[3]

Similarly, in the more recent case of *G Percy Trentham Ltd v Archital Luxfer Ltd*[4], which concerned a battle of the forms problem, the Court of Appeal recognised that a contract could come into existence in stages, without there being a particular moment at which a comprehensive offer was definitively accepted and a contract (as classically conceived) materialised. As Steyn LJ (as he then was) put it, the courts 'ought not to yield to Victorian times in realism about the practical application of rules of contract formation'[5]. In other words, if (in *The Eurymedon*) the understanding of contractors involved in the carriage of goods by sea is that the protection of carriage contracts normally extends to the stevedores who unload the goods, and if (in the *Trentham* case) the understanding of contractors involved in the construction industry is that they have a contractual relationship under which work has actually been carried out (and, in fact, in *Trentham* itself, completed), then classical contract doctrine must be repositioned to accommodate such commercial expectations[6].

1   Cf eg Lord Devlin 'The Relation between Commercial Law and Commercial Practice' (1951) 14 MLR 249, esp at 266; and The Rt Hon Sir Robert Goff 'Commercial Contracts and the Commercial Court' (1984) LMCLQ 382, esp at 391.
2   *New Zealand Shipping Co Ltd v AM Satterthwaite and Co Ltd, The Eurymedon* [1975] AC 154.
3   [1975] AC 154 at 167.
4   [1993] 1 Lloyd's Rep 25.
5   [1993] 1 Lloyd's Rep 25 at 29.
6   Cf Buckley '*Walford v Miles*: False Certainty About Uncertainty—An Australian Perspective' (1993) 6 Journal of Contract Law 58; and Eisenberg 'Relational Contracts' in Beatson and Friedmann (eds) *Good Faith and Fault in Contract Law* (1995) 291.

6.7   We can highlight the contrast between the static and the dynamic approaches by considering one of the most maligned doctrines (and decisions) of English contract law, the so-called principle of vicarious immunity as elaborated in the *Elder Dempster* case[1]. There, one of the issues was whether shipowners could rely on exceptions contained in a contract of carriage to which they were not a party in order to answer a claim brought by cargo-owners who were party to the carriage contract in question. In the Court of Appeal, Scrutton LJ held that the shipowners were protected by the exception on the basis of vicarious immunity[2]; and this approach enjoyed some support in the House of Lords[3]. *Elder Dempster*, however, elicited two quite different reactions. For many years, the prevailing view was that it was a puzzling and essentially rogue authority, apparently ignoring the fundamental principle of privity of contract laid down in *Dunlop Pneumatic Tyre Co v Selfridge and Co Ltd*[4] only a few years before. As Lord Reid was to put it in *Scruttons Ltd v Midland Silicones Ltd*[5]:

> [*Elder Dempster* represents] an anomalous and unexplained exception to the general principle that a stranger cannot rely for his protection on provisions in a contract to which he is not a party.

Other judges were more forthright, Donaldson J saying that it was 'something of a judicial nightmare'[6], and Ackner LJ referring to it as 'heavily comatosed, if not long-interred'[7]. The judges who supported the principle of vicarious immunity, however, were mindful of the commercial sense of the doctrine in the particular context of carriage of goods by sea, and in many ways they anticipated the tide of more recent thinking. Thus, reflecting on the fate of *Elder Dempster*, Lord Goff has said:

> In more recent years the pendulum of judicial opinion has swung back again, as recognition has been given to the undesirability, especially in a commercial context, of allowing plaintiffs to circumvent contractual exception clauses by suing in particular the servant or agent of the contracting party who caused the relevant damage, thereby undermining the purpose of the exception, and so redistributing the contractual allocation of risk which is reflected in the freight rate and in the parties' respective insurance arrangements. Nowadays, therefore, there is a greater readiness, not only to accept something like Scrutton LJ's doctrine of vicarious immunity ... but also to rehabilitate the *Elder Dempster* case itself ... .[8]

Indeed, so much so has *Elder Dempster* been accepted that it has been described as 'a pragmatic legal recognition of commercial reality'[9]. Thus, whereas those who reject *Elder Dempster* as inconsistent with basic principle evince a static approach, those who accept it as a necessary adjustment if doctrine is to fit better with commercial expectations take the pragmatic approach of dynamic market-individualism.

1   *Elder Dempster and Co Ltd v Paterson Zochonis and Co Ltd* [1924] AC 522.
2   See [1923] 1KB 420 at 441–442.
3   See the account given by Lord Goff in *The Mahkutai* [1996] AC 650.
4   [1915] AC 847.
5   [1962] AC 446, 479.
6   See *Johnson Matthey and Co Ltd v Constantine Terminals Ltd* [1976] 2 Lloyd's Rep 215, 219.
7   See *The Forum Craftsman* [1985] 1 Lloyd's Rep 291, 295.
8   See *The Mahkutai* [1996] AC 650, 661.
9   See *Dresser UK Ltd v Falcongate Freight Management Ltd: The Duke of Yare* [1992] QB 502, 511 (per Bingham LJ).

6.8   When we turn to the individualist dimension, for the static market-individualist, the law of contract should set up a stable framework within which contractors can agree to exchanges that promise to maximise their individual utility. Contractors, on this view, are licensed to act as self-interested utility maximisers and, having so acted, they are required by the principle of sanctity of contract to respect the bargains that they have struck. However, the market-individualist view of contract as a freely agreed exchange imposes some constraints on the unbridled pursuit of self-interest. In particular, the law of contract must regulate against fraud and coercion, the former because it undermines the reality of agreement, the latter because it is inconsistent with the notion of a *free* transaction. For present purposes, the question of whether or not there is ultimately any coherent deep justification for these minimal restrictions on the advancement of self-interest need not trouble us[1]. Rather, what we should note is the importance to static market-individualism that the regulation of fraud and coercion should respect two principles: first, that the lines between fraud and non-fraud, and between coercion and non-coercion, should be drawn clearly so that the ground rules for contracting remain bright and sharp; and, secondly, that the lines should be drawn in such a position that they offer no encouragement to contractors who, having made bad bargains, are looking for excuses for non-performance.

1   Cf Kronman 'Contract Law and Distributive Justice' (1980) 89 Yale LJ 472; and, generally, see para 2.18.

6.9   By contrast, in the case of dynamic market-individualism, the paradigms of market-individualism—contracting as self-interested dealing; contract as exchange; contract as free agreement—are qualified by commercial practice and opinion. One conspicuous example of such qualification can be seen in the adoption of an overriding requirement of good faith in the performance and enforcement of contracts. Thus, in his seminal paper on the good faith provisions of the Uniform Commercial Code, E. Allan Farnsworth argued that the criterion of good faith should be constituted by reasonable commercial standards of fair dealing in the trade[1]. Similarly, in the Australian case of *Renard Constructions (ME) Property Ltd v Minister for Public Works*[2], Priestley JA said:

> [P]eople generally, including judges and other lawyers, from all strands of the community, have grown used to the courts applying standards of fairness to contract which are wholly consistent with the existence in all contracts of a duty upon the parties of good faith and fair dealing in its performance. In my view this is in these days the expected standard, and *anything less is contrary to prevailing community expectations.*[3]

In other words, there is a general expectation that contractors should deal fairly and act in good faith which crystallises into more specific views about how far self-interested opportunism, shirking, manipulation and the like, should be restricted. Of course, the expectations of commercial contractors might fluctuate and, indeed, might reflect underlying economic pressures—for example, we might find that commercial opinion expects quite high levels of co-operation where trading conditions are stable but that its expectation of co-operation is significantly lower where the economy is in recession[4]. At all events, the dynamic market-individualist will judge it appropriate that the law should follow the general drift of commercial expectation whether it be relatively restrictive or relatively permissive in relation to contractors prioritising their self-interest.

The concept of free agreement, too, may be qualified in a dynamic market-individualist regime. For example, whereas static market-individualism takes a transaction as being freely made in the absence of very obvious forms of coercion, dynamic market-individualism must make provision for those more subtle forms of pressure that commercial opinion regards as improper. Such provision could be made within the terms of a broad-ranging good faith requirement. In the modern English law of contract, however, provision has been made in the form of a doctrine of economic duress. Ever since the landmark decision in *The Atlantic Baron*[5], when the doctrine was first accepted, there has been a difficult question about how the line is to be drawn between economic duress and legitimate commercial pressure. Naturally, for the static market-individualist, such doctrinal indeterminacy is a cause for concern. However, for the dynamic market-individualist, such indeterminacy is a mark of doctrinal sophistication as the law attempts to be more sensitive to commercial opinion.

Another example of the law taking a harder look at whether agreement is free can be found in the modern regulation of unfair terms—an area that we have touched on several times already[6]. For static market-individualists, there are obvious dangers in conferring a judicial discretion to strike out unreasonable terms. However, for dynamic market-individualists such a discretion (as ever guided by commercial opinion) may be justifiable where the terms have not been freely agreed. Generally, it is accepted that standardised transacting is efficient and precludes individually negotiated agreement. Moreover, it is accepted that there are various kinds of standard terms (or arrangements of terms) that would pass as normal. However, where particular terms stand out as abnormal, a question is raised about whether such terms have been freely agreed and the onus passes to the party seeking to rely on such terms to demonstrate that they were freely agreed upon. There are a number of doctrinal expressions of this idea but, in England, the 'reasonableness requirement' of the Unfair Contract Terms Act 1977 is the most significant double-check on whether agreement has been genuinely free.

1   Farnsworth, 'Good Faith Performance and Commercial Reasonableness Under the Uniform Commercial Code' (1962–63) 30 U Chi LR 666; and, generally, see the discussion of a good faith requirement in chapter 5.
2   (1992) 26 NSWLR 234.
3   (1992) 26 NSWLR 234 at 268, emphasis supplied.
4   See eg Galanter and Rogers 'The Transformation of American Business Disputing? Some Preliminary Observations' (paper presented at the Annual Meeting of the Law and Society Association, Colorado, 1988); and Vincent-Jones 'Contract Litigation in England and Wales 1975–91: A Transformation in Business Disputing?' [1993] Civil Justice Quarterly 337.
5   *North Ocean Shipping Co v Hyundai Construction Co, The Atlantic Baron* [1979] QB 705.
6   See esp paras 2.11–2.16, 3.1–3.4 and 4.7–4.9.

Case law indications

6.10   One of the pillars of static market-individualism is the idea that contract is constituted by exchange. Where there is no exchange, there is no contract. From this simple idea, two doctrinal consequences of enormous importance follow. First, it follows that there is no contract where the parties have not yet reached the moment of exchange (even though they are working towards it). And, secondly, it follows that, even though the parties are already joined by an exchange, there is no fresh contract where the terms are modified without there being a fresh exchange. In the recent case law, these consequences (and the central idea itself) have been significantly qualified by two major decisions of the Court of Appeal, the *Blackpool and Fylde Aero Club*[1] case and *Williams v Roffey Bros & Nicholls (Contractors) Ltd*[2].

In the *Blackpool and Fylde Aero Club* case, it will be recalled, the Court of Appeal held that the club could hold the defendant council to its advertised procedures for the consideration of tenders submitted in relation to a local airport concession. According to Sir Thomas Bingham, the council was not free to ignore its own published tendering guidelines (for example, by accepting a tender well before the deadline for tenders to be submitted had been reached, or by accepting a tender received well after the deadline) otherwise 'there would in my view be an unacceptable discrepancy between the law of contract and the confident assumptions of commercial parties'[3]. Moreover, in holding that the club's understanding of the tendering process raised an entitlement, 'not as a matter of mere expectation but of contractual right'[4], that the council should abide by its own rules, the court followed the line taken in a number of other jurisdictions that the law of contract is capable of giving at least some protection to the interests of commercial parties who are working their way towards an exchange[5].

If the *Blackpool and Fylde Aero Club* case breaks new ground in relation to pre-contractual reliance and expectation, *Williams v Roffey Bros & Nicholls (Contractors) Ltd* follows suit in relation to reliance and expectation encouraged during the performance of a contract. As is well known, the question in *Williams v Roffey* was whether the main contractors were contractually bound by their promise to pay the carpenter sub-contractors *additional* sums (over and above the agreed contractual price) for the contract work. In holding that the main contractors were so bound, provided that their promise was freely given and procured some practical advantage to the promisors, the Court of Appeal departed from the settled principle that A's promise to perform (or the actual performance of) his existing contractual duty to B is no consideration for a promise by B to pay additional sums to A[6]. Although the decision gives rise to a host of doctrinal concerns[7], for present purposes, we need not agonise about whether it is better to say that the Court of Appeal revised the traditional concept of an 'exchange' (as embedded in the English doctrine of consideration) or simply that it effectively dispensed with the requirement of an exchange for a binding variation within an existing contractual relationship— for, either way, the court must be seen as taking its lead from the expectations of commercial contractors rather than from the classical rule-book associated with the static form of market-individualism[8].

1   [1990] 3 All ER 25; and see para 1.10.
2   [1990] 1 All ER 512; and see para 1.14.
3   [1990] 3 All ER 25, 30.
4   [1990] 3 All ER 25, 30.
5   The standard examples of protecting pre-contractual reliance are *Hoffman v Red Owl Stores* 26 Wis 2d 683 (1965) and *Walton's Stores (Interstate) Ltd v Maher* (1988) 76 ALR 513. See, too, the Canadian Supreme Court decision

in *The Queen in Right of Ontario et al v Ron Engineering and Construction Eastern Ltd* (1981) 119 DLR (3d) 267.

6   See Adams and Brownsword 'Contract, Consideration and the Critical Path' (1990) 53 MLR 536; and Halson 'Sailors, Sub-Contractors and Consideration' (1990) 106 LQR 183.

7   See eg Chen-Wishart 'Consideration: Practical Benefit and the Emperor's New Clothes' in Beatson and Freedman (eds) *Good Faith and Fault in Contract Law* (1995) 123; and Carter, Phang, and Poole 'Reactions to *Williams v Roffey*' (1995) 8 JCL 248.

8   See, too, *Anangel Atlas Compania Naviera SA v Ishikawajima-Harima Heavy Industries Co Ltd (No 2)* [1990] 2 Lloyd's Rep 526.

6.11   With the weakening of the consideration requirement, we might also expect some qualification of the privity doctrine. In both Canada and Australia, there have been some important head-on confrontations with the privity principle (particularly invited by the linked involvement of many contracting parties in commercial projects such as construction and carriage)[1]; and, in England, the recent case law takes place in the knowledge that the Law Commission has recommended legislative reform of the doctrine[2]. So, for example, in both *The Pioneer Container*[3] and *White v Jones*[4], we find Lord Goff remarking that it is now open to question how long the basic privity principles will be maintained in all their strictness; and we will consider these two cases at some length in a later section[5]. Here, we can review another of the recent departures from strict privity thinking, the decision of the Court of Appeal in *Darlington Borough Council v Wiltshier Northern Ltd*[6].

The essential dispute in *Darlington* concerned alleged defects in a building, the Dolphin Centre, built for the council by Wiltshier. However, before this dispute could be settled, a preliminary issue arose: namely, even if Wiltshier were in breach of the building contract, would Darlington be entitled to recover substantial damages? This preliminary question arose because Darlington were not actually a party to the building contract—to avoid (quite lawfully) the borrowing constraints of the Local Government Act 1972, Darlington financed the deal via Morgan Grenfell who thus became parties to the building contract with Wiltshier. However, as Steyn LJ (as he then was) emphasised, the building contract was for the benefit of Darlington and there was no doubt that 'that is how all three parties saw it[7].' Accordingly, but for the doctrine of privity of contract, Darlington could simply have sued on the contract made for its benefit.

Given that there was de facto a tripartite arrangement here— which, to repeat Steyn LJ's emphasis, was how the parties themselves saw it—the privity doctrine involved breaking up the contracts in a somewhat artificial way (particularly bearing in mind that the benefit of the building contract had been duly assigned to Darlington by Morgan Grenfell). Ignoring privity, one might simply have argued that Darlington had a free-standing direct claim on the building contract. However, the court took a less radical step, holding that, in principle, Morgan Grenfell could have claimed substantial damages (even though they suffered no loss) and so Darlington, as assignees, had a similar claim. In so holding, the court adopted the approach ventured by the House of Lords in *Linden Gardens Trust Ltd v Lenesta Sludge Disposals Ltd*[8] according to which there are, exceptionally, some circumstances in which a plaintiff may recover damages for the benefit of a third party—quite what those circumstances are remains to be fully determined, but the underlying idea is that the exception will apply to provide 'a remedy where no other would be available to a person sustaining loss which under a rational legal system ought to be compensated by the person who has caused it[9].' No doubt, there is room for debate about what a rational legal system might require[10]. In the context of the *Darlington* case, however, it is pretty clear that a rational system will not tolerate a meritorious claim falling down some doctrinal black-hole, as counsel put it[11], not least where such an outcome is out of line with reasonable commercial expectations[12].

1   See Adams and Brownsword 'Privity and the Concept of a Network Contract' (1990) 10 Legal Studies 12; and 'Privity of Contract—That Pestilential Nuisance' (1993) 56 MLR 722.
2   See *Privity of Contract: Contracts for the Benefit of Third Parties* (Law Com Consultation Paper No 121) (1991); *Privity of Contract: Contracts for the Benefit of Third Parties* (Law Com No 242) (Cm 3329, July 1996); and Adams, Beyleveld, and Brownsword, 'Privity of Contract—the Benefits and the Burdens of Law Reform' (1997) 60 MLR 238. At the time of writing, the Contracts (Rights of Third Parties) Bill is making its way through Parliament.
3   *KH Enterprise (cargo owners) v Pioneer Container (owners), The Pioneer Container* [1994] 2 All ER 250, 255–256.
4   [1995] 1 All ER 691, 705.
5   See chapter 8.
6   [1995] 1 WLR 68.
7   [1995] 1 WLR 68 at p 76.
8   [1993] 3 All ER 417.
9   See Lord Diplock in *Albacruz (cargo owners) v Albazero (owners), The Albazero* [1977] AC 774, 846–847.
10 See chapter 9; and see Adams and Brownsword *Key Issues in Contract* (1995) passim but esp ch 10.
11 [1995] 1 WLR 68, 79. See, too, *Alfred McAlpine Construction Ltd v Panatown Ltd* (1998) 58 Con LR 46.
12 Of course, to the extent that expectations are judged to be reasonable or unreasonable relative to formal contract doctrine, the expectations of the claimants in *Darlington* might be thought to be unreasonable (*Linden Gardens* not having been decided at the time of the *Darlington* contracts. Cf para 9.21).

6.12   Before we turn from the traces of dynamic market-individualism evident in the recent case law, we should not forget the willingness of the Court of Appeal in the *BSkyB* case[1] to imply a term for good faith in the performance of the contract. Although this did not affect the outcome of the case, it symbolises a readiness to adjudicate from within the structure of the parties' own relationship rather than from a perspective external to the context and purpose of the transaction. This, it is suggested, is the sign of a court ready to move from the static to the dynamic market-individualist approach.

1 *Philips Electronique Grand Public SA v British Sky Broadcasting Ltd* [1995] EMLR 472; *Philips International BV v British Satellite Broadcasting Ltd* (19 October 1994, unreported) (see para 5.16).

6.13 If the recent case law bears some imprints of dynamic market-individualist thinking, it equally bears the continuing imprint of static market-individualism. Three illustrations will suffice: *Walford v Miles*[1], *Regalian Properties plc v London Dockland Development Corpn*[2], and *Re Selectmove Ltd*[3].

1 [1992] 1 All ER 453.
2 [1995] 1 All ER 1005.
3 [1995] 2 All ER 531.

6.14 In *Walford v Miles*, as is well known, the House of Lords emphatically rejected the suggestion from the Court of Appeal that English law might recognise the validity of an agreement to negotiate in good faith. In a particularly striking speech, Lord Ackner proclaimed that the very idea of 'a duty to carry on negotiations in good faith is inherently repugnant to the adversarial position of the parties when involved in negotiations[1].' Whilst, therefore, English law recognises the validity of clearly defined 'lock-out' agreements[2], it does not recognise the validity of 'lock-in' agreements even when backed by an understanding that negotiations are to be conducted in good faith. For orthodox contract lawyers, not only are such agreements too uncertain to enforce, they are at odds (as Lord Ackner reminds us) with the adversarial ethic that is the underpinning of static market-individualism[3].

1 [1992] 1 All ER 453, 460–461.
2 *Pitt v PHH Asset Management Ltd* [1993] 4 All ER 961.
3 Cf *Coal Cliff Collieries Property Ltd v Sijehama Property Ltd* (1991) 24 NSWLR 1, and *Queensland Electricity Generating Board v New Hope Collieries Pty Ltd* [1989] 1 Lloyd's Rep 205. For discussion of the latter in contrast to *Walford v Miles*, see McKendrick, 'The Regulation of Long-Term Contracts in English Law' in Beatson and Friedmann (eds) *Good Faith and Fault in Contract Law* (1995) 305, 317–321.

6.15 The thinking in *Walford v Miles* indicates that contractors are largely expected to look after their own interests during the negotiation of a contract. At this stage, the risk is not simply that one's fellow negotiator might prefer to close the deal with a third party (as in *Walford v Miles* itself); for, even if no third party is involved, an expected contract may fail to eventuate, leaving the negotiating party with considerable pre-contractual expenses. Such a situation arose in *Regalian Properties plc v London Dockland Development Corpn.* There, in summer 1986, Regalian had entered into an agreement 'subject to contract' with London Dockland Development Corporation for a proposed residential development of land in Wapping. Some two years later, for a variety of reasons, the contract had not been finalised—in part, this was because of difficulties in securing vacant possession of the whole of the site, in part, it was because the fluctuations in land values prompted a number of reviews of the price to be paid by Regalian. At all events, by late 1988, the slump in the residential property market was such that Regalian realised that it would be unwise to proceed with the project and negotiations between the parties duly lapsed. The question to which the failed negotiations gave rise was whether Regalian were entitled to be reimbursed by London Dockland Development Corporation for just under £2.9m spent on professional fees (particularly architects' fees in respect of preparing the designs) in pursuance of the agreement 'subject to contract' and in anticipation of the contract itself.

Regalian pleaded their claim for reimbursement in restitution, conceding that there could be no straightforward contractual action on an agreement 'subject to contract'. The restitutionary claim, however, was no more straightforward, for Rattee J declined to hold that Regalian's expenses were incurred for the benefit of London Dockland Development Corporation—rather, the expenses were incurred with a view to putting Regalian into a position to start work on the development if and when the contract was finalised. This left Regalian to clutch at the principle of good faith, particularly as applied in this context by Sheppard J in *Sabemo Pty Ltd v North Sydney Municipal Council*[1], the gist of which is that negotiating parties are to be protected where one party 'unilaterally decides to abandon the project, not for any reason associated with bona fide disagreement concerning the terms of the contract to be entered into, but for reasons which, however valid, pertain only to his own position and do not relate at all to that of the other party.' Rattee J. ruled that this principle was not applicable on the facts, because the Corporation had not unilaterally abandoned the project. More significantly, however, he suggested that the *Sabemo* principle should not be extended to situations where the parties realised that they incurred negotiation costs at their own risk:

I appreciate that the English law of restitution should be flexible and capable of continuous development. However, I see no good reason to extend it to apply some such principle as adopted by Sheppard J in the *Sabemo* case to facts such as those of the present case, where, however much the parties expect a contract between them to materialise, both enter negotiations expressly ... on terms that each party is free to withdraw from the negotiations at any time. Each party to such negotiations must be taken to know ... that pending the conclusion of a binding contract any cost incurred by him in preparation for the intended contract will be incurred at his own risk in the sense that he will have no recompense for those costs if no contract results.[2]

Although it was agreed in *Regalian* that negotiations covered by the rubric 'subject to contract', entailed that either party 'was free to walk away from [the] negotiations, however little [the other party] expected it to do so'[3], there is an important difference in principle between walking away for any reason whatsoever and walking away for a reason that keeps faith with the integrity of the negotiating situation. What Sheppard J sought to draw out in the *Sabemo* case was just this point, that a bad faith withdrawal from negotiations (just like a bad faith withdrawal from a concluded contract) is defined by the reasons motivating that withdrawal[4]—which, of course, is not to say that an inquiry into a party's reasons for withdrawal will always prove to be straightforward in practice[5]. Whereas static market-individualist thinking prefers to cling to the certainties supposedly associated with key doctrinal signals—such as 'subject to contract' or, in the context of withdrawal for breach, breach of 'condition'—it is distinctive of dynamic market-individualist thinking that the law should attempt to track the way in which commercial people themselves discriminate between legitimate and illegitimate reasons for action.

1   [1977] 2 NSWLR 880, esp at 900–903.
2   [1995] 1 All ER 1005, 1024.
3   Per Rattee J [1995] 1 All ER 1005, 1024.
4   See Burton 'Breach of Contract and the Common Law Duty to Perform in Good Faith' (1980–81) 94 Harv LR 369; and Brownsword, 'Retrieving Reasons, Retrieving Rationality? A New Look at the Right to Withdraw for Breach of Contract' (1992) 5 JCL 83.
5   See Cohen 'Pre-Contractual Duties: Two Freedoms and the Contract to Negotiate' in Beatson and Friedmann (eds) *Good Faith and Fault in Contract Law* (1995) 25; Waddams 'Good Faith, Unconscionability and Reasonable Expectations' (1995) 9 JCL 55, 63–64; and generally, see paras 5.6 and 5.24.

6.16   The third case is *Re Selectmove*, where the principal question was whether the Inland Revenue was bound by a promise allegedly made that it would allow Selectmove Ltd. to pay off tax arrears at a rate of £1,000 a month. At first instance, it was held that, in the absence of any consideration moving from the company to the Revenue for this concession, the promise was not contractually binding—indeed, given the decision of the House of Lords in *Foakes v Beer*[1], such was trite law. On appeal, counsel for the company argued that, in the light of the reasoning in *Williams v Roffey*, and *Foakes v Beer* notwithstanding, the point could no longer be regarded as settled. To this, Peter Gibson LJ (giving judgment on behalf of the court) responded:

> I see the force of the argument, but the difficulty that I feel with it is that if the principle of *Williams'* case is to be extended to an obligation to make payment, it would in effect leave the principle in *Foakes v Beer* without any application. When a creditor and a debtor who are at arm's length reach agreement on the payment of the debt by instalments to accommodate the debtor, the creditor will no doubt always see a practical benefit to himself in so doing. In the absence of authority there would be much to be said for the enforceability of such a contract. But that was a matter expressly considered in *Foakes v Beer* yet held not to constitute good consideration in law. *Foakes v Beer* was not even referred to in *Williams'* case, and it is in my judgment impossible, consistently with the doctrine of precedent, for this Court to extend the principle of *Williams'* case to any circumstances governed by the principle of *Foakes v Beer*. If that extension is to be made, it must be by the House of Lords or, perhaps even more appropriately, by Parliament after consideration by the Law Commission.[2]

On one reading, given a free hand, the court might have brought the law into line with practical commercial sense; but, in fact, the court's formalistic approach precluded any deviation from the static market-individualist approach represented by the precedents. For the present, then, dynamic market-individualism must give way to the authority of the cases, leaving the law in a somewhat contradictory state. On the one hand, *Williams v Roffey* seems to cover (freely agreed but gratuitous) variations in favour of the creditor; yet, on the other hand, (freely agreed but gratuitous) variations in favour of the debtor remain covered by *Foakes v Beer* and the classical requirement of exchange[3]. One of the cornerstone features of static market-individualism thus retains a tenuous grip on the doctrine of consideration but, for the dynamic market-individualist, there is little doubt that the Court of Appeal in *Re Selectmove* must be seen as having missed an opportunity presented by *Williams v Roffey* to keep contract law closer in touch with commercial practice.

1   (1884) 9 App Cas 605.
2   [1995] 2 All ER 531, 538.

3   See, too, *Re C (a debtor)* (11 May1994, unreported, CA), discussed in Carter, Phang, and Poole, 'Reactions to *Williams v Roffey*' (1995) 8 JCL 248 at 257–258.

Dynamic market-individualism as the ruling ideology

6.17   There are two principal respects in which dynamic market-individualism departs from static market-individualism. First, the former takes a more flexible view of the situations in which contractual obligations may arise; and, secondly, it takes a potentially more restrictive view of the extent to which a contracting party may privilege its own economic interests (articulated doctrinally in the form of requirements of good faith, fair dealing, reasonableness, and the like). In both respects, however, dynamic market-individualism takes its lead from the commercial community—on the market side, it is as flexible as the relevant community allows and, on the individualistic side, it is as liberal or as restrictive as that community requires.

6.18   It is tempting to see the significance of dynamic market-individualism in its recognition of the concept of legitimate expectation—indeed, not merely in its recognition of this concept, but in its placing of legitimate expectation at the core of its scheme of values. After all, within dynamic market-individualism, it is the expectations of the commercial community that determine where contractual obligation arises and where the line is to be drawn between permissible and impermissible transactional behaviour. It is possible, however, to present static market-individualism, too, as having a concern with legitimate expectation, in the sense that it is recognised that parties may form legitimate expectations on the basis of the declared (static) ground rules for contracting. Putting the matter this way, both static and dynamic market-individualism are concerned with the protection of legitimate expectations; but the difference is that the former treats the formal law as the exclusive source of such expectations, while the latter treats the informal practice of the commercial community as the relevant source (the formal law simply reinforcing such expectations).

6.19   Even if the simple recognition of the concept of legitimate expectation is not directly the key to distinguishing between static and dynamic market-individualism, *the way in which this concept is implicated in the ideologies* highlights an important distinction. In principle, contract doctrine (and its accompanying ideology) might try to set a framework for (and channel) commercial practice or it might try merely to formalise practice. If we call an ideology of the former kind an independent contractual ideology and an ideology of the latter kind a dependent contractual ideology then, whereas static market-individualism is an independent contractual ideology, dynamic market-individualism is largely a dependent contractual ideology—and this gives us a fundamental insight into the complex way in which the modern law of contract seeks to protect the parties' reasonable expectations by reference not only to an imposed regime of background rights and obligations but also by reference to the understandings encouraged by particular contractual settings and by specific inter-personal dealings[1].

1   Cf Steyn 'Contract Law: Fulfilling the Reasonable Expectations of Honest Men' (1997) 113 LQR 433.

6.20   As the doctrinal landmarks associated with static market-individualism are gradually eroded (the doctrine of precedent notwithstanding), we can expect the tides of dynamic market-individualism to run ever more strongly. Does it follow, therefore, that dynamic market-individualism is set to become the ruling ideology of contract? Again, to return to our opening remarks in this section, the general law of contract in the present century has been dominated by two ideologies, market-individualism and consumer-welfarism. The consumer side of consumer-welfarism does not, however, present any serious opposition to the rise of dynamic market-individualism; for the law of consumer contracts must be seen nowadays as a regulatory regime in its own right, severable for the most part from the general law of contract; and the welfarist side of consumer-welfarism is under-developed in its application to commercial contracting[1]. It should not be thought, however, that the rise of dynamic market-individualism might occur, so to speak, faute de mieux. On the contrary, the shift to dynamic market-individualism (in conjunction with the severability of the law of consumer contracts) is very much in line with the modern view that legal doctrine should at least be 'acceptable' without necessarily being underwritten by any detached theory that renders it legitimate in a free-standing sense[2]. It follows that if there is to be a ruling ideology on the commercial wing of contract law, dynamic market-individualism is quite plainly the leading contender to emerge from the modern period.

1   See Brownsword 'The Philosophy of Welfarism and its Emergence in the Modern English Law of Contract' in Brownsword, Howells and Wilhelmsson (eds) *Welfarism in Contract Law* (1994) 21.
2   See eg Teubner 'Substantive and Reflexive Elements in Modern Law' (1983) 17 Law and Society Review 239; and Brownsword, 'The Limits of Freedom of Contract and the Limits of Contract Theory' (1995) 22 Journal of Law and Society 259.

Beyond dynamic market-individualism

6.21 The rise of dynamic market-individualism and the (relative) decline of its static counterpart should caution us, however, against assuming that the ideologies of contract are written in the skies. The ideologies of contract are subject to the ebb and flow of contemporary beliefs, values and attitudes[1]; and, already, some contract theorists are speculating about the shape of the 'post-modern' law of contract[2]. In the present context, this invites speculation about what might lie beyond dynamic market-individualism.

1   See eg Atiyah *From Principles to Pragmatism* (1978); and *The Rise and Fall of Freedom of Contract* (1979).
2   See eg Wilhelmsson 'Questions for a Critical Contract Law—and a Contradictory Answer: Contract as Social Cooperation' in Wilhelmsson (ed) *Perspectives of Critical Contract Law* (1993) 9; and *Social Contract Law and European Integration* (1995).

6.22   Consider, for example, art 1.107 of the Lando Commission's Principles of European Contract Law, according to which '[e]ach party owes the other a duty to co-operate in order to give full effect to the contract'[1]. The Commission gives four illustrative examples of where there is a duty to co-operate[2]. In the first two examples, one party's ability to perform is contingent on 'co-operative' performance by the other party—one illustration being a sale of goods contract under which the buyer must co-operate by nominating the vessel on which the goods are to be carried, and the other being a building contract under which the client must co-operate by obtaining a building licence (even if the contract does not impose an express obligation on the client to obtain the licence). These examples, like the Commission's fourth example of a buyer who refuses to accept delivery, are fairly conservative illustrations of a co-operative requirement. The Commission's third illustrative example, however, is less straightforward:

> *Illustration 3*: Subcontractor S of country A is about to send some of his staff to perform his duty to Contractor C, also from A, to assist in building a dam in country Y. C learns that the government of Y intends to detain any citizens from A who are found in Y as hostages, in order to exert pressure on the government of A to release some of Y's citizens who have been detained in A charged with terrorism. C has a duty to inform S of the risks involved in sending his staff to Y.

If C's information is accurate, it looks as though the dam project will have to be abandoned anyway. However, if we try to generalise this illustrative example, the question is how far the duty of co-operation requires one contractor to disclose information to a fellow contractor where that information is material to the latter's (physical and/or economic) interests. If the duty to co-operate is employed within a framework of dynamic market-individualist thinking, the scope and depth of the duty to co-operate will vary from one business context to another[3]. However, on a more ambitious reading, art 1.107 might be taken as a pointer to a thoroughgoing co-operativism, in which the institution of contract itself is seen as a vehicle for solidifying trust and mutual support and assistance[4]. As Hugh Collins has said:

> If ... one regards the law of contract as offering an opportunity for entering into binding long-term commitments with others, an opportunity which augments the freedom of the individual, then ... calculations of self-interest at every stage in the transaction should not be permitted to subvert the value of the institution of contracts. Instead, the law must impose certain duties of co-operation in the formation and performance of contracts, which reflect the need to secure reliable and worthwhile opportunities for market exchanges.[5]

Such an expanded concept of co-operation, of course, is not the only possibilty. Indeed, far from moving in this direction, the law might go into reverse, reacting against the uncertainties of commercial practice and opinion and returning to a detached bright line rule ideology based on the classical model of self-interested exchange.

1   Lando and Beale (eds), *The Principles of European Contract Law: Part I* (1995).
2   Lando and Beale at pp 59–60. The Commission also gives two illustrative examples of co-operation that lie beyond the duty. One example is of a contract under which a party buys a ticket for the theatre: having paid for the ticket, the buyer has no duty to 'co-operate' by collecting the ticket or attending the performance. The other example is the sale of goods contract mentioned in the text except that the buyer's duty to nominate the vessel does not arise until the buyer has the seller's notification of intention to ship the goods: until the buyer is so notified, the buyer has no duty to 'co-operate' by nominating the vessel.
3   In the accompanying notes (Lando and Beale at p 61), the duty to co-operate in English law is tied to the business efficacy test for implied terms. As we have seen, in para 1.72, this can be related to a dynamic market-individualist approach. The notes also state that the 'strongest recognition perhaps has been in relation to contracts of employment', citing *Secretary of State for Employment v ASLEF (No 2)* [1972] 2 QB 455. More recently, the obvious contrast in employment contexts, at least in relation to an employer's duty to co-operate, is between *Reid v Rush and Tompkins Group plc* [1989] 3 All ER 228 (weak duty to co-operate) and *Scally v Southern Health and Social Services Board* [1992] 1AC 294 as well as *Malik v Bank of Credit and Commerce International SA (in liquidation)* [1997] 3 All ER 1 (strong duty to co-operate). See further, Collins 'Implied Duty to Give Information During Performance of Contracts' (1992) 55 MLR 556; and Rideout, 'Implied Terms in the Employment Relationship' in Halson (ed) *Exploring the Boundaries of Contract Law* (1996) 119.

4   Cf Reiter, 'Good Faith in Contracts' (1983) 17 Valparaiso ULR 705.
5   Collins, *The Law of Contract* (3rd edn, 1997) 33. And, see, Brownsword, '"Good Faith in Contracts" Revisited' (1996) 49 CLP 111, 134–151.

6.23   As for the present, we can be less speculative: two tendencies are definitely at work in shaping the modern law. First, the commercial law of contract is working its way free of the mould set by static market-individualism to become a regulatory regime dictated to a considerable extent by the informal expectations embedded in commercial practice and opinion—in other words, the emerging regime is inspired by a dynamic market-individualist approach. It must be remembered, too, that the modern law of contract is shaped as much by legislation as by precedent, and that Parliamentary time is readily available to meet pressing commercial needs[1]. Secondly, the modern law of contract on the commercial side, no less than on the consumer side, is subject to the pressures created by what we might term the 'globalisation' of contract law. Whether we are considering regional pressure to harmonise contract law in Europe, or the pressure to justify English doctrine when (as increasingly happens) it is set alongside the regulatory features of other legal systems, it is no longer plausible to suppose that English law can be immunised against change occurring elsewhere in the legal world. It is to pressures of this kind that we turn in the next section.

1   Cf Lord Goff's depiction of the Carriage of Goods by Sea Act 1992 as 'a sweeping statutory reform, powered by the needs of commerce': *White v Jones* [1995] 2AC 207, 265.

CHAPTER 7

The Globalisation of Contract Law

The phenomenon of globalisation

7.1 We concluded the last section by suggesting that the English law of contract is subject to pressures created by 'globalisation'. The phenomenon of globalisation, however, can be understood in several senses. It can mean, for instance, that it is possible nowadays for contractors to simulate face-to-face dealing even though they are physically separated by great distances—an observation that perhaps seems all too obvious when parties commonly use telephones and fax machines to negotiate and conclude contracts. However, in the late twentieth century, globalisation implies rather more than this: for, the development of sophisticated computer, telecommunications, and information technology is putting in place a revolutionary new electronic worldwide marketplace. As a recent report from the World Trade Organization[1] puts it:

> These modern technologies are being combined, especially through the Internet, to link millions of people in every corner of the world. Communications are increasingly unburdened from the constraints of geography and time. Information spreads more widely and more rapidly than ever before. Deals are struck, transactions completed, and decisions taken in a time-frame that would have seemed simply inconceivable a few years ago.[2]

In this world of electronic commerce (which, in a broad sense, covers the use of telephones and faxes, television shopping channels, electronic payment and money transfer systems, Electronic Data Interchange, and the Internet), it is the Internet in particular that is seen as opening up new contractual possibilities:

> [W]ith the Internet all elements of a commercial transaction can be conducted on an interactive basis with one or many people, unconstrained by time and space, in a multimedia environment with sound, image and text transmission, and at relatively low (and still declining) costs.[3]

With these new possibilities, however, there also come new challenges; and, already, the literature on the regulation of electronic forms of commerce is growing apace[4].

Because electronic commerce will make cross-border shopping viable at the flick of a switch, one of the challenges will be to put in place a calculable and secure legal superstructure that meets the needs of those contractors who make use of the emerging technological infrastructure[5]. Although our concern, in the present section, is not with electronic commerce as such, it is with globalisation in the sense of a process of putting in place a unified law of contract to regulate transactions wherever they occur[6].

1   Bacchetta Low, Mattoo, Schuknecht, Wager, and Wehrens *Electronic Commerce and the Role of the WTO* (1998).
2   *Electronic Commerce and the Role of the WTO* p 1.
3   *Electronic Commerce and the Role of the WTO* p 5.
4   The most important international regulatory guide is the UNCITRAL Model Law on Electronic Commerce. Its influence can be seen in many local draft laws: see e g the Report of the Electronic Commerce Expert Group to the Attorney General of Australia *Electronic Commerce: Building the Legal Framework* (31 March 1998); and the New Zealand Law Commission's *Report 50: Electronic Commerce* (http://www.lawcom.govt.nz/EComm/R50). The importance of consumer confidence and protection is a theme of the OECD's work: see eg *Gateways to the Global Market: Consumers and Electronic Commerce* (1998); and it is an issue highlighted in the Australian Competition and Consumer Commission's Discussion Paper *The Global Enforcement Challenge: the Enforcement of Consumer Protection Laws in a Global Marketplace* (August 1997) (http://www.accc.gov.au/docs/ global/httoc.htm). For general academic surveys, see eg Edwards and Waelde (eds) *Law and the Internet* (1997) Part III; de Zwart, 'Electronic Commerce: Promises, Problems and Proposals' (1998) 21 UNSWLJ 305; and Brownsword and Howells 'When Surfers Start to Shop: Internet Commerce and Contract Law' (1999) 19 LS (forthcoming).
5   The European Union, for example, having declared its intention to create a coherent legal framework for the Single Market by the year 2000 (COM (97) 157 final, 16.04.97) has published a draft Directive on a Common Framework for Electronic Signatures (OJ C325, 23.10.98, p5) as well as a draft Directive on Certain Legal Aspects of Electronic Commerce in the Internal Market (OJ C30, 5.2.99, p4).
6   Cf Collins *The Law of Contract* (3rd edn, 1997) 41–45.

7.2   Unification can arise in more than one way. One way is for there to be a spontaneous convergence as contract law in different jurisidictions evolves towards a common position. To some extent, convergence of this kind can be expected as cross-border transport and trade develops; but such natural processes may be facilitated and accelerated in various ways, particularly (or so one would suppose) by increasing familiarity with the jurisprudence of other legal systems. Another way in which unification might be promoted is by the adoption of a harmonising programme of the kind employed within the EU[1]; and, closely linked to this, harmonisation can be facilitated and supported by the articulation of model codes and restatements—for example, the Principles of European Contract Law[2] (to which we have referred on several occasions in earlier sections). Most directly, of course, unification can be promoted through the offices of bodies such as the International Institute for the Unification of Private Law (UNIDROIT), reflected most recently in the UNIDROIT Principles for International Commercial Contracts[3].

1 See paras 7.7–7.10.
2 See Lando and Beale (eds) *The Principles of European Contract Law* (Part I: Performance, Non-Performance and Remedies) (1995). See, too, the Resolution of the European Parliament on the Harmonization of Certain Sectors of the Private Law of the Member States, OJ C 205/518, 6 May 1994, in which the Parliament called on the Commission, inter alia, to commence work on the possibility of drawing up a Common European Code of Private Law, as well as endorsing continuing support for the work of the Lando Commission.
3 See Furmston 'Unidroit General Principles for International Commercial Contracts' (1996) 10 JCL 11.

7.3 In Europe, the work of the Lando Commission in conjunction with the EU single market programme can be seen as the outstanding pressures for harmonisation; and it is with these developments that we can begin. We can turn then to convergence within the common law world and to the unification of the law concerning international contracts[1].

1 It should not be assumed, of course, that everyone agrees that harmonisation is a good thing. Some argue that each particular legal system has its own distinctive culture, coherence, and identity. See, eg Legrand, 'Against a European Civil Code' (1997) 60 MLR 44; and Hobhouse, 'International Conventions and Commercial Law: The Pursuit of Uniformity' (1990) 106 LQR 530 (discussed at para 1.140). Nor should it be assumed that harmonisation is an unproblematic project: see, eg Teubner, 'Legal Irritants: Good Faith in British Law or How Unifying Law Ends Up in New Divergences' (1998) 61 MLR 11.

The Lando Commission

7.4 The Lando Commission began its work in the mid-1970s, initially attempting to draft a European Uniform Commercial Code, which in due course became the Principles of European Contract Law. In 1995, the Commission published its first volume of the Principles[1], comprising 59 Articles divided into four chapters (namely, General Provisions; Terms and Performance of the Contract; Non-Performance and Remedies in General; and Particular Remedies for Non-Performance). The work of the Commission is far from complete, however. It plans to publish further Principles dealing with 'formation, interpretation and validity of contracts as well as with the authority of agents'[2].

1   Lando and Beale, para 1.126 note 2.
2   Lando and Beale at pxxi.

7.5   According to the Commission, the Principles can be regarded as having 'both immediate and longer-term objectives'[1]. Thus:

> They are available for immediate use by parties making contracts, by courts and arbitrators in deciding contract disputes and by legislators in drafting contract rules whether at the European or the national level. Their longer-term objective is to help bring about the harmonisation of general contract law within the European Community.[2]

The way in which contracting parties might, at once, use the Principles is simply by incorporating a clause to the effect that the contract is to be governed by the Principles of European Contract Law. Similarly, where parties have adopted the *lex mercatoria* (or one of its cognates) to govern their contract, arbitrators could have recourse to the Principles. The Principles are available, too, as a model from which those charged with reforming contract law—whether in the EU or in Central and Eastern Europe—can take their lead. Above all, though, the Commission has been inspired by the need to establish an infrastructure of generally accepted principles on which the harmonisation of contract law within the EU can be grounded. In other words, while the lawmaking bodies within the EU are generating Directives dealing with specific issues, the programme of harmonisation lacks a foundation of agreed general principles and common terminology, and it is this weakness in the process of unification that Lando hopes to repair[3].

1   Lando and Beale pxix.
2   Lando and Beale pxix.
3   See Lando and Beale pxvi.

7.6   Although it is the Commission's intention to articulate principles that enjoy broad acceptance already within Europe, in some respects Lando is playing a vanguard role. Thus, according to Lando:

> The Principles are also intended to be progressive. On many issues covered by national law they may be found to offer a more satisfactory

answer than that which is reached by traditional legal thinking. For example, their provisions relating to the assurance of performance and to the grant of relief where a change of circumstances renders performance of the contract excessively onerous deal in a balanced way with recurrent difficulties on which most national laws are silent.[1]

Covering an omission is one thing. How progressive can the Principles be, though, where the European civilian and common law systems take significantly different views on a particular question, say, with regard to a general doctrine of good faith or the validity of penalty clauses? Here, Lando's aspiration is to offer the Principles as 'a bridge between the civil law and the common law by providing rules designed to reconcile their differing legal philosophies[2]'. So, to take the case of penalty clauses, whereas art 4.508(1) defers to the civilian view by providing that a sum specified to be paid by the contract-breaker to the innocent party in the event of breach is to be awarded irrespective of the latter's actual loss, art 4.508(2) defers to the common law position by providing that the specified sum 'may be reduced to a reasonable amount where it is grossly excessive in relation to the loss resulting from the non-performance and the other circumstances[3]'. With regard to the doctrine of good faith, it is arguable that the Commission has built something of a one-way bridge favouring the civilian view. However, at least within the EU, it might be said that the foundations for this particular bridge had already been laid before the publication of the Principles; for good faith had already been received in English law in the train of the Directives dealing with commercial agents and unfair terms in consumer contracts[4].

1   Lando and Beale pxvi.
2   Lando and Beale pxvii.
3   Similarly, see the Commission's compromise strategy with regard to the remedy of specific performance in relation to non-monetary obligations. Thus, art 4.102(1) defers to the civilian view by providing for the availability of specific performance; but art 4.102(2) defers to the common law view by excluding the remedy where performance would be unlawful or impossible, where it would cause the party in breach unreasonable effort or expense, where it consists in work or services of a personal nature (or depends upon a personal relationship), or where the innocent party may reasonably obtain performance from another source.
4   Directives 86/653/EEC and 93/13/EEC; see para 5.2.

Harmonisation within the European Union

7.7   In *HP Bulmer v J Bollinger SA*[1], Lord Denning MR famously remarked that European Community law 'is like an incoming tide. It flows into the estuaries and up the rivers. It cannot be held back'[2].

Certainly, contracting has not been untouched by this new source of regulation—the public procurement Directives[3], for example, cover the letting of many forms of public contract. Above all, though, it has been in the field of consumer contracting that there has been no holding back the stream of Community law[4]. Directives have been issued dealing with such matters as doorstep selling[5], consumer credit[6], product liability[7], package holidays[8], unfair terms[9]; and distance selling[10]; and a draft Directive is presently under consideration dealing with the sale of consumer goods and associated guarantees[11].

1   [1974] 2 All ER 1226.
2   [1974] 2 All ER 1226 at 1231.
3   Principally, see the Public Works Contracts Regulations 1991, SI 1991/2680, implementing Directive 71/305/EEC as amended by Directive 89/440/EEC, together with Directive 89/665/EEC (so far as material); the Public Services Contracts Regulations 1993 (SI 1993/3228), implementing Directive 92/50/EEC, together with Directive 89/665/EEC (as amended by the former Directive to the extent that it relates to the latter); and the Public Supply Contracts Regulations 1995, SI 1995/201 implementing Directive 93/36/EEC (which Directive consolidates the provisions of Directive 77/62/EEC, as amended, and amends the procedures for awarding public supply contracts so that they conform more closely to similar measures for public services and works contracts (as in Directives 92/50/EEC and 93/37/EEC respectively)). See further, Arrowsmith, 'The Impact of Public Law on the Private Law of Contract' in Halson (ed) *Exploring the Boundaries of Contract* (1996) 3, at pp 11–12.
4   See Beale, 'The "Europeanisation" of Contract Law' in Halson (ed) *Exploring the Boundaries of Contract* (1996) 23.
5   Directive 85/577/EEC.
6   Directive 87/102/EEC, amended by 90/88/EEC.
7   Directive 85/374/EEC, implemented by the Consumer Protection Act 1987.
8   Directive 90/314/EEC, implemented by the Package Travel, Package Holidays and Package Tours Regulations 1992, SI 1992/3288.
9   Directive 93/13/EEC, implemented by the Unfair Terms in Consumer Contracts Regulations 1994, SI 1994/3159.
10   Directive 97/7/EC.
11   See the Commission's Green Paper on *Guarantees for Consumer Goods and After-Sales Services* COM(93) 509; and, subsequently, see COM(95) 520. For discussion, see Beale and Howells 'EC Harmonisation of Consumer Sales Law—A Missed Opportunity?' (1997) 12 JCL 21.

7.8   Norbert Reich, one of the leading commentators on European consumer law, has identified two principal concerns in EC consumer policy: the completion of the internal market and the protection of consumer rights[1]. With regard to the former, having removed the more obvious economic barriers to trade between member states, the Commission needed to remove less obvious barriers, such as uncertainty about the terms of the governing legal regime. Linked to this, securing a fair deal for consumers may be regarded as a good thing in itself; but it, too, is instrumental in establishing a culture in which consumers are sufficiently confident of their position to cross borders and trade anywhere in the market. Such overlapping concerns are clearly apparent in the Directive on Unfair Terms in Consumer Contracts, the Recitals to which declare that, in line with the Community programmes for consumer protection and information policy,

> acquirers of goods and services should be protected against the abuse of power by the seller or supplier, in particular against one-sided standard contracts and the unfair exclusion of essential rights in contracts.

In other words, the Directive is concerned to protect consumer contractors (presumptively weaker parties) against abuses of power. However, the Recitals also declare that where consumers are unaware of the rules of law governing transactions in other member states, such 'lack of awareness may deter them from direct transactions for the purchase of goods or services in another Member State'. And, the Recitals continue:

> Whereas, in order to facilitate the establishment of the internal market and to safeguard the citizen in his role as consumer when acquiring goods and services under contracts which are governed by the laws of Member States other than his own, it is essential to remove unfair terms from those contracts.

Fairly clearly, therefore, the model of the market presupposed by this Directive is one in which consumer rights are respected in all areas of the European internal market, and where the legal regime is standardised so that consumers can cross borders confident in the knowledge that they lose no legal protection by so doing[2].

Given that English contract law already reflects a strong domestic commitment to consumer protection, one view is that we should not expect there to be serious problems in accommodating this aspect of EC consumer policy[3]. Certainly, Directives might occasionally identify and then cover (unintended) gaps in domestic provision; but, generally, they will introduce regulatory frameworks which overlap with and complement the protections already available in English law. Thus, for example, when 'one-sided standard contracts' and 'the unfair exclusion of essential rights' are identified in the Directive on Unfair Terms in Consumer Contracts as particular forms of abuse, this echoes the long-standing concern that consumer contractors should be protected against unfairness arising from standard forms and from exclusion clauses. Accordingly, on this view, if there is a difficulty with EU provisions of this kind, then, it is not so much that they reflect policies or values rejected in English law but simply that they introduce fresh layers of regulation on top of existing provisions. If the European and domestic regimes are not then consolidated in a single piece of legislation, this is untidy and less than satisfactory—indeed, it might even provoke strong critical comment[4]. However, in the long run, the pressure created is to clean up contract law rather than to modify it.

By contrast, where Directives are driven by internal market considerations, they might not stop at consumer protection; and they might not fit so readily into the existing body of domestic contract law. Thus, according to Hugh Beale:

> I anticipate that there will be pressure, at least, to extend direct intervention from Brussels from merely consumer sales to at least some business sales. The rationale which seems to underlie both the Unfair Terms Directive and the proposals on legal guarantees applies just as much to business sales. Here too a form of market failure caused by the cost of discovering the law of other Member States, or of negotiating terms, is likely to hinder the development of the Single Market.[5]

If this is correct, there are likely to be some difficulties as the European programme meets resistance in the English law of contract.

1 Reich 'From Contract to Trade Practices Law: Protection of Consumers' Economic Interests by the EC' in Wilhelmsson (ed) *Perspectives of Critical Contract Law* (1993) 55. See, too, Beale and Howells, para 1.131 note 11, at pp 22–24.
2 See further Brownsword, Howells, and Wilhelmsson, 'Between Market and Welfare: Some Reflections on Article 3 of the EC Directive on Unfair Terms in Consumer Contracts' in Willett (ed) *Aspects of Fairness in Contract* (1996) 25.
3 For a different view, see para 7.10.
4 See Reynolds, 'Unfair Contract Terms' (1994) 110 LQR 1.
5 Beale 'The "Europeanisation" of Contract Law' in Halson (ed) *Exploring the Boundaries of Contract* (1996) 23, at p 31.

7.9 Some indication of the likely impact of EU law outside the field of consumer contracting can be seen in *Page v Combined Shipping and Trading Co Ltd*[1], the first reported case under the Commercial Agents Directive. In *Page*, the plaintiff commercial agent lawfully terminated his agency agreement with the defendants (who had committed a repudiatory breach). The plaintiff claimed compensation for the loss of commission that he would have earned had the defendants properly performed their contractual obligations. Under English common law principles, in cases of this kind, where the defendant contract-breaker has some control over (or choice about) how the contract would have been performed, the assumption is made that the defendant would have performed 'in the way most favourable to himself, that is in the way which most reduces the sum which he will have to pay as damages'[2]. The defendants argued that, under the contract, they could have prevented the plaintiff earning any commission and so his claim should be dismissed.

However, the plaintiff relied on the Commercial Agent (Council Directive) Regulations 1993[3], reg 17(7), to argue that he was entitled to be compensated on the basis of 'proper performance' by the defendants. Bearing in mind that reg4(1) provides that the principal must act in good faith, the plaintiff contended that he was entitled to substantial damages. Given that this was an appeal on a preliminary point of law, the Court of Appeal did not need to decide any more than that the plaintiff had an arguable case for substantial damages—and the court so held.

1   [1997] 3 All ER 656.
2   [1997] 3 All ER 656 at 659 (per Staughton LJ).
3   SI 1993/3053.

7.10 It is not the case, though, that pressure for change might be experienced only where EU law pushes harder for a standard legal umbrella regulating the internal market. For instance, in relation to the Directive on Unfair Terms in Consumer Contracts, art 3.1, which defines a term as unfair if 'contrary to the requirement of good faith, it causes a significant imbalance in the parties' rights and obligations arising under the contract to the detriment of the consumer', there has been considerable speculation about the impact that the concept of good faith might have elsewhere in English contract law[1]. At one level, this is a matter for English judges to decide—although the active enforcement of the implementing Regulations by the Office of Fair Trading probably means that it will be some time before the courts have the opportunity to address the concept of good faith directly[2]. At another level, however, this is a matter for the European Court of Justice to decide; and that court might flesh out the concept of good faith in a way that takes it beyond procedural questions of disclosure and notice currently favoured by English lawyers[3]. In other words, once European concepts find a place in English law, albeit initially in the law of consumer contracts, we cannot be sure that their influence will not spread[4].

1   Generally, see section E above; and see, in particular, Collins, 'Good Faith in European Contract Law' (1994) 14 OJLS 229.
2   See the bulletins issued regularly by the Office of Fair Trading, starting with *Unfair Contract Terms* (Issue No 1, May 1996); and see especially *Unfair Contract Terms* (Issue No. 4, December 1997), which is in the nature of a compendium issue. However, for the view that the OFT's approach to the enforcement of the Regulations is too light, see Colbey, 'Unfair Terms and the OFT' (1998) 148 NLJ 46.
3   Cf Collins, *The Law of Contract* (3rd edn, 1997) 271. The equation of good faith with disclosure and notice, however, is not uniquely English. Thus, art

4(2) of Directive 97/7/EC (on distance selling) prescribes that prior information (as required by art 4(1)) is to be 'provided in a clear and comprehensible manner in any way appropriate to the means of distance communication used, with due regard, in particular, to the principles of good faith in commercial transactions ... '

4   See, too, Mason 'The Impact of Equitable Doctrine on the Law of Contract' (1998) 27 Anglo-Am LR 1 at 3 (on the effect of closer integration with Europe).

Convergence within the common law world

7.11   Having splintered from the evolving contract jurisprudence of civilian Europe[1], English contract law has largely gone its own way from the Nineteenth Century onwards. During this time, not only has English law insulated itself against civilian influence, it has taken little interest in doctrinal developments in other common law jurisdictions. Increasingly, though, English contract lawyers are both aware of such developments and accept that it would be wrong not to be so aware. English law might be special; but parochialism is no longer acceptable[2]. Moreover, where English law is out of line with the position in other common law jurisdictions, this places a question mark against the defensibility of the English view. Two areas in which pressure from other common law systems has created precedents for change in English law are the doctrine of privity of contract and the protection of pre-contractual reliance.

1   Cf Gordley, *The Philosophical Origins of Modern Contract Doctrine* (1991). It should not be thought, however, that the legal systems of civilian Europe were any less inward-looking; there, too, centrifugal forces were at work (see Basedow, 'The Renascence of Uniform Law: European Contract Law and its Components' paper presented to SPTL Annual Conference, University of Warwick, September 1997, p 1).

2   See eg Reynolds 'Drawing the Strings Together' in Birks (ed) *The Frontiers of Liability: Volume 2* (1994) 156; and see Beatson and Friedmann 'Introduction: From "Classical" to Modern Contract Law' in Beatson and Friedmann (eds) *Good Faith and Fault in Contract Law* (1995) 3.

7.12   In the case of privity, models for relaxation of the doctrine abound in the common law world; and, in fact, the Law Commission has proposed relaxation along the lines of the New Zealand Contracts (Privity) Act 1982[1]. Moreover, advocates of reform in England have been encouraged by the bold decision of the High Court of Australia in *Trident General Insurance Co Ltd v McNiece Bros Pty Ltd*[2], and by that of the Canadian Supreme Court in *London Drugs Ltd v Kuehne and Nagel International Ltd*[3].

In the *Trident* case, the question was whether McNiece, a contractor employed by Blue Circle, could rely on an insurance policy written by Trident for Blue Circle. The policy was to cover Blue Circle and all its subsidiaries, contractors and subcontractors involved in specified construction contracts. Although McNiece was within the category covered, it was not directly in contract with Trident. Despite this lack of privity, the majority of the High Court ruled in favour of McNiece. In the words of Toohey J[4]:

> [W]hen a rule of the common law harks back no further than the middle of the last century, when it has been the subject of constant criticism and when, in its widest form, it lacks a sound foundation in jurisprudence and logic and further, when that rule has been so affected by exceptions or qualifications, I see nothing inimical to principled development in this Court now declaring the law to be otherwise in the circumstance of the present case.

More recently, in the *London Drugs* case, the Canadian Supreme Court has followed the example of *Trident* by openly relaxing the privity doctrine in the particular circumstances of the dispute presented to the court. The facts of *London Drugs* were as follows. Pursuant to a warehousing contract, London Drugs delivered a transformer to Kuehne and Nagel for storage. Section 11(b) of the contract provided:

> The warehouseman's liability on any one package is limited to $40 unless the holder has declared in writing a valuation in excess of $40 and paid the additional charge specified to cover warehouse liability.

Instead of making the appropriate declaration and paying the additional charge, London Drugs included the transformer in its own all-risks insurance cover. The transformer was unloaded safely enough. However, when London Drugs gave the order for the transformer to be loaded up for delivery to their new factory, two of Kuehne and Nagel's employees negligently damaged the transformer by attempting to lift it with forklift trucks. The transformer toppled over, occasioning damage of nearly $34,000. London Drugs sued *inter alios* both Kuehne and Nagel (in contract and in negligence) and the two careless employees (in negligence)[5].

The trial judge, Trainor J, having found that the two employees were negligent, and having ruled that Kuehne and Nagel's liability was limited to $40 (in accordance with s 11(b) of the warehousing contract), declared that the main issue was whether the negligent employees were entitled to invoke s 11(b) to limit their liability[6]. Whilst Trainor J had some sympathy for the employees' submission (that they, too, should be shielded by s 11(b)), he ruled that the employees were liable to London Drugs for the full amount of the loss[7]. On appeal to the British Columbia Court of Appeal, this sympathy for the employees was translated into hard legal support by a variety of indirect stratagems[8]. However, when the case reached the Supreme Court, a more direct approach was preferred. According to Iacobucci J, who delivered the majority opinion[9]:

> Except for a rigid adherence to the doctrine of privity of contract, I do not see any compelling reason based on principle, authority or policy demonstrating that this Court, or any other, must embark upon a complex and somewhat uncertain 'tort analysis' [ie the indirect approach] in order to allow third parties such as the respondents to obtain the benefit of a contractual limitation of liability clause, once it has been established that they breached a recognized duty of care. In my view, apart from privity of contract, it is contrary to neither principle nor authority to allow such a party, in appropriate circumstances, to obtain the benefit directly from the contract (ie in the same manner as would the contracting party) by resorting to what may be referred to as a 'contract analysis'.

As in the *Trident* case, the central issue in *London Drugs* was whether the particular circumstances were appropriate ones in which to relax the privity doctrine. The majority had little doubt that the circumstances were eminently appropriate[10]:

> When all the circumstances of this case are taken into account, including the nature of the relationship between employees and their employer, the identity of interest with respect to contractual obligations, the fact that the appellant knew that employees would be involved in performing the contractual obligations, and the absence of a clear indication in the contract to the contrary, the term 'warehouseman' in s.11(b) of the contract must be interpreted as meaning 'warehousemen'. As such, the respondents are not complete strangers to the limitation of liability clause. Rather, they are unexpressed or implicit third party beneficiaries with respect to this clause.

On this basis, the court held that there should be a general exception to the privity doctrine where: (i) a limitation of liability clause, either expressly or impliedly, extends its benefit to the employees (or employee) seeking to rely on it; and (ii) the employees (or employee) seeking the benefit of the limitation of liability clause were acting in the course of their employment and were performing the very services provided for in the contract between their employer and the plaintiff (customer) when the loss occurred[11].

1   *Privity of Contract: Contracts for the Benefit of Third Parties* (Law Com No 242) (Cm 3329, July 1996). In fact, the Commission's proposed test of enforceability is not quite identical to that in the New Zealand legislation, and this could occasion some nice points of interpretation: see Adams, Beyleveld, and Brownsword 'Privity of Contract—the Benefits and the Burdens of Law Reform' (1997) 60 MLR 238. At the time of writing, the Contracts (Rights of Third Parties) Bill is making its way through Parliament.

2 (1988) 165 CLR 107. See Reynolds 'Privity of Contract, the Boundaries of Categories and the Limits of the Judicial Function' (1989) 108 LQR 1.
3 [1993] 1 WWR 1.
4 (1988) 165 CLR 107, 170–171.
5 London Drugs also sued the manufacturers of the transformer. This part of the claim failed at trial, however, it being held that the manufacturers were not negligent in manufacturing and packaging the transformer.
6 (1986) 2 BCLR (2d) 181, [1986] 4 WWR 183.
7 Cf *Muller Martini Canada Inc. v Kuehne and Nagel International Ltd.* (1990) 73 DLR (4th) 315, where Isaac J refused, on materially similar facts, to allow employees the benefit of the limitation clause in the warehousing contract.
8 See Adams and Brownsword 'More Answers than Questions: The *London Drugs* Case' (1991) 55 Saskatchewan LR 441; also 'Privity of Contract—That Pestilential Nuisance' (1993) 56 MLR 722.
9 [1993] 1 WWR 1, 25.
10 [1993] 1 WWR 1, 52.
11 [1993] 1 WWR 1, 50.

7.13 Turning to pre-contractual reliance, the common law courts have again pointed the way ahead. Thus, in the famous case of *Hoffman v Red Owl Stores Inc*[1], the plaintiffs, wanting to open a Red Owl Store, approached the defendant with a view to acquiring a franchise. The plaintiffs were encouraged to believe that they would be given a franchise for a particular store and, with the defendant's knowledge, they sold their house and existing business and moved to the town in which the new store was to be situated. In doing so, they incurred considerable expenditure. Shortly before they were due to open the new store, however, the defendant told the plaintiffs that they were not after all going to be given the franchise. The Hoffmans claimed compensation, not on the basis that they had a contract with the defendant, but on the ground that it would be unfair if they were not compensated for the substantial expenditure incurred in reliance on the expectation induced by the defendant that they would be granted a franchise. Drawing on paragraph 90 of the *American Restatement of Contracts* 2d, the court found in favour of the Hoffmans[2]. Similarly, in the Australian case of *Walton's Stores (Interstate) Ltd v Maher*[3], the High Court turned to the doctrine of estoppel to protect the pre-contractual reliance of Maher (who had demolished a building and started redeveloping the site in anticipation of a contract with Walton's); and, in Canada, in the *Canamerican Auto*[4] case, the idea of a preliminary (collateral) contract was employed[5] in order to protect the pre-contractual reliance of a company bidding for car rental concessions at nine major Canadian airports—the company having put in an unnecessarily high bid in reliance on its understanding that concessions would be awarded to the highest bidders[6].

1 133NW 2d 267 (1965).

2   Paragraph 90 provides:
     A promise which the promisor should reasonably expect to induce action
     or forbearance on the part of the promisee ... and which does induce such
     action or forbearance is binding if injustice can be avoided only by
     enforcement of the promise. The remedy granted for the breach may be
     limited as justice requires.
3   (1988) 76 ALR 513.
4   *R v Canamerican Auto Lease and Rental Ltd* (1987) 37 DLR (4th) 591.
5   Here, the court took its lead from the Canadian Surpeme Court decision in
     *The Queen in Right of Ontario et al v Ron Engineering and Construction Eastern
     Ltd* (1981) 119 DLR (3d) 267. In the *Ron Engineering* case (where tenders had
     been invited for the construction of a water and sewage plant), the Supreme
     Court said that the 'integrity of the bidding system must be protected where
     under the law of contract it is possible to do so' (per Estey J at 273).
6   The Federal Court of Appeal compensated Canamerican for their reliance
     losses (the margin of their overbidding), but rejected their claim for expectation
     losses as too remote.

7.14   Convergence within the common law world, of course, is not
entirely a one-way process. For example, in *Musumeci v Winadell Pty
Ltd*[1], Santow J had occasion to refine the principle of practical benefit
set out by the Court of Appeal in *Williams v Roffey Bros & Nicholls
(Contractors) Ltd*[2]. In *Musumeci*, the plaintiff lessee of a shop in a
shopping centre renegotiated the rent payable to the defendant lessor
when the latter let premises at the shopping centre to a party who would
compete with the plaintiff. The question was whether the renegotiated
agreement yielded any practical benefit for the lessor. Restating the
principles of *Williams v Roffey*, Santow J inter alia broadened their
scope to cover not only the situation where a contractor promises
additional payment (as in *Williams v Roffey* itself) but also the case of
a contractor making a concession by reducing the original contractual
obligation (as occurred in *Musumeci*); but, at the same time, the judge
increased the promisor's protection against unfair dealing by extending
the circumstances in which the renegotiated agreement could be
avoided[3]. On the facts, it was held that, because the rent concession
meant that the plaintiff had a better chance of staying in business
despite the additional competition, the defendant thereby benefitted
from 'uninterrupted successful trade overall in [the] shopping centre',
at the same time enhancing its 'reputation for fairness'[4]. Of course,
whilst the narrow version of *Williams v Roffey* will export readily to
jurisdictions in which there is little commitment to a strict (mutual
benefit and detriment) theory of consideration, it does not follow that
we will import the broader version of *Musumeci* quite so quickly.

1   [1994] 34 NSWLR 723.
2   [1990] 1 All ER 512; see para 1.14.
3   [1994] 34 NSWLR 723, 747.
4   [1994] 34 NSWLR 723 at 748.

An international law of contract: esperanto or lingua franca?

7.15 International trade has long been facilitated by the use of Conventions establishing a regulatory framework for contracting. The Hague and Hague-Visby Rules (regulating the carriage of goods by sea) and the New York Arbitration Convention of 1958 are obvious examples. Similarly, the Uniform Customs and Practice for Documentary Credits, if not quite an international uniform law, is not far short of that. However, whilst no one disputes the desirability of establishing an internationally agreed infra-structure for commerce, not everyone is persuaded that the pursuit of uniformity for its own sake is a good thing. A test case in point is the UN Convention on Contracts for the International Sale of Goods, 1980 (the so-called Vienna Convention)[1], the history of which goes back to 1928 when UNIDROIT declared that its first programme of work was to be on the unification of the law of the international sale of goods[2]. Views about the practical sense of such unificatory initiatives range from extremely negative to highly positive.

1   For commentary on the Convention, see eg Feltham, 'The United Nations Convention on Contracts for the International Sale of Goods' [1981] JBL 346; and Nicholas 'The Vienna Convention on International Sales Law' (1989) 105 LQR 201.

2   Many years later, the work of the drafting committees culminated in the Hague Conference in 1964 and the Hague Conventions which came into force in 1972. Even before the Hague Conventions were ratified, however, their longer term significance had been thrown into question by UNCITRAL's (the UN Commission for International Trade Law) decision in 1968 to make the unification of sales law one of its responsibilities. It was then UNCITRAL's reworking of the Hague Conventions that led to the Vienna Convention on Contracts for the International Sale of Goods, which came into force in 1988. See Schlechtriem 'Some Observations on the United Nations Convention on Contracts for the International Sale of Goods' in Birks (ed) *The Frontiers of Liability: Volume 2* (1994) 29, at 29–30.

7.16 A well-known example of the negative view is Sir John Hobhouse's complaint[1] that many modern Conventions (such as the Vienna Convention)[2] represent an ill-conceived attempt to impose 'stark uniformity'[3] on commercial people, albeit in the name of removing legal barriers and promoting the development of international trade. Such Conventions, Sir John argued, performed no service to commercial contractors, for whom a certain and calculable legal framework is the first priority. Thus:

> These conventions are inevitably and confessedly drafted as multi-cultural compromises between different schemes of law.

Consequently they will normally have less merit than most of the individual legal systems from which they have been derived. They lack coherence and consistency. They create problems about their scope. They introduce uncertainty where no uncertainty existed before. They probably deprive the law of those very features which enable it to be an effective tool for the use of international commerce.[4]

In general, Sir John portrayed the modern quest for uniformity as a case of misguided utopianism—akin to the quest for Esperanto—and he argued that international commerce was best promoted, not by imposing upon it unsatisfactory legal regimes, but by 'encouraging the development of the best schemes in a climate of free competition and choice'[5].

Focusing specifically on the Vienna Convention, Professor Reynolds, too, has expressed reservations about its suitability for the regulation of large-scale international sales, where we are dealing not with 'disputes concerning consignments of shoes sent from Italy to England or Germany' but with 'documentary sales of commodities and other goods carried, often for long distances, by sea on c.i.f. or f.o.b. terms'[6]. As to whether the Convention should be adopted, Professor Reynolds, having echoed Sir John Hobhouse's concerns about the need for certainty, and having underlined his own concern that the Convention 'almost totally ignores the documentary aspects of international sales'[7], concluded that there are sound practical reasons for ratifying the Convention (to 'ignore [it would be] to bury one's head in the sand')[8]. However, Professor Reynolds qualified this by arguing that those who are parties to documentary-based international sales should be advised to exclude the Convention; that a reservation should be made in respect of transactions with non-Convention countries; and that the Convention should not be adopted for purely domestic sales.

1   Hobhouse, 'International Conventions and Commercial Law: The Pursuit of Uniformity' (1990) 106 LQR 530.
2   Sir John's targets were: the UN Convention on the Limitation Period in the International Sale of Goods, New York 1974; the EEC Convention on the Law Applicable to Contractual Obligations, Rome 1980; the UN Convention on Contracts for the International Sale of Goods, Vienna 1980; and the UNIDROIT Convention on Agency in the International Sale of Goods, Geneva 1983.
3   Hobhouse (1990) 106 LQR 530 at 532.
4   Hobhouse (1990) 106 LQR 530 at 533.
5   Hobhouse (1990) 106 LQR 530 at 535.
6   Reynolds, 'A Note of Caution' in Birks (ed) *The Frontiers of Liability: Volume 2* (1994) 18, at 24.
7   Reynolds, 'A Note of Caution' in Birks (ed) *The Frontiers of Liability: Volume 2* (1994) 18, at 27.
8   Reynolds, 'A Note of Caution' in Birks (ed) *The Frontiers of Liability: Volume 2* (1994) 18, at 27.

7.17 Responding to Sir John's strictures against the modern pressure for uniformity, Johan Steyn has taken a rather different view[1]. English lawyers, Lord Steyn observes, have a tradition of scepticism about multi-lateral international Conventions, tending to over-state both the negative impact of such agreements and the supposed calculability of domestic contract law. Whilst Lord Steyn is prepared to concede that the text of the Vienna Convention is not always clear[2], he shares Professor Reynolds' judgment that, in the context of widespread adoption of the Convention, it is in 'the best interests of the United Kingdom as a trading nation to ratify'[3].

For a more positive assessment of the Convention's unificatory aspirations, we can turn to Peter Schlechtriem's contribution to this debate[4]. According to Schlechtriem, quite apart from the fact that the Convention has been ratified by a large proportion of those countries that have an extensive foreign trade, it has played a significant role, too, in shaping the domestic law of a number of these countries. Thus:

> This sort of influence confirms and reinforces the role of Uniform Sales Law as a kind of *lingua franca* among lawyers with different training and traditions. It could become, therefore, a model for the development and transformation of domestic contract laws and may bring about legal harmonization extending beyond the field of international goods traffic.[5]

When the Convention is placed alongside the unificatory statements now available in the Lando Commission's Principles of European Contract Law and the UNIDROIT Principles for International Commercial Contracts, we can discern a 'common core of solutions for issues of contract law'[6]. We might surmise, therefore, that while the English language outdid the unifying aspirations of Esperanto, it is unlikely that a version of English contract law, designed for Victorian Empire, will enjoy the same degree of success[7].

1 Steyn, 'A Kind of Esperanto?' in Birks (ed) *The Frontiers of Liability: Volume 2* (1994) 11.
2 Lord Steyn gives as an example art 16(2)(a) of the Convention, which provides that an offer cannot be revoked 'if it indicates, whether by stating a fixed time for acceptance or otherwise, that it is irrevocable'. To a civilian lawyer, this introduces a firm (irrevocable) offer provision; but, to a common lawyer, it simply means that the (revocable) offer will definitely lapse after the stated time.
3 Steyn, 'A Kind of Esperanto?' in Birks (ed) *The Frontiers of Liability: Volume 2* (1994) 11 at 17.
4 See Schlechtriem 'Some Observations on the United Nations Convention on Contracts for the International Sale of Goods' in Birks (ed) *The Frontiers of Liability: Volume 2* (1994) 29.
5 Steyn, 'A Kind of Esperanto?' in Birks (ed) *The Frontiers of Liability: Volume 2* (1994) 11 at 31.

6   Steyn, 'A Kind of Esperanto?' in Birks (ed) *The Frontiers of Liability: Volume 2* (1994) 11 at 45.
7   Nor, some might think, should it do so. As Steyn LJ (as then was) put it in another context: the courts 'ought not to yield to Victorian times in realism about the practical application of rules of contract formation' (see *G Percy Trentham Ltd v Archital Luxfer Ltd* [1993] 1 Lloyd's Rep 25, 29).
    See, too, McKendrick 'English Contract Law: A Rich Past, An Uncertain Future' in (1997) 50 CLP 25 at 57–61.

CHAPTER 8

The Interfaces of Contract Law

Contract in the context of domestic law

8.1   If the development of the domestic law of contract can no longer be understood in isolation from the evolution of contract law both regionally and internationally, then neither can it be understood in isolation from other areas of English law. Most importantly, contract law must be seen as one element of the so-called common law of obligations, this regime comprising contract law, tort law, and the law of restitution, with the elements being concerned respectively with the protection of lost expectation, the restoration of the status quo (sometimes expressed as protection of the reliance interest)[1], and the correction of unjust enrichment[2]. Moreover, just as pressures for change in domestic contract law can arise from doctrinal positions taken beyond the boundaries of England, so too pressures can be exerted on (or relieved with regard to) contract law by positions taken in the domestic law of tort and restitution. For example, pressure can be put on contract law to protect pre-contractual reliance and expectation where a party's interests are not adequately covered by tort law or the law of restitution, and vice versa[3]; and, in the context of third-party claims, it is well known that a restrictive law of tort can result in pressure being put on contract law, and vice versa[4].

1   See Burrows 'Contract, Tort and Restitution—A Satisfactory Division or Not?' (1983) 99 LQR 217, 219–221, for a compelling statement of the reasons why 'status quo' is to be preferred to 'reliance'.

2   Seminally, for the terminology of expectation, reliance, and restitution interests, see Fuller and Perdue 'The Reliance Interest in Contract Damages' (1936) 46 Yale LJ 52 and 373. Fuller and Perdue treat compensation relative to the expectation interest as designed 'to put the plaintiff in as good a position as he would have occupied had the defendant performed his promise' (at 54); relative

to the reliance interest, compensation is concerned 'to put the plaintiff in as good a position as he was in before the promise was made' (at 53–54); and, relative to the restitution interest, compensation is concerned with 'the prevention of gain by the defaulting promisor at the expense of the promisee' or with forcing 'the defendant to disgorge the value he received from the plaintiff' (at 53–54).

Although Fuller and Perdue's trichotomy was developed with reference to the award of compensatory damages in contract law, writers have drawn on it (with some plausibility) to analyse the function of damages more generally and (more problematically) to identify the basis of obligation in contract (expectation), tort (reliance), and restitution (unjust enrichment). See eg Atiyah 'Promises, Obligations and the Law of Contract' (1978) 94 LQR 193; and Burrows (1983) 99 LQR 217.

3 See eg *Regalian Properties plc v London Dockland Development Corpn* [1995] 1 All ER 1005; discussed at para 1.116. See, too, Ball 'Work Carried out in Pursuance of Letters of Intent: Contract or Restitution?' (1983) 99 LQR 572; Bernard Rudden, 'The Domain of Contract' in Harris and Tallon (eds) *Contract Law Today* (1989) 81; and Collins, *The Law of Contract* (3rd edn, 1997) 165–167, and ch 10.

4 See Markesinis 'An Expanding Tort Law—The Price of a Rigid Contract Law' (1987) 103 LQR 354; see, too, Lord Goff in *White v Jones* [1995] 2AC 207, 262–264.

8.2 The relationship between contract, on the one hand, and tort and restitution, on the other, is not the only interface of interest. Quite apart from the relationship between contract law and other bodies of private law (for example, property law and family law)[1], we need to map contract alongside public law (where the emergence of the modern contracting state together with the constant re-drawing of the boundary between the public and the private, makes this a difficult field to plot). These are large matters, however, and some selection is essential. Accordingly, in this section, we will concentrate on the relationship between contract, tort, and restitution (but particularly contract and the law of negligence), before dealing with contract and public law.

1 Cf Freeman, 'Contracting in the Haven: *Balfour v Balfour* Revisited' in Halson (ed) *Exploring the Boundaries of Contract* (1996) 68; Hedley, 'Keeping Contract in its Place—*Balfour v Balfour* and the Enforceability of Informal Agreements' (1985) 5 OJLS 391; and Collins The Law of Contract (3rd edn, 1997) 91–94.

The common law of obligations

8.3 We saw in an earlier section[1] that the classical view took contract to be distinctive in the common law of obligations. According to this view, whereas contract law focuses on intentions and deals with 'things', tort and restitution focus on actions and we do not conceive of their operations as involving 'thing-like' phenomena. Although the modern view may share the classical idea that contract is distinctively about the voluntary assumption of obligation, it expresses this idea more directly. So, for example, the standard modern account of the distinction between contract and tort has it that, whereas in tort the duties are fixed by law and are owed to persons generally, in contract the obligations are fixed by the parties themselves and are owed to specific persons[2]. Or, putting the distinction in the language of expectation, whilst contract law protects expectations triggered by the actions (including the promises) of specific parties, tort law—insofar as it makes sense to conceive of tort law as having any concern with the protection of expectations— protects general expectations about right conduct (such as the expectation that manufacturers of drinks will not allow the decomposed remains of snails to get into their products). Clear-cut contrasts of this kind, however, soon break down. Many contractual obligations, for example, are fixed by the law rather than by the parties[3]; the idea of duties in tort being owed to persons generally fits poorly with the way that the law regulates (via the duty of care and its concomitant concepts of proximity and neighbourhood) which plaintiffs are eligible; and, on occasion, tort law is used in preference to contract law not only to protect reliance based on expectations triggered by specific actions[4] but also to protect highly specific expectations[5]. Nevertheless, the insight that, while some common law obligations are fixed by law, others are fixed by contract, offers a helpful basis for organising our thoughts about the relationship between contract, tort, and restitution.

1 See chapter 2.
2 See *Chitty on Contracts: Volume 1, General Principles* (27th edn, 1994) para 1–043.
3 See, eg Collins The Law of Contract (3rd edn, 1997), at pp 9–10.
4 See *Hedley Byrne and Co Ltd v Heller & Partners Ltd* [1964] AC 465; and the many authorities building on the *Hedley Byrne* head of liability.
5 See eg *Ross v Caunters* [1980] Ch 297; *White v Jones* [1995] 2AC 207.

Background (fixed) obligations and contractual obligations

8.4 In principle, the starting point for the law of obligations is a (fixed, or imposed) background regime of rights and duties between citizens, this regime articulating the governing notions of wrongdoing within a particular politico-legal order. Some of these obligations may involve strict liability; others may adopt a negligence standard. Either way, though, these obligations are treated as independent of any contractual relationship between the parties: such rights and obligations, in other words, do not originate in contract; and claims are not limited to parties who have a contractual relationship with one another. Victims of wrongdoing (as defined by the background regime) are to be compensated, whether by restoring them to the position that they were in prior to the occurrence of the wrongdoing (in the way that we associate with the tort system) or by reversing dealings in which there has been unjust enrichment (in the way that we associate with the law of restitution).

8.5   The next step for the law of obligations is to specify how far, if at all, private contractual arrangements can modify the rights and duties prescribed by the background regime. This entails that the law must determine: (i) whether it is permissible for parties to contract out of some or all of the background obligations; and, if so, which background obligations (if any) are non-excludable by contract and which excludable; and (ii) whether it is permissible for the parties to add to (increase) their background obligations by contract.

For the sake of illustration, let us suppose that the law specifies these matters in the following way. First, it designates some background obligations as non-excludable (for example, in English law, this is the effect of some of the provisions in the Unfair Contract Terms Act 1977). Secondly, it provides that all other background obligations are excludable: to this extent, the background regime simply constitutes a default position that the parties are free to bargain around. And, thirdly, it takes the position that contractors are permitted to add to their background obligations (for example, where the background obligation is simply to take reasonable care, a contractor may agree to take all possible care or to warrant a particular outcome)[1].

1   Cf eg *Greaves and Co (Contractors) Ltd v Baynham Meikle & Partners* [1975] 1 WLR 1095.

8.6   Now, where the obligations prescribed by the background regime are settled, where the relationship between the background regime and private contractual arrangements is clearly and fully specified, and where exclusion of or addition to negotiable background obligations must be based on express provision, the legal position is relatively clear and calculable. Difficulties arise, however, where there is room for argument about the obligations within the background regime as well as the relationship between these obligations and private contractual arrangements, and where the law allows exclusion of or addition to background obligations on the basis of *implied* contractual provision.

Difficulties at the interface between contract and negligence

8.7   Where the extent of (background) negligence liability is contestable, where the relationship between the (background) negligence regime and private contractual agreement is unclear, and where it is arguable that the contractual effects arise by implication, then the interface between contract and negligence is likely to be problematic. Essentially, three types of dispute may arise. These are:

  (i)   various kinds of dispute between contracting parties where there is potentially a dual track argument about liability in contract and/or in tort;
 (ii)   disputes between a plaintiff contractor and a non-contracting third party defendant; and
(iii)   disputes between a non-contracting third party plaintiff and a defendant contractor. We can consider each of these types of dispute in turn.

Disputes between contracting parties

8.8   In the leading case of *Tai Hing Cotton Mill Ltd v Liu Chong Hing Bank Ltd*[1], the question was whether the company was entitled to recover sums debited against its current account with the bank, following a fraud perpetrated by an accounts clerk employed by the company. Over a period of years, the clerk had forged the signature of the company's managing director on some 300 cheques. The bank denied liability on a number of grounds, including reliance on an express term purporting to treat the debit items recorded in the regular statements as correct and conclusive unless challenged by the customer within a specified time limit. The Privy Council having ruled that the bank had not given the company sufficient notice of such an onerous provision, the principal issue was whether the bank could avoid liability on the ground that the company had failed to comply with a duty of care (based either on an implied term of the contract or in tort) pertaining to the detection of a long-running fraud committed by its own employee.

1   [1986] AC 80.

8.9   Dealing with the implied term argument, the Privy Council followed the general principles established by *London Joint Stock Bank Ltd v Macmillan*[1] and *Greenwood v Martins Bank Ltd.*[2] What these cases establish is that a customer has a duty, first, to refrain from drawing cheques in such a manner as may facilitate fraud or forgery and, secondly, to inform the bank of any forged cheque as soon as he becomes aware of it. Adopting the emphasis in *Macmillan* that no further responsibility could be contended for as a *necessary* incident of the bank/customer relationship, the Privy Council rejected the bank's case for a broader implied term duty of care.

1   [1918] AC 777.
2   [1933] AC 51.

8.10   If the bank failed to establish a broader duty of care in contract, could it nevertheless succeed with the same argument but based in tort? In rejecting the bank's claim, Lord Scarman set down the following seminal guidance:

> Their Lordships do not believe that there is anything to the advantage of the law's development in searching for a liability in tort where the parties are in a contractual relationship. This is particularly so in a commercial relationship. Though it is possible as a matter of legal semantics to conduct an analysis of the rights and duties inherent in some contractual relationships including that of banker and customer either as a matter of contract law when the question will be what, if any, terms are to be implied or as a matter of tort law when the task will be to identify a duty arising from the proximity and character of the relationship between the parties, their Lordships believe it to be correct in principle and necessary for the avoidance of confusion in the law to adhere to the contractual analysis: on principle because it is a relationship in which the parties have, subject to a few exceptions, the right to determine their obligations to each other, and for the avoidance of confusion because different consequences do follow according to whether liability arises from contract or tort, eg in the limitation of action. ... Their Lordships do not, therefore, embark on an investigation as to whether in the relationship of banker and customer it is possible to identify tort as well as contract as a source of the obligations owed by the one to the other. Their Lordships do not, however, accept that the parties' mutual obligations in tort can be any greater than those to be found expressly or by necessary implication in their contract.[1]

The thrust of these observations is that contractual provisions (express or implied) take priority over the tort regime—or, at strongest, that where parties are in a contractual relationship disputes between the parties are governed exclusively by the law of contract. However, as will be apparent from our earlier remarks in this section, such a robust statement of the relationship between contract and tort is obviously too simplistic, not to say misleading. For example, it cannot be right to suggest that the bank, having contracted with the company to administer a current account, would not be liable in tort to the company if it published a defamatory statement about its customer, or if one of the bank's employees negligently damaged property belonging to the customer, simply because these (background) obligations were not found expressly or by necessary implication in the contract between the parties. What principle, therefore, can we take from the *Tai Hing Cotton Mill* case? In what sense does contract take priority over (or exclude) tort?

To answer this question, we need to distinguish the following four types of disputes between the contracting parties, assuming in each case (for the sake of simplifying the analysis) that it is agreed that the material provisions within the background regime are simply default rules that the contractors are at liberty to vary (whether by exclusion, restriction, or addition):

  (i) one of the contracting parties contends that the contract *excludes or restricts* a particular *settled* background tort obligation;
 (ii) one of the contracting parties contends that the contract *excludes or restricts* a particular *contestable* background tort obligation;
(iii) one of the contracting parties contends that the contract *adds to* a particular *settled* background tort obligation; and
 (iv) one of the contracting parties contends that the contract *adds to* a particular *contestable* background tort obligation.

In the first case, provided that the contract expressly and unequivocally purports to exclude or restrict the particular background tort obligation, then the contractual position prevails because we are assuming that we are dealing with background default rules; and, in this sense, contract takes priority. So much is unproblematic. However, if the contract does not make express provision for exclusion or restriction of the particular background tort obligation, the argument will turn on whether exclusion or restriction is effected by an implied term. On the *Tai Hing* approach to implied terms (which is highly orthodox), the question will be whether exclusion or restriction is a necessary implication; and, although this is something of a generalisation, in the absence of express provision, we might expect the courts to be rarely persuaded that background tort obligations have been excluded or restricted by necessary implication.

By and large, the pattern of the second kind of case is similar to that of the first. Where the contract expressly excludes or restricts a contestable background tort obligation, it will be so excluded or restricted; where the contract does not expressly so provide, and where exclusion or restriction turns on necessary implication, we would not normally expect the background tort obligation to be excluded or restricted. However, in this latter case, precisely because the background tort obligation is contestable, the fact that the contract has not succeeded in excluding or restricting the obligation does not close the dispute.

In the third case, provided that the contract expressly and unequivocally purports to add to the background tort obligations, then the contractual position prevails because we are assuming that we are dealing with background default rules; and, thus, contract takes priority. So much is plain; but, as *Tai Hing* itself demonstrates, we should not assume that the courts will readily agree that the express terms of the contract are sufficiently clear to succeed in adding to the background obligations. If the contract does not make express provision for addition to the background regime of obligations, or if (as in *Tai Hing*) the express terms are held to be insufficient, then the argument will turn on whether addition is effected by an implied term. Following the *Tai Hing* approach, the question will be whether addition is a necessary implication; and, again, in the absence of express provision, we might expect the courts to be rarely persuaded that background tort obligations have been added to by necessary implication. If the case for addition is not made out in contract, then *Tai Hing* distinctively holds that no parallel argument (pleaded in tort) for extension of the scope of background tort liability should be entertained. If a contractor claims that background tort obligations have been increased, the *Tai Hing* view is that he must make out this argument in contract or not at all.

Finally, in the fourth kind of case, the analysis largely follows that of the third. Where the contract expressly adds to a contestable background tort obligation, the addition will be binding; the fact that the background tort obligation is contestable is immaterial. However, where the contract fails to make (or fails to make successful) express provision, so that the argument for addition turns on necessary implication, we would not normally expect the background obligation (which is contestable anyway) to be added to. If the contract argument fails, *Tai Hing* directs that this is the end of the matter: the failed contract argument cannot now be re-presented as a tort-based argument for extending background (contestable here) tort liability.

At one level, then, where we are dealing with background default rules, the priority of contract over tort is very straightforward. Ex hypothesi, where contractual provision is clear and explicit, and irrespective of whether it subtracts from or adds to the background (default) regime of obligations, it should prevail. Where contractual provision is not clear and explicit, the effect of the contract will turn on a test of necessary implication. Generally, we would expect the courts to be slow to hold that the background regime has been modified by necessary implication; and, where a court holds that the contract has not modified background obligations, then of course, so far as the background regime applies, it remains in place without alteration. At another level, however, *Tai Hing* goes beyond this in according priority to contract. What *Tai Hing* distinctively holds is that where a contracting party (the bank) fails to make out its argument for addition to settled background obligations (whether regarded as essentially tortious or contractual obligations) by relying on express contractual provision or necessary implication, then that is the end of the case: if the case cannot be made out in contract, then neither can it be made out in tort.

Precisely what this distinctive ruling in *Tai Hing* amounts to, however, is itself open to interpretation. The broad reading of *Tai Hing* is that the Privy Council presupposed what we might term 'contractual exclusivity'. On this view, where the parties have a contractual relationship, and where the dispute is essentially connected with or arises out of that relationship, then the dispute must be settled exclusively according to contract law. Such a view might be seen as having some conceptual elegance[2]. However, in practice, it invites argument about whether a particular dispute is 'essentially' connected with the contract; and its effect is to close off access to argument in tort, not only where the tort position is speculative (as in *Tai Hing* itself) but also where it is settled that the tort position is more advantageous to the claimant (for example, in relation to limitation periods)[3]. The narrower reading of *Tai Hing* is that it simply precludes access to tort where this would be 'inconsistent' with the contract between the parties[4]. The key issue on this reading is how we understand inconsistency. The most obvious case of inconsistency is found where the contract expressly excludes a background (excludable) tort obligation. As we have said already, the priority of contract over tort is unproblematic in such a case. In *Tai Hing*, though, the question was not whether the contract succeeded in excluding or restricting background obligations but whether it *added* to such obligations— the bank was arguing for a duty on the part of the customer that was more (not less) extensive than that set by the background default rules. On this (narrower) reading, therefore, it follows that the particular sense in which the Privy Council thought that recourse to tort would be inconsistent with the contract must have been more subtle. In what sense, then, might the Privy Council (without presupposing contractual exclusivity) have thought that allowing the bank to argue the case in tort would be inconsistent with the contractual position?

The answer to this question lies in the Privy Council's traditional (and, thus, relatively parsimonious) approach to the implication of terms. In line with *Liverpool City Council v Irwin*[5], terms are to be implied only where they are strictly necessary. Had the bank argued that the obligations that it contended for should be implied as a matter of reasonableness, this would surely have been rejected as inconsistent with the approach in *Irwin* (unless the obligations could be presented as a standard implication in all current account banking contracts)[6]. Accordingly, to allow the bank to re-present an argument based on reasonableness under the guise of extending established tort liability (or in a contested domain of tort liability) would be to invite the use of tort law as a way round the standards set by contract law. Putting the matter in these terms, the *Tai Hing* view is not so much that recourse to tort should be barred where this would be inconsistent with particular contractual provisions, but that contractors should not be allowed to subvert the (background) standards set by contract law by appealing to the more favourable standards set by tort law in relation to essentially the same question. Moreover, given that *Tai Hing* fell for decision at a time when the courts were having second thoughts about the implications of *Junior Books Ltd v Veitchi Co Ltd*[7]—namely, that *Junior Books* invited plaintiff contractors to seek recovery of their economic losses from third-party linked contractors in tort when such recovery was barred in contract—it is conceivable that the Privy Council was anxious to avoid setting up any further inconsistencies of this kind.

Drawing these threads together, we can see that the *Tai Hing* view is doubly restrictive: it adopts a restrictive view towards a particular doctrinal issue in contract law (namely, the implication of terms); and then it adds the restrictive corollary that tort cannot be used to by-pass the restrictions adopted in contract. Just how restrictive *Tai Hing* is in relation to the latter point is moot. If *Tai Hing* presupposes contractual exclusivity, then contract and tort are mutually exclusive domains such that, once a dispute is characterised as essentially contractual, contract alone rules. If, however, *Tai Hing* simply restricts access to tort claims where this would be inconsistent with the contractual position (as expressly provided for by the parties or as provided for by background contractual rules), then access to tort depends on how stringently the idea of inconsistency is interpreted. For example, although *Tai Hing* disallows the bank from shopping around in contract and tort to find the most advantageous duty of care, it is open to question whether the bank might have been allowed to choose tort over contract for some different kind of advantage (for instance, to take advantage of a more favourable limitation period or a better chance of recovering consequential losses)[8]. These moot points take us directly to the vexed question of concurrent liability.

1   [1986] AC 80, 107.
2   Cf *Henderson v Merrett Syndicates Ltd* [1995] 2AC 145, 186.
3   See the discussion of concurrent causes of action, para 8.12.

4 See eg Whittaker 'The Application of the "Broad Principle of *Hedley Byrne*" as between Parties to a Contract' (1997) 17 *Legal Studies* 169.
5 [1977] AC 239. See chapter 4.
6 Of course, if the Privy Council had adopted a reasonableness test on the implied term question, this would probably have closed the gap between the contract position and the tort position with regard to the customer's duty of care to the bank.
7 [1983] 1 AC 520.
8 See further, para 8.15.

8.11 Thus far, in our discussion of *Tai Hing*, we have assumed for the most part that the issue is whether a contract modifies the background regime of rights and obligations. However, a contract might provide for rights and obligations which replicate extant background tort obligations (as might be the case, for example, where a contract stipulates that reasonable care is to be taken in the performance of the contract). This gives rise to the related question of (established) concurrent causes of action (or concurrent liability)[1]. Where contractual and tortious obligations coincide in this way, in principle, the law might regulate the plaintiff's remedy in one of three ways:

> (i) the plaintiff is permitted to cumulate, coordinate, or combine features of the contract and tort claims in the manner most advantageous to his case;
>
> (ii) the plaintiff's remedy is exclusively in contract or exclusively in tort, the law prescribing whether the claim lies in contract or in tort; or
>
> (iii) the plaintiff has the choice or election of pursuing a remedy in either contract or tort[2].

Legal systems have rarely adopted cumulation, although it has been supported in Germany; but both contractual exclusivity and the principle of plaintiff election have enjoyed support in a number of legal systems[3]. In English law, the issue has lain between the second and third of these positions. Following the decision of the House of Lords in *Henderson v Merrett Syndicates Ltd*[4], though, it seems that the third position now represents English law.

1 The possibility of concurrence might also be mooted where the tort action is for negligent breach of a strict contractual obligation: see Swanton, 'Concurrent Liability in Tort and Contract: the Problem of Defining the Limits' (1996) 10 JCL 21.
2 See van Aswegen, 'The Concurrence of Contractual and Delictual Liability for Damages: Factors Determining Solutions' *Acta Juridica* (1997) 75.
3 See van Aswegen, 'The Concurrence of Contractual and Delictual Liability for Damages: Factors Determining Solutions' *Acta Juridica* (1997) 75 at 79–85. See, too, Schlechtriem, 'Some Observations on the United Nations Convention on Contracts for the International Sale of Goods' in Birks (ed) *The Frontiers of Liability: Volume 2* (1994) 29, at p 35.
4 [1995] 2AC 145.

8.12 As we have seen, one interpretation of *Tai Hing* is that it favours what we have called contractual exclusivity. On this reading, *Tai Hing* straightforwardly supports the second position—that, in cases of concurrence, the plaintiff's remedy lies exclusively in contract[1]. We have also seen, however, that *Tai Hing* can be interpreted more narrowly, as disallowing a tort claim only where it would be inconsistent with contract. On this latter interpretation, there is room for debate about how far *Tai Hing* bears on the concurrence question with which we are now concerned. Strictly speaking, *Tai Hing* was not itself a case of concurrence, at any rate, not in the sense that the contractual position for which the bank contended clearly corresponded to the background tort position, and nor in the sense that the bank sought to argue its case in tort rather than in contract. Rather, as we have emphasised, it was a case where the bank sought to argue in both contract and in tort for an additional obligation, over and above the settled background obligations[2]. Even so, if the bank had attempted to argue its defence exclusively in tort (because it thought that tort law was more flexible than contract law and, thus, more likely to support its argument for an extended duty of care), we can be confident that the Privy Council would have disallowed any such strategy. Accordingly, even on the narrower interpretation, *Tai Hing* places some restrictions on a contractor being permitted to argue the case in tort rather than in contract. What *Tai Hing* does not settle, however, is quite how far these restrictions reach. In particular, it does not settle whether in a case of concurrent obligations in the strict sense, a contractor can choose the tort remedy with a view to taking advantage of some procedural rule, such as a more generous limitation period. On this particular issue, prior to *Henderson v Merrett*, the authorities were divided as between the second and third positions[3]; but, in *Henderson*, the House of Lords came down firmly in favour of the third position.

1   Cf Burrows 'Solving the Problem of Concurrent Liability' (1995) 48 CLP 103.
2   Cf *Lloyd's Litigation: Merrett, Gooda Walker and Feltrim Cases* [1994] 2 Lloyd's Rep 468, 476 (Sir Thomas Bingham, MR).
3   Amongst the modern English authorities supporting contractual exclusivity (the second position) are: *Groom v Crocker* [1939] 1KB 194; *Bagot v Stevens Scanlan and Co Ltd* [1966] 1QB 197; *Cook v S* [1967] 1 All ER 299; *Heywood v Wellers (a firm)* [1976] QB 446; and, on one interpretation, *Tai Hing*. On the other side, modern English authorities against contractual exclusivity (and in support of the third position) include: *Esso Petroleum Co Ltd v Mardon* [1976] QB 801; *Batty v Metropolitan Property Realisations Ltd* [1978] QB 554; *Midland Bank Trust Co Ltd v Hett Stubbs and Kemp (a firm)* [1979] Ch 384; *Forsikrigsaktieselskapet Vesta v Butcher* [1989] AC 852; and, in *Henderson* ([1995] 2AC 145, 186–187) Lord Goff took *Hedley Byrne & Co Ltd v Heller & Partners Ltd* [1964] AC 465, as the first and most important sign of a

recognition of concurrent remedies in contract and tort. For further citation, see *Lloyd's Litigation: Merrett, Gooda Walker and Feltrim Cases* [1994] 2 Lloyd's Rep 468, 475–476; and Burrows 'Solving the Problem of Concurrent Liability' (1995) 48 CLP 103 at 116, footnote 26.

8.13 *Henderson v Merrett* involved a number of appeals arising out of claims made by underwriting members at Lloyd's (the so-called Names) against the agents who managed the syndicates of which the Names were members. The Names were seeking to minimise their personal underwriting liability by alleging that the agents had failed to exercise due care in the running of the business. Essentially, the appeals, and the relationship between the Names and their agents, fell into two categories. Some of the claimants were 'direct Names', these Names having a direct contractual link with the managing agents; other claimants were 'indirect Names', these Names having no direct contractual link with their managing agents (only an indirect link through intermediaries who placed the Names with syndicates run by managing sub-agents). The claims made by direct Names gave rise to the concurrent liability question because the Names wished to take advantage of a more favourable limitation period in relation to a tort claim; and, whilst the claim made by the indirect Names did not give rise to a concurrent liability question in the strict sense (because they had no contractual action against the managing agents), they too sought to establish the availability of a tort claim, partly in order to establish a direct cause of action against the managing agents but also in some cases for limitation period reasons[1]. The principal defence argued by the managing agents was that the imposition of a duty of care in tort would be inconsistent with the contractual position. As Lord Goff spelled out the defence:

> In the case of direct Names, where there was a direct contract between the Names and the managing agents, the argument was that the contract legislated exclusively for the relationship between the parties, and that a parallel duty of care in tort was therefore excluded by the contract. In the case of indirect Names, reliance was placed on the fact that there had been brought into existence a contractual chain, between Name and members' agent, and between members' agent and managing agent; and it was said that, by structuring their contractual relationship in this way, the indirect Names and the managing agents had deliberately excluded any direct responsibility, including any tortious duty of care, to the indirect Names by the managing agents. In particular, the argument ran, it was as a result not permissible for the Names to pray in aid, for limitation purposes, the more favourable time for accrual of a cause of action in tort. To do so, submitted the managing agents, would deprive them of their contractual expectations, and would avoid the policy of Parliament that there are different limitation regimes for contract and tort.[2]

We will defer consideration of the claim made by the indirect Names, for this comes under the heading of a dispute between a contracting party plaintiff and a non-contracting third-party defendant. However, the dispute between the direct Names and their managing agents is focal for our present discussion.

1   See [1995] 2AC 145, 174.
2   [1995] 2AC 145 at 177.

8.14   So far as the claim of the direct Names was concerned, the central question was whether they were confined to their contractual action against the managing agents. As we have said, the English authorities were divided on this question[1]; and authorities either way could be found in other jurisdictions[2]. Having reviewed the precedents, Lord Goff concluded:

> My own belief is that, in the present context, the common law is not antipathetic to concurrent liability, and that there is no sound basis for a rule which automatically restricts the claimant to either a tortious or a contractual remedy. The result may be untidy; but, given that the tortious duty is imposed by the general law, and the contractual duty is attributable to the will of the parties, I do not find it objectionable that the claimant may be entitled to take advantage of the remedy which is most advantageous to him, subject only to ascertaining whether the tortious duty is so inconsistent with the applicable contract that, in accordance with ordinary principle, the parties must be taken to have agreed that the tortious remedy is to be limited or excluded.[3]

The thrust of *Henderson*, therefore, is that background tort obligations (and their accompanying procedural rules) remain available to a contracting party plaintiff unless the parties have clearly signalled that the tort remedy is to be excluded or restricted.

1   See para 8.12 note 3.
2   For example, authorities in support of contractual exclusivity include: *McLaren Maycroft and Co v Fletcher Development Co Ltd* [1973] 2 NZLR 100. And, authorities against contractual exclusivity (and in favour of the third position) include: *Finlay v Murtagh* [1979] IR 249; *Central Trust Co v Rafuse* (1986) 31 DLR (4th) 481; *Rowlands v Collow* [1992] 1 NZLR 178; *Aluminium Products (Qld) Pty Ltd v Hill* [1981] Qd R 33; *Macpherson and Kelley v Kevin J Prunty & Associates* [1983] 1VR 573; but cf *Hawkins v Clayton* (1988) 164 CLR 539, 584–6 (Deane J). See further in Australia, *Bryan v Maloney* (1994) 69 AJLR 375, 378; and Swanton, 'Concurrent Liability in Tort and Contract: the Problem of Defining the Limits' (1996) 10 JCL 21.
3   [1995] 2AC 145, 193–194.

8.15   Granted that *Tai Hing* and *Henderson* are rather different types of case (the latter, unlike the former, involving concurrent liability in the strict sense, the potential exclusion or restriction of background obligations, and potentially vulnerable contractors on the one side), where does this leave the law? Certainly, *Henderson* rejects contractual exclusivity; from which it follows that Lord Scarman's remarks in *Tai Hing* must now either be disregarded or given the narrower interpretation (namely, that tort claims or defences are barred where this would be inconsistent with contract)[1]. If we take the narrower interpretation of *Tai Hing*, can the cases be reconciled? Without question, the cases tally in holding that where the contracting parties expressly exclude or restrict background tort obligations, the tort regime is so excluded or restricted; and the same probably holds where exclusion or restriction arises by necessary implication. Beyond this, when would the cases hold that it would be inconsistent with contract to allow a party to access the tort regime? If we treat *Tai Hing* as holding that access to tort is precluded where a contractor seeks to take advantage of a more favourable substantive law position in tort (for example, an enhanced performance requirement), and *Henderson* as holding that access to tort is permissible where a contractor seeks to take advantage of a more favourable procedural position in tort, then the cases can be squared. To put this the other way round, if the Privy Council in *Tai Hing* would have allowed the bank to raise the tort defence where the same substantive defence was time-barred in contract, and if the House of Lords in *Henderson* would have rejected the direct Names' claim in tort if they had been arguing for a higher standard of care than that set by the contract, then there is no contradiction between the two authorities. Whether or not the resulting law, which Lord Goff concedes to be untidy[2], can be defended as rational is another matter[3].

1   Cf Burrows, (1995) 48 CLP 103 at 105, for the view that *Henderson* justifiably rejected 'Lord Scarman's infamous and influential dictum.'
2   Similarly, when *Henderson* was argued before the Court of Appeal, Sir Thomas Bingham conceded that the law was untidy, the courts having little option other than to make pragmatic responses where necessary for the avoidance of injustice: *Lloyd's Litigation: Merrett, Gooda Walker and Feltrim Cases* [1994] 2 Lloyd's Rep 468, 476.
3   Cf Burrows (1995) 48 CLP 103, esp at 122–124; and generally, see chapter 9.

Disputes between a contracting party plaintiff and a non-contracting third-party defendant

8.16   The disputes that we have been considering between contracting parties can be seen as falling into two categories: some such disputes relate to alleged contractual modification to background obligations (as in the *Tai Hing* case); other disputes relate to the availability of tort as an alternative recourse (as in the direct Names part of the *Henderson* case). Where the dispute lies between a contracting party plaintiff and a non-contracting third-party defendant, these two categories of inter-contracting party dispute have their analogues. In other words, the dispute can centre on the effect of an alleged contractual modification to the background regime of obligations, or (as in the indirect Names part of the *Henderson* case) it can focus on a question akin to that of concurrent liability. The involvement of a non-contracting third party in the dispute does, however, introduce a significant new element. For, according to the doctrine of privity of contract, such a third party can neither take the benefit of the plaintiff's contract nor be burdened by it[1]. This means that, where the dispute lies between a contracting party plaintiff and a non-contracting third-party defendant, two principles are liable to be in play. First, there is the 'general regulative principle' (as we can call it), namely that a contracting party may have recourse to tort provided that this is not inconsistent with the contractual position; and, secondly, there is the specific principle of privity of contract. Further complicating matters, we will also find that, *Henderson* notwithstanding, a principle resembling that of contractual exclusivity (at any rate, in outcome) retains some force in confining those who are parties to contractual networks (such as the structures commonly found in construction and carriage) to contractual remedies where the negligence of a third-party defendant contractor occasions financial loss to a plaintiff contractor within the network[2].

1   See BCLS: CL (1999) chapter 6.
2   For the idea of a contractual network see Adams and Brownsword, 'Privity and the Concept of a Network Contract' (1990) 10 LS 12.

8.17   Consider, first, the case of alleged contractual modification to the background tort regime. If the plaintiff contends that the contract (between the plaintiff and his co-contractor) purports to *add to* the third-party defendant's background tort liability, the plaintiff will fail. Technically, such an argument will be defeated by the burden limb of the privity principle; and, as a matter of principle, there is no good reason to give contracting parties private legislative powers of this kind[1]. If, however, the argument is that the contract (between the plaintiff and his co-contractor) purports to *exclude or restrict* the third-party defendant's background tort liability to the plaintiff, this raises more complex issues.

1   See further para 8.32, for discussion of *The Mahkutai* [1996] AC 650.

8.18   Let us suppose that a contract expressly purports to exclude or restrict a contracting party's (otherwise entirely straightforward) background tort claim against a non-contracting third party. The general regulative principle suggests that the contracting party's claim in tort will be barred (as inconsistent with the contract); and it might well be the case that an action by the contracting party could be stayed by the other contractor[1]. However, so far as the third-party defendant is concerned, an orthodox application of the doctrine of privity of contract will preclude taking the benefit of the contractual exclusion or restriction. Or, to put this another way, an orthodox application of the doctrine of privity of contract will disable the defendant from challenging the plaintiff's tort claim as inconsistent with the contract. Yet, it is not immediately obvious that such an application of the privity principle is either fair or rational; and, indeed, this sentiment has become increasingly apparent in the modern case law.

In many of the leading cases on the doctrine of privity of contract, the dispute has been precisely whether the defendant can argue for the exclusion or restriction of liability in relation to a straightforward tort claim by reference to contractual terms to which the plaintiff, but not the defendant, is a party. Commonly, though, the defendant is not a complete stranger to the contractual network; on the contrary, the third-party defendant is acting in a sub-contracting capacity. So, for example, in *Scruttons Ltd v Midland Silicones Ltd*[2], the defendants were negligent stevedores, seeking to limit their liability to the plaintiff cargo owners by setting up protective terms in the head contract of carriage. In principle, the issue could have been approached 'contractually' (the doctrine of privity of contract barring the defence) or 'tortiously' (the plaintiffs' consent to limited liability restricting the tort claim). Whilst Lord Denning alone espoused the latter approach, the majority of the House of Lords famously followed the former approach. From a contractual standpoint, however, the outcome was less than satisfactory; for the contractual structure provided a basis for the parties to insure against various risks, and this was destablised by allowing the cargo owners (or their insurers) to access an unrestricted tort remedy directly against the stevedores (or their insurers)[3]. It followed that, if the tort claim was to be allowed to run, commercial convenience demanded that the third-party defendant be allowed to rely on protective contractual provisions. In *The Eurymedon*[4], the majority of the Privy Council engineered a contractual solution to the problem by implying a bridging contractual link between the plaintiff cargo owners and the defendant stevedores. Since then, with the doctrine of privity of contract losing its hold in the common law world[5], it has become progressively easier for the third party to argue that the plaintiff's tort claim should be read in the light of the overall contractual structure[6].

1   Cf *Gore v Van der Lann* [1967] 2QB 31; on which (and subsequent cases) see
     Davies 'Mrs Gore's Legacy to Commerce' (1981) 1 LS 287. And see BCLS:
     CL (1999) ch 6.
2   [1962] AC 446.
3   Cf *Marc Rich and Co AG v Bishop Rock Marine Co Ltd: The Nicholas H* [1996]
     AC 211; para 8.21 below. In *The Nicholas H*, the majority of the House of
     Lords also followed a contractual approach but in such a way that *barred* the
     cargo-owners' claim against a third party, the thinking being precisely that
     the claim must be barred to prevent destabilisation of the settled framework
     for carriage of goods by sea.
4   *New Zealand Shipping Co Ltd v AM Satterthwaite and Co Ltd* [1975] AC 154.
     Similarly, see *Port Jackson Stevedoring Pty Ltd v Salmond and Spraggon (Australia)
     Pty Ltd, The New York Star* [1980] 3 All ER 257. For helpful analysis of these two
     decisions, see Lord Goff in *The Mahkutai* [1996] AC 650, 662–665.
5   See eg *Trident General Insurance Co Ltd v McNiece Bros Pty Ltd* (1988) 165
     CLR 107; and *London Drugs Ltd v Kuehne and Nagel International Ltd* [1993]
     1 WWR 1. See Reynolds, 'Privity of Contract, the Boundaries of Categories
     and the Limits of the Judicial Function' (1989) 108 LQR 1; and Adams and
     Brownsword, 'More Answers than Questions: The *London Drugs* Case' (1991)
     55 Saskatchewan LR 441, and 'Privity of Contract—That Pestilential
     Nuisance' (1993) 56 MLR 722.
6   See eg *Southern Water Authority v Carey* [1985] 2 All ER 1077; *Norwich City
     Council v Harvey* [1989] 1 All ER 1180. But cf *British Telecommunications plc
     v James Thomson & Sons (Engineers) Ltd* [1999] 1 WLR 9.

8.19   Turning to the claim by the indirect Names in *Henderson v
Merrett*, this, too, involved disputants in a contractual network; but it
was rather a different kind of case. First, the defendant sub-contracting
agents in *Henderson* were not seeking to rely on contractual provisions
in the plaintiffs' contracts; the defence did not rest on alleged
contractual modification to the background regime; the dispute was a
three-party analogue to the concurrent liability issue raised directly
between contracting parties. Secondly, the plaintiffs were not arguing
an otherwise straightforward tort claim for physical damage. Their
loss was purely financial. The tort question, therefore, was whether
the defendants had assumed responsibility should the plaintiffs incur
losses as a result of the negligent running of the business; and this
gave rise to the question whether the contractual structure precluded
the plaintiffs having such a tort claim against the defendants. As we
will explain shortly, if privity of contract presented a problem to either
of the parties, here it was to the *plaintiffs* rather than to the defendants.

   In *Henderson*, the House held unanimously that the contractual
structure did not militate against the plaintiffs' tort claim and that there
was no reason, in principle, why the defendants should not owe a
contractual duty to the intermediaries and a concurrent tort duty to
the plaintiffs. As Lord Goff put it:

   I can see no inconsistency between the assumption of responsibility
   by the managing agents to the indirect Names, and that which arises

under the sub-agency agreement between the managing agents and the members' agents, whether viewed in isolation or as part of the contractual chain stretching back to and so including the indirect Names.[1]

As with the direct Names, therefore, the indirect Names were not denied access to the tort regime.

1 [1995] 2AC 145, 196.

8.20 If we view *Henderson* in terms of the managing agents owing a contractual duty to the intermediaries as well as a tortious duty to the indirect Names, this might seem relatively unexceptional. However, if we look at the relationships from the plaintiffs' perspective, the result is that they are given the option of pursuing a tort claim against the defendants as well as having a potential contractual claim against the intermediaries. Moreover, the tort claim, just like the contract claim, is for the very same purely financial loss. In effect, is this not allowing the plaintiffs to enforce the sub-agency agreements, lack of privity of contract notwithstanding? As Sir Thomas Bingham observed when *Henderson* was before the Court of Appeal, simply to state the argument for recovery 'is enough to indicate that one is entering the Flanders of the modern English law of tort'[1].

Significantly, therefore, Lord Goff emphasises that allowing the indirect Names to pursue a tort claim for financial loss, despite their already having a contractual claim in relation to the same financial loss, might be exceptional:

> I strongly suspect that the situation which arises in the present case is most unusual; and that in many cases in which a contractual chain comparable to that in the present case is constructed it may well prove to be inconsistent with an assumption of responsibility which has the effect of, so to speak, short circuiting the contractual structure so put in place by the parties. It cannot therefore be inferred from the present case that other sub-agents will be held directly liable to the agent's principal in tort.[2]

By way of illustration, the contractual structure typically associated with construction projects is given. According to Lord Goff, sub-contractors or suppliers are generally not directly accountable (in tort) to client building owners for financial losses occasioned by their contractual breaches, 'the parties having so structured their relationship that it is inconsistent with any such assumption of responsibility[3]'. Of course, *Junior Books Ltd v Veitchi Co Ltd*[4] must still be reckoned with—a decision which, in a masterpiece of understatement, Lord Goff acknowledges as having created 'some difficulty'[5]. However, the thrust of the law since *Junior Books* has been to treat the decision as exceptional, and to confine the authority of the case to its own special facts[6].

Let us take stock. Where there is a network of contracts, and where the disputants are parties to the network but not to the same contract, then the general rule is that a plaintiff contractor will not be permitted to sue in tort for purely financial losses arising from negligent performance by the defendant (third party) contractor[7]. The standard way of expressing this restriction is in terms of the contractual structure being inconsistent with the plaintiff having recourse to the tort action. Exceptionally, however, as both *Henderson* and *Junior Books* demonstrate, the restriction may be relaxed; but precisely why these exceptions were made is unclear. At the time, the majority of the House probably did not think that the decision in *Junior Books* was creating an exception—rather, it was following the logic of a principled approach to liability. As for *Henderson*, we probably cannot improve on the view that the exception was necessary in order to give effect to 'the commercial common sense of the situation'[8]. Nevertheless, the decision in *Henderson* leaves the law somewhat uncertain and one might anticipate it serving to encourage argument on further exceptions to the general rule—a possibility underlined by the subsequent case of *The Nicholas H*[9].

1   *Lloyd's Litigation: Merrett, Gooda Walker and Feltrim Cases* [1994] 2 Lloyd's Rep 468, 474.
2   [1995] 2AC 145, 195.
3   [1995] 2AC 145 at 196.
4   [1983] 1 AC 520.
5   [1995] 2AC 145 at 196.
6   Lord Goff relies on *Simaan General Contracting Co v Pilkington Glass Ltd* (No 2) [1988] QB 758: [1995] 2AC 145 at 196.
7   As we have seen above, straightforward tort claims for personal injury or directly occasioned damage to property are another matter.
8   *Lloyd's Litigation: Merrett, Gooda Walker and Feltrim Cases* [1994] 2 Lloyd's Rep 468, 475.
9   *Marc Rich and Co AG v Bishop Rock Marine Co Ltd: The Nicholas H* [1996] AC 211. And see BCLS: CL (1999) ch 6.

8.21   In *The Nicholas H*, the question of legal principle was whether the plaintiff cargo owners had a tort claim against the defendant classification society where the negligence of the latter allowed a vessel with a cracked hull to put to sea with only temporary repairs, leading shortly thereafter to the sinking of the vessel with a total loss of cargo. From the tort perspective, the critical issue was whether it would be fair, just, and reasonable to allow such a claim; and, from the contract perspective, the material question was whether it would be consistent to allow the plaintiffs to pursue a tort claim when they already had a contractual claim against the shipowners (and, indeed, had already settled that claim up to the tonnage limitation applicable to the vessel). By a majority of four to one, the House of Lords ruled that the classification society did not owe a duty of care to the cargo owners.

Speaking for the majority, Lord Steyn took it as a key factor militating against the recognition of a duty of care that the plaintiff was party to a contractual network regulated by international conventions for the carriage of goods by sea[1]. This settled contractual structure was the basis on which efficient insurance arrangements were made by the parties. Thus:

> The result of a recognition of a duty of care in this case will be to enable cargo owners, or rather their insurers, to disturb the balance created by the Hague Rules and Hague-Visby Rules as well as by tonnage limitation provisions, by enabling cargo owners to recover in tort against a peripheral party to the prejudice of the protection of shipowners under the existing system. For these reasons I would hold that the international trade system tends to militate against the recognition of the claim in tort put forward by the cargo owners against the classification society.[2]

Concluding, Lord Steyn held 'that the recognition of a duty would be unfair, unjust and unreasonable as against the shipowners who would ultimately have to bear the cost of holding classification societies liable, such consequence being at variance with the bargain between shipowners and cargo owners based on an internationally agreed contractual structure'[3].

Lord Lloyd, dissenting, took a rather different view. His Lordship was not impressed by the argument that the classification societies would pass on the cost of insuring against a new liability risk to the shipowners (this was 'mere guess work')[4]; nor was his Lordship persuaded that, even if this did happen, 'it would be a significant factor in upsetting the balance of rights and liabilities under the Hague Rules'[5]. More generally, though, Lord Lloyd was anxious that the tort regime should not be unduly cramped by concerns about contract; and, in this respect, he drew support from Lord Goff's speech in *Henderson*. Thus:

> I am unable to see why the existence of a contract of carriage should 'militate against' a duty of care being owed by a third party in tort. The function of the law of tort is not limited to filling in gaps left by the law of contract, as this House has recently affirmed in *Henderson* ... The House rejected an approach which treated the law of tort as supplementary to the law of contract, ie as providing for a tortious remedy only where there is no contract. On the contrary: the law of tort is the general law, out of which the parties may, if they can, contract.[6]

Significantly, though, the underlying premise in Lord Lloyd's dissent (unlike in the majority opinion) is that the cargo owners suffered physical damage to their goods, directly tied to the negligence of the defendants, from which it follows that their claim requires no extension of ordinary negligence principles but simply 'a straightforward application of *Donoghue v Stevenson*'[7]. Lord Lloyd concluded:

> In physical damage cases proximity very often goes without saying. Where the facts cry out for the imposition of a duty of care between the parties, as they do here, it would require an exceptional case to refuse to impose a duty on the ground that it would not be fair, just and reasonable. Otherwise there is a risk that the law of negligence will disintegrate into a series of isolated decisions without any coherent principles at all ... .[8]

From the majority's standpoint, the response to this tort-led view is not to get dragged into a debate about whether the cargo owners' loss was or was not a case of direct physical damage, but to recognise that the implication of the contract must be that the cargo owners' loss (however classified in tort law) is at their own risk over and above the compensatory levels set by the international conventions.

1   [1996] AC 211 at 238–240. Cf Lord Donaldson MR in *Leigh and Sillivan Ltd v Aliakmon Shipping Co Ltd, The Aliakmon* [1985] QB 350, 368.
2   [1996] AC 211, 240.
3   [1996] AC 211, at 242. See further Clarke 'Misdelivery and Time Bars' [1990] LMCLQ 314; and Cane 'The Liability of Classification Societies' [1994] LMCLQ 363.
4   [1996] AC 211 at 222. Cf Hepple 'Negligence: The Search for Coherence' (1997) 50 CLP 69 at 82–84.
5   [1996] AC 211 at 222.
6   [1996] AC 211 at 223.
7   [1932] AC 562.
8   [1996] AC 211 at 230.

8.22   Can we make some sense of this difficult case law by focusing on the expectations of contracting parties? At one level, the background tort regime reflects community expectations (inter alia) about people taking reasonable care and about compensation being available where carelessness results in injury or loss; at another level, the expectations of particular persons can be modified by contractual agreement. In *Henderson*, the background expectation is that the managing agents should take care in running the business and should be accountable to the Names for their careless management. In the absence of contractual provision modifying the background regime (or access thereto), or of a clear understanding amongst the parties to the contractual network that the principle of contractual exclusivity applies to claims for economic loss, the mere fact that the indirect

Names are parties to a particular contractual structure does not affect their ability to cash the background expectation. In *The Nicholas H,* by contrast, we can interpret the majority view as holding that, even though background tort claims might not have been specifically excluded, nevertheless the settled expectation of parties to carriage of goods' contractual networks is that questions of financial risk are governed exclusively by contractual regulations. Put this way, the question of whether participation in a contractual network implies contractual exclusivity in relation to claims for negligently caused economic loss will depend on the expectations of the parties and will vary from one context to another. In this light, what makes the decision in *Junior Books* suspect, is not so much that it rejects contractual exclusivity in the context of the particular construction network, but that the presumption now is that construction networks generally *do imply* contractual exclusivity[1].

1   Cf Lord Mustill in *White v Jones* [1995] 2AC 207, 279. His Lordship, having noted that, after *Henderson,* it cannot be argued that 'contractual and tortious responsibilities occupy exclusive domains' continues:

> This is certainly not to deny that where the act or omission complained of occurs between persons who have deliberately involved themselves in a network of commercial or professional contractual relations, such for example as may exist between the numerous parties involved in contracts for large building or engineering works, the contractual framework may be so strong, so complex and so detailed as to exclude the recognition of delictual duties between parties who are not already connected by contractual links ... *This aspect of the law is far from being fully developed.* (emphasis added).

Then, anticipating the outcome in *The Nicholas H,* Lord Mustill continued (at 279):

> Whatever rationalisation is preferred as a means of justifying tortious liability for a failure to act causing pure financial loss—whether a voluntary assumption of an obligation, or the existence of a special situation, or the simple filling of an unacceptable gap—there may be situations where the parties have erected a structure which leaves no room for any obligations other than those which they have expressly chosen to create. On this view, *the express and impied terms of the various contracts amount between them to an exhaustive codification of the parties' mutual duties.* (emphasis added)

Cf, too, *Privity of Contract: Contracts for the Benefit of Third Parties* (Law Com No 242) (Cm 3329, July 1996) para 7.18(iii) for the view that privity restrictions will continue to apply in construction networks.

Disputes between a non-contracting third-party plaintiff and a contracting party defendant

8.23   What kind of disputes might arise between a non-contracting third-party plaintiff and a contracting party defendant? First, there may be cases where the plaintiff pursues a tort claim against a contractor, but where the contractor defends on the basis that the (tort) claim is inconsistent with the contract. In such cases, unless the particular tort claim depends upon the defendant having specifically assumed responsibility towards the plaintiff, in which event contractual provisions might bear on whether such responsibility has been assumed[1], the contractor's defence will be defeated by the principle of privity of contract: for there is no good reason to allow contracting parties to burden third parties by excluding or restricting their ordinary tort remedies (say, for negligently inflicted physical injury)[2]. Secondly, the plaintiff might argue that the contract has modified the background regime by adding to the defendant contractor's obligations. If orthodox privity principles are applied to such a dispute, the third party will be unable to take the benefit of the contractual provisions. Where the third party fails in contract in such a case, it is arguable that no equivalent tort claim should then be permitted. However, as we shall see shortly, in *White v Jones*[3], which is reported immediately after *Henderson*, the majority of the House of Lords thought otherwise. Finally, within a contractual network, various kinds of dispute can arise. Where the dispute involves purely financial loss, it fits the pattern of several of the cases already discussed. However, where the (tort) claim is straightforwardly for physical damage, reliance on sub-contract (rather than head-contract) defences can pose fresh questions with regard to privity of contract. When we have considered *White v Jones*, we can look briefly at this network privity point.

1   In *Smith v Eric S Bush (a firm)* [1990] 1AC 831, the defendant contractor surveyors were unsuccessful in arguing that contractual disclaimers in building society survey reports were inconsistent with an assumption of responsibility to the third-party plaintiffs. The surveyors were prima facie liable in tort and the question was whether the disclaimers succeeded in meeting the reasonableness test under the Unfair Contract Terms Act 1977. The House held that the disclaimers failed to satisfy the test. But, cf Lord Goff's short remarks on this general question in *White v Jones* [1995] 2AC 207, 268.
2   See eg *Haseldine v CA Daw and Son Ltd* [1941] 3 All ER 156.
3   [1995] 2AC 207. And see BCLS: CL (1999) ch 6.

8.24   In some respects, *White v Jones* is the *Donoghue v Stevenson*[1] of the 1990s. The short point at issue was whether the intended beneficiaries of a will should have a remedy in tort (or, possibly, in contract) against a solicitor who negligently failed to carry out the instructions of the testator client. In the earlier case of *Ross v Caunters (a firm)*[2], where the will failed because it was not properly attested, Megarry V-C controversially ruled that the beneficiaries had a tort remedy against the negligent solicitors; in *White v Jones*, the facts were slightly different, the testator's intentions being frustrated by the solicitor's undue delay in acting on the client's instructions, but the essential question of law was the same. As in *Donoghue v Stevenson*, in *White v Jones* the House divided three to two in favour of the plaintiff. Also as in *Donoghue*, the general issue in *White v Jones* is seen as involving a choice between considerations of practical justice (favouring the beneficiaries) and the conceptual integrity of the law of obligations (favouring the defendant solicitor); against Lord Goff's bold reliance on the *Hedley Byrne*[3] principle (evoking shades of Lord Atkin), we have Lord Mustill's measured dissent[4]; and, in the event, the conflict is resolved in favour of practical justice—the majority using, as some might see it, tort law to repair the shortcomings of contract law[5].

1   [1932] AC 562.
2   [1980] Ch 297.
3   *Hedley Byrne & Co Ltd v Heller & Partners Ltd* [1964] AC 465.
4   See eg [1995] 2AC 207, 291, where Lord Mustill says:
     A broad new type of claim may properly be met by a broad new type of rationalisation, as happened in the *Hedley Byrne* case ... ; but rationalisation there must be, and it does not conduce to the orderly development of the law, or to the certainty which practical convenience demands, if duties are simply conjured up as a matter of positive law, to answer the apparent justice of an individual case.
5   Others might argue that the restrictiveness of the law relating to wills is the villain of the piece: [1995] 2AC 207, 278.

8.25   The fundamental premise of Lord Goff's argument is that practical justice demands that the intended beneficiaries have their remedy[1]. If they are denied a remedy, they might suffer a hardship, the testator's intentions are frustrated, and the negligent solicitor avoids having to answer for professional incompetence. The bizarre outcome of denying a remedy to the beneficiaries is that while the testator (and his estate) have a claim in contract, but no actual loss, the intended beneficiaries have suffered a loss but they have no claim[2]. For Lord Goff, this was 'a point of cardinal importance'[3]; and the impulse to do practical justice is a recurring theme in his judgment. Against this consideration, Lord Goff recognises a fundamental conceptual objection, namely that the beneficiaries' claim is essentially contractual (not least because it seeks to put the plaintiffs in the position that they would have been in had the solicitor properly performed his contract with the client)[4]; that a contract claim is unavailable to the plaintiffs because of the doctrine of privity of contract; and that it must, therefore, be misconceived to permit the plaintiffs to succeed in their contractual claim via tort when they cannot succeed in contract. Following the House's decision in *Henderson*, this conceptual point could not be sustained in terms of contractual exclusivity, but it could be pressed in terms of the principle of inconsistency. In a succinct dissenting judgment, Lord Keith rested his case on just this point:

The contractual duty which Mr Jones [the solicitor] owed to the testator was to secure that his testamentary intention was put into effective legal form promptly. The plaintiffs' case is that precisely the same duty was owed to them by Mr Jones in tort. If the intended effect of the contract between Mr Jones and the testator had been that an immediate benefit, provided by Mr Jones, should be conferred on the plaintiffs, and by reason of Mr Jones's deliberate act or his negligence the plaintiffs had failed to obtain the benefit, the plaintiffs would have had no cause of action against Mr Jones for breach of contract, because English law does not admit of jus quaesitum tertio. Nor would they have had any cause of action against him in tort, for the law would not, I think, allow the rule against jus quaesitum tertio to be circumvented in that way. To admit the plaintiffs' claim in the present case would in substance, in my opinion, be to give them the benefit of a contract to which they were not parties.[5]

In *White v Jones*, therefore, the nub of the objection to the tort claim is that it exposes the contracting party defendant to a liability that contract law presently shields contractors against. Whether the restrictive contract rule is the principle of privity, or (as in *Tai Hing*) necessity as the basis for implied terms, these are the rules for the time being; and the essence of the counter-argument is that the courts should not allow these contract rules to be circumvented (and eroded) by encouraging tort claims. How, then, does Lord Goff deal with this conceptual objection?

1   Lord Mustill was altogether less impressed by the merits: see [1995] 2AC 207, at 277–279; and, at 290, his Lordship acknowledged that he did not share the majority view that denying the plaintiffs a remedy 'will leave a wholly unacceptable gap in the law.'

2   An anomaly highlighted in *Ross v Caunters* [1980] ch 297 at 303. As to when a contracting party who has suffered no loss will be permitted to recover substantial damages on behalf of a third party who has suffered loss, see BCLS: Cl (1999) ch 6.

3   [1995] 2AC 207 at 260. Cf Lord Mustill, at 290, who took 'the cardinal feature' of the *Hedley Byrne* principle to be that the defendant assumed responsibility (or undertook the job) specifically towards the plaintiff.

4   [1995] 2AC 207 at 261: Lord Goff also mentions the fact that the claim is for purely economic loss; the need for the defendant solicitor to be able to rely on terms of his contract which purport to exclude or limit liability to a third party; and the fact that the claim arises from a pure omission.

5   [1995] 2AC 207 at 251.

8.26   One way of overcoming the conceptual objection would be to rework the law of contract so that the third parties are able to enforce the testator's contract with the solicitor. Lord Goff deals at some length with the legal position in Germany, where the doctrine of protective effects enables third-party beneficiaries to access a contractual remedy; and he reviews some of the more ambitious ways in which the modern law of contract in England has been manipulated to alleviate some of the practical problems presented by the privity doctrine[1]. However, he concludes that, to give the intended beneficiaries a contractual claim would probably be criticised as 'an illegitimate circumvention of [the] long-established doctrines [of consideration and privity of contract]'[2]. Accordingly, the solution must lie in tort[3]. In the absence of special circumstances, the *Hedley Byrne* principle will not ground liability on the part of a negligent solicitor with regard to an intended beneficiary. Undeterred, though, Lord Goff continued:

> Even so it seems to me that it is open to your Lordships' House ... to fashion a remedy to fill a lacuna in the law and so prevent the injustice which would otherwise occur on the facts of cases such as the present ... In my opinion, therefore, your Lordships' House should in cases such as these extend to the intended beneficiary a remedy under the *Hedley Byrne* principle by holding that the assumption of responsibility by the solicitor towards his client should be held in law to extend to the intended beneficiary who (as the solicitor can reasonably foresee) may, as a result of the solicitor's negligence, be deprived of his intended legacy in circumstances in which neither the testator nor his estate will have a remedy against the solicitor.[4]

By so fashioning a tort remedy for the intended beneficiaries, Lord Goff maintains: 'There is no unacceptable circumvention of established principles of the law of contract.'[5] What are we to make of this?

1   [1995] 2AC 207 at 262–267. Here, Lord Goff discusses the theory of transferred loss, and the remedial strategies developed in *The Albazero, Albacruz (cargo owners) v Albazero (owners)* [1977] AC 774, and *Linden Gardens Trust Ltd v Lenesta Sludge Disposals Ltd* [1994] 1 AC 85.
2   [1995] 2AC 207, 266.
3   The Law Commission, too, is prepared to settle for the tort solution: see *Privity of Contract: Contracts for the Benefit of Third Parties* (Law Com No 242) (Cm 3329, July 1996) paras 7.19–7.27. However, because claims by prospective beneficiaries involve liability for omission and for purely economic loss, the Commission takes the view that, 'at a theoretical level ... the right of the prospective beneficiaries more properly belongs within the realm of contract than tort' (para 7.27).
4   [1995] 2AC 207, 268.
5   [1995] 2AC 207 at 268.

8.27   The natural reading of Lord Goff's speech is that the third party's tort claim does involve a circumvention of established principles of contract; and, thus, the minority Law Lords are correct in saying that the inconsistency principle is violated. However, Lord Goff, moved by the merits, contends that there is 'no unacceptable circumvention', that is, that the circumvention is acceptable. If we generalise this approach, the inconsistency principle must be qualified in an important respect to read: a party may have recourse to tort law provided that this is not inconsistent with the contractual position, *unless the contractual position is so unjust that tort law may be used to relieve the injustice*[1]. Quite apart from rendering the interface of contract and tort even less calculable than it already is—for example, Lord Denning sitting in *Tai Hing* might have thought the contractual position in relation to implied terms so unfair that the bank should be permitted to present a tort argument—the *White v Jones* rider encourages contradictory doctrines to develop on essentially the same matter and it discourages attention being given directly to the problem. Ideally, if the contract rules do produce injustice, it is suggested that they (not the rules of tort) should be revised[2].

1   Cf Lord Steyn in *Williams v Natural Life Health Foods Ltd* [1998] 2 All ER 577, 586, for the view that '[coherence] must sometimes yield to practical justice'; that the backcloth to *Hedley Byrne* and its development in *Henderson v Merrett* and *White v Jones* was 'the restricted conception of contract in English law, resulting from the combined effect of the principles of consideration and privity of contract'; and that, in these circumstances, the law of tort must 'fulfil an essential gap-filling role'. See, too, Smith, 'Rights, Remedies, and Normal Expectations in Tort and Contract' (1997) 113 LQR 426, 430: 'If [*White v Jones*] demonstrates any general principle, it is the principle that [it] is sometimes acceptable to ignore principles in one area of the law in order to get around unjust rules in other areas of the law'; and Schlechtriem, 'Some Observations on the United Nations Convention on Contracts for the International Sale of Goods' in Birks (ed) *The Frontiers of Liability: Volume 2* (1994) 29 at 35: 'The circumvention of one liability system by relying on concurring actions ... might be welcome and therefore not regarded as a problem at all. This is true especially if the superseded rules of liability are outdated, inadequate and need correction.'

2   Cf Lord Mustill, in *White v Jones* [1995] 2 AC 207 at 282:
     Notwithstanding an instinctive preference for a contractual solution I am satisfied that it would not [provide such an obvious way through the woods that the law of tort can safely be ignored as a blind alley.] The conclusion is not of course that because there may well be no contractual right, there must be a duty in tort: for there may be no duty at all.

8.28   Turning to contractual networks, where a head contractor has a prima facie straightforward tort claim (say, for damage to property) against a sub-contractor, the latter may seek to rely on protective provisions in either the head contract or in the sub-contract—or, indeed, as in *Scruttons Ltd v Midland Silicones Ltd*[1], in both contracts. We have already considered the situation where the sub-contractor relies on a head contract defence (this being a dispute between a contracting party plaintiff and, as it were, a non-contracting third-party defendant). What is the position, however, if the sub-contractor relies on a sub-contract term?

1   [1962] AC 446. See BCLS: CL (1999) ch 6.

8.29   In the *Midland Silicones* case, the majority of the House of Lords, taking a contractual approach, ruled that the stevedores were barred by privity of contract from relying on the sub-contract in response to the cargo-owners' tort claim. From a privity-informed contractual perspective, to allow the stevedores to set up a sub-contract defence would be to authorise contractors to legislate away the (background) legal rights of others. Clearly, third parties should not be so burdened by private contractual arrangements. Even if the situation is viewed in a more tortious spirit, it is not obvious that a different answer emerges. Although, if the plaintiff has clearly consented to the risk of the stevedores' negligence, it might then be argued that it would not be fair, just, and reasonable to allow the tort claim to proceed—in this sense, it would be inconsistent with contract; and, provided that the consent was beyond dispute, then arguably it should not matter whether the consent was expressed in the head contract or in the sub-contract.

8.30 As the traditional privity restrictions in contract are relaxed, however, we might expect sub-contractors to enjoy more success in relying on sub-contract provisions that exclude, restrict, or qualify the remedies of third-party plaintiff network contractors. And, indeed, the decision of the Privy Council in *The Pioneer Container*[1] indicates that this is so. It also indicates, though, that the distinctive characteristics of the law of bailment must be taken into account when the facts fit a bailment pattern (as, of course, they will in disputes arising from carriage of goods contracts).

The plaintiffs in *The Pioneer Container* were various groups of cargo owners; the defendants were the owners of a container vessel which sank while carrying the plaintiffs' cargo. Some of the plaintiffs had a direct contractual link with the defendants, but others did not, having contracted with intermediary parties. So far as the latter plaintiffs were concerned, the defendants were in the position of sub-contractors. The principal question was whether the defendants could rely on a choice of law (Chinese) and exclusive jurisdiction (Taiwan) provision in their sub-contract. Effectively this broke down into two sub-questions. First, given that there was no privity of contract between the parties, was it open to the defendants to have recourse to their sub-contract to answer the cargo-owners? Secondly, if the defendants were able to have recourse to their sub-contract, were they able to rely specifically on the exclusive jurisdiction clause?

Dealing with the first of these questions, Lord Goff (speaking for the Privy Council) characterised the defendants' argument as an attempt to invoke the law of bailment to circumvent the difficulties presented by contract law[2]. Within the law of bailment, there were two views in relation to this matter. According to one view, captured in a much-cited obiter dictum by Lord Denning MR in *Morris v CW*

Martin & Sons Ltd[3], 'the owner is bound by the conditions if he has expressly or impliedly consented to the bailee making a sub-bailment containing those conditions, but not otherwise'. In *Johnson Matthey and Co Ltd v Constantine Terminals Ltd*[4], however, Donaldson J took a different view, holding that the owner could not assert the bailment without relying on the sub-bailment contract, from which it followed that the owner was bound by the sub-contract even in the absence of consent or authorisation. In *The Pioneer Container*, the Privy Council preferred the former view; on the particular facts, the cargo-owners had expressly authorised their co-contractors (the head bailees) to sub-contract on any terms; and, thus, the only question was whether the express authorisation was broad enough to entail consent to the specific provision on which the defendants relied.

On the second question, the plaintiffs argued that it could not reasonably be thought that their authorisation to the carriers implied consent to the exclusive jurisdiction clause. However, this elicited a sharp rebuttal by the Privy Council:

> On the contrary, [their Lordships] consider that the relevant clause in the sub-bailment would be in accordance with the reasonable commercial expectations of those who engage in this type of trade, and that such incorporation will generally lead to a conclusion which is eminently sensible in the context of the carriage of goods by sea, especially in a container ship, in so far as it is productive of an ordered and sensible resolution of disputes in a single jurisdiction, so avoiding wasted expenditure in legal costs and an undesirable disharmony of differing consequences where claims are resolved in different jurisdictions.[5]

The shipowners, therefore, were successful in qualifying the third-party plaintiffs' claim by reference to the exclusive jurisdiction clause; and there is no reason to think that the sub-contract could not have been relied upon for other protective purposes, provided that the provision in question fell within the terms of the consent.

1   [1994] 2AC 324.
2   [1994] 2AC 324 at 335.
3   [1966] 1QB 716, 729. See, too, *Cia Portorafti Commerciale SA v Ultramar Panama Inc, The Captain Gregos (No 2)* [1990] 2 Lloyd's Rep 395, 405; and *Singer Co (UK) Ltd v Tees and Hartlepool Port Authority* [1988] 2 Lloyd's Rep 164.
4   [1976] 2 Lloyd's Rep 215.
5   [1994] 2AC 324, 347.

8.31   *The Pioneer Container* is significant in two respects. First, it suggests that the general regulative principle applies equally at the interface of contract and bailment. In other words, a contractor may have recourse to the principles of bailment, provided that this is not inconsistent with contract, unless the contractual position is itself manifestly unfair or inconvenient. Thus, in *The Pioneer Container*, although the shipowners' bailment defence circumvented the strict application of the principle of privity of contract, it was consistent with the deeper contractual principle of holding contractors to their agreements, and anyway it was (as in *White v Jones*) another acceptable circumvention. Secondly, the way in which the Privy Council rejects the plaintiffs' argument on what we have referred to as the second question (above), by resting on the expectations of reasonable commercial people in the carriage of goods business, supports the view that both within contract law itself, and at the interface of contract with other doctrinal elements in the law of obligations, the modern judicial project is to bring the law into line with the reasonable expectations of transactors[1].

1   See chapter 6.

8.32   Before gathering together the threads of our discussion, we must add a coda to *The Pioneer Container*. This concerns the apparently similar case of *The Mahkutai*[1], where the Privy Council (again led by Lord Goff) held that the defendant shipowners were not entitled to rely (either as a matter of contract or bailment) on an exclusive jurisdiction clause in the head contract of carriage (hence, strictly speaking, *The Mahkutai* is a case belonging in our second category, that is, it involves a dispute between a contracting party plaintiff and a non-contracting third-party defendant). How is this to be explained alongside the decision in favour of the shipowners in *The Pioneer Container*? When this question is posed directly, Lord Goff distinguishes the cases in the following terms:

> The present case is ... concerned not with a question of enforceability of a term in a *sub-bailment* by the sub-bailee against the head bailor, but with the question whether a sub-contractor is entitled to take the benefit of a term in the *head contract*. The former depends on the scope of the *authority* of the intermediate bailor to act on behalf of the head bailor in agreeing on his behalf to the relevant term in the *sub-bailment*; whereas the latter depends on the scope of the *agreement* between the head contractor and the sub-contractor, entered into by the intermediate contractor as agent for the sub-contractor, under which the benefit of a term in the *head contract* may be made available by the head contractor to the sub-contractor. It does not follow that a decision in the former type of case provides any useful guidance in a case of the latter type; and their Lordships do not therefore find *The Pioneer Container* of assistance in the present case.[2]

On the face of it, such a formalistic distinction is unpersuasive, particularly so when the decision in *The Pioneer Container* drew so explicitly on the expectations of reasonable commercial contractors versed in the custom and practice of carriage of goods by sea. Lord Goff's remarks, however, must be read in conjunction with an earlier, and altogether more telling, distinction. As Lord Goff interprets it, an exclusive jurisdiction clause is to be distinguished from the exceptions and limitations on which sub-contractors often wish to rely, 'in that it does not benefit only one party, but embodies a mutual agreement under which both parties agree with each other as to the relevant jurisdiction for the resolution of disputes. It is therefore a clause which creates mutual rights and obligations'[3]. An exclusive jurisdiction clause, in other words, potentially imposes a burden on those who are bound by it. Now, as it happened, the shipowners in *The Mahkutai* regarded the exclusive jurisdiction clause as operating in their favour; but Lord Goff's point is that, in principle, such a clause imposes a burden. This being the case, the general stance of the law must be to protect third parties against contractors who seek to impose burdensome arrangements upon them—which is precisely what the burden limb of the privity doctrine purports to do. Accordingly, the critical feature of *The Mahkutai* is that the contractual provision at issue involves a burden, from which it follows, as Lord Goff says, that the consent of the contracting cargo-owners (as in *The Pioneer Container*) is irrelevant; moreover, it is irrelevant whether the matter is argued in contract or in bailment. What matters is whether the sub-contractors have agreed to accept the burden (ie the derogation from their background legal rights). Thus, whilst some might find the decision in *The Mahkutai* unsatisfactory in denying the shipowners access to the exclusive jurisdiction clause when, as it proved, they found it suited them—and perhaps lacking, too, in failing to explore whether the shipowners would have been taken to have consented given reasonable commercial expectations—the decision would seem a lot less puzzling if the boot had been on the other foot, with the shipowners disputing the right of the cargo-owners to rely on an exclusive jurisdiction provision in a head contract to which they, but not the shipowners, were a party.

1   [1996] AC 650.
2   [1996] AC 650 at 667–668.
3   [1996] AC 650 at 666.

An intelligible mosaic?

8.33   In *White v Jones*, Lord Mustill explains his preference for taking a hard look at a few key authorities, rather than stringing together one citation after another, by saying that '[t]he construction of an intelligible mosaic becomes impossible if there are too many pieces. Many of them will not fit. A full account of all the previous decisions would be endless and useless.'[1] Similar sentiments apply with regard to our discussion of the interface of contract and negligence. We have been relatively sparing in our citation of the numerous authorities in the hope that the larger picture of principle will emerge. Is there, however, an intelligible mosaic at this important legal interface?[2]

1   [1995] 2AC 207, 292.
2   See, too, Hepple 'Negligence: The Search for Coherence' (1997) 50 CLP 69.

8.34   To begin with, we should recall our opening remark that, in principle, the interface between contract and tort is liable to be problematic if the background rules are unclear, if the relationship between the background rules and contractual provision is unclear, and if the background regime can be modified by implied contractual provision. Having reviewed the leading authorities, we can see that the key uncertainties distinctively shaping the interface in English law are: the lack of clarity about the general regulative principle itself (exacerbated by the *White v Jones* rider to the inconsistency principle, allowing for circumvention where it is acceptable in the interests of justice); the lack of clarity within tort law about the circumstances in which a duty of care will lie in relation to purely economic loss (including a lack of clarity about the circumstances in which particular contractual structures will militate against tort claims for purely economic loss); and the relative willingness or unwillingness of particular judges to defend the cornerstones of classical contract doctrine (particularly, the requirements of consideration and privity, and the restrictive approach to implied terms).

8.35   Insofar as we can suggest more specific guidelines, the following seem to be salient features of the mosaic. First, following the decision in *Henderson*, the general regulative principle must be formulated in terms of inconsistency rather than contractual exclusivity. Secondly, where the dispute lies between contracting parties, the inconsistency principle dictates that a tort claim will not be available where this is incompatible with the express or implied terms of the contract, or where it would circumvent a feature of contract law that the court wishes to defend[1]. Hence, in *Tai Hing*, where the court prefers that contractual performance requirements are governed by contract, the tort defence is disallowed; but, in *Henderson*, the court sees no particular virtue in defending the limitation periods set for contract claims. Thirdly, where the dispute lies between a contracting party plaintiff and a non-contracting third-party defendant, the inconsistency principle operates alongside the privity principle. The latter principle entails that third parties are shielded against potentially burdensome contractual provisions (as is the intention of the Privy Council in *The Mahkutai*), but it also means that they might have problems in accessing beneficial contractual provisions and thereby qualifying a contracting party's claim (although, as the case law from *The Eurymedon* onwards indicates, this is rather less of a problem in the evolving regime of contract law). However, it is a feature of the modern law that, where the plaintiff's (tort) claim is for purely economic loss, and where both plaintiff and defendant are parties to a contractual network, then the contractual structure might be deemed to militate against the availability of the tort claim—the tort claim is, as it were, inconsistent with the expectations generated by participation in a network. Since *Junior Books*, this idea has been rehearsed on many occasions with reference to construction contracts, and *The Nicholas H* applied it (arguably with a slight extension, in the sense that the classification society serviced, rather than was a party to, the network) in the context of carriage of goods networks. In *Henderson*, the claim by the indirect Names was judged not to fall foul of this aspect of the inconsistency principle, possibly because access to more favourable tort limitation periods was thought not to defeat network expectations in the way that would happen if tort claims were used to modify performance requirements or to alter the risk allocation set by exclusion and limitation clauses. Fourthly, where the dispute lies between a non-contracting third-party plaintiff and a contracting party defendant, we again have the privity principle operating alongside the general regulative principle. Standard applications of the privity principle protect non-contracting third-parties against ostensible contractual derogations from the background regime, but they also hinder attempts by third parties to enforce contracts that are made for their benefit. Exceptionally, *White v Jones* permits tort to be used to circumvent contractual restrictions, but only because the contract position is thought to be out of line both with the requirements of justice as well as the needs of a modern regime of contract law. As we have said, the emergence of precisely such a modernised regime is apparent in a number of cases, particularly where the orthodox privity restrictions are relaxed to give effect to the expectations of those who participate in contractual networks—and this includes holding a third-party (network) plaintiff to the restrictions stipulated by the defendant's network contract (as in *The Pioneer Container*).

1   Sed quaere: would the *White v Jones* rider to the inconsistency principle allow for circumvention in two party cases, where it was judged to be acceptable in the interests of justice? And, for the non-circumvention principle viewed from the *tort* side of the contract/tort divide, see Lord Nicholls in *Malik v Bank of Credit and Commerce International SA (in liquidation)* [1997] 3 All ER 1, 10:

'The boundaries set by the tort of defamation are not to be side-stepped by allowing a claim in contract that would not succeed in defamation' (citing Dillon LJ in *Lonrho plc v Fayed* (No 5) [1994] 1 All ER 188, 195).

8.36 In the final analysis, it is suggested that the baseline for this area of law is that of reasonable expectation. The background tort regime reflects the reasonable expectations of the community in relation to compensation for wrongdoing. The background contract regime should reflect, inter alia, the reasonable expectations of contractors who deal regularly in particular business sectors and markets. Other things being equal, specific contract provision can be made to modify these background rules, and the parties' reasonable expectations are then tied to their own specific contractual provision. Where questions about access to tort are raised at the interface of contract and negligence, the trajectory of the law is to endeavour to keep faith with these layers of reasonable expectation. Perhaps most strikingly, where the dispute arises within a contractual network, the courts are now prepared to enforce the expectation that, at least in relation to claims for financial loss, the network has its own regulatory code. Accordingly, deviant tort claims must be disallowed; or, if they are allowed, restrictive contractual rules must be relaxed to enable defendants to raise defences that are consistent with the network code.

Contract and public law

8.37 The relationship between contract and public law, despite having many important facets, has not always been a matter in which private lawyers have taken a particularly keen interest[1]. However, with the emergence in England of a modern contracting state[2], in which there is extensive public procurement from the private sector, privatised supply of public utilities, and a strong contract culture within the public sector itself, it is clear that contract lawyers can no longer afford to ignore the interface between contract and public law. And, nor are they so doing[3]. For the configuration of the modern State is such that it is increasingly difficult to draw a bright line dividing 'the public' from 'the private'[4]. Furthermore, it is possible to detect a number of doctrinal parallels—for example, ideas of due process and protection of reasonable (practice-based) expectation—that are becoming apparent in both public law and contract law[5]. Arguably, in these several respects, as public law moves closer to private law, private law, too, moves closer to public law.

Predictably, as dealing in and around the public sector begins to look 'contractual', and as disputing parties detect some advantage (procedural or substantive) in putting their case in contract law rather than in public law, *or* vice versa, the interface between these two bodies of law can prove problematic. In principle, if we imagine a dispute between a 'public contractor' and a 'private contractor'[6], an interface question might arise in the following four forms:

   (i) the private contractor argues that contract law governs (and/or that private law procedures are appropriate);

  (ii) the public contractor argues that public law governs (and/or that public law procedures must be followed);

 (iii) the public contractor argues that contract law governs (and/or that private law procedures are appropriate); and

 (iv) the private contractor argues that public law governs (and/or that public law procedures must be followed).

We can simplify this by combining (i) with (ii), and (iii) with (iv), for (ii) is the denial of (i) (and vice versa), and (iv) is the denial of (iii) (and vice versa). So simplified, we can focus on two types of dispute: the one where the private contractor argues that contract law governs (often in opposition to the public contractor's argument that this will involve an abuse of process), and the other where the public contractor argues that contract law governs (often in opposition to the private contractor's argument that this will license an abuse of right).

1   See, eg Arrowsmith, 'The Impact of Public Law on the Private Law of Contract' in Halson (ed) *Exploring the Boundaries of Contract* (1996) 3. In this paper, Arrowsmith focuses on the particular question of how the law deals with (private law) contractual liability where a contract has been made in breach of background public law rules. This question was prompted by the House of Lords' ruling in *Hazell v Hammersmith and Fulham London Borough Council* [1992] 2AC 1, to the effect that local authorities had no power to enter into 'interest rate swap' transactions which, accordingly, were held to be void. The repercussions of *Hazell* were considerable, involving nice points of the law of restitution (see especially *Westdeutsche Landesbank Girozentrale v Islington London Borough Council* [1996] AC 669 and *Kleinwort Benson Ltd v Lincoln City Council* [1998] 4 All ER 513) and jurisdiction (see *Kleinwort Benson Ltd v Glasgow City Council* [1997] 4 All ER 641).

2   See, eg Harden, *The Contracting State* (Buckingham, Open University Press, 1992); Barron and Scott 'The Citizen's Charter Programme' (1992) 55 MLR 526; and Birkinshaw 'By Command of Her Britanic Majesty's Government: Let There be Government by Contract', in Olszewskiego and Popowskiej (eds) *Economy, Administration and Self-Government* (1997) 55.

3   Seminally, see Turpin, *Government Procurement and Contracts* (1989). See, too, eg Freedland 'Government by Contract and Public Law' [1994] PL 86; the papers in Part 2 of Campbell and Vincent-Jones (eds) *Contract and Economic Organisation* (1996); the papers in Part II of Deakin and Michie (eds) *Contracts, Co-operation, and Competition* (1997); Flynn and Williams (eds) *Contracting for Health* (1997); and for an overview drawing on the last two books cited, see Milne *Making Markets Work* (Economic and Social Research Council, 1997).

4   See eg Fredman and Morris 'The Costs of Exclusivity: Public and Private Re-examined' [1994] PL 69; and Collins *The Law of Contract* (3rd edn, 1997) 247–250 (commenting on the corporatist regulatory patterns straddling the public/private divide).

5   See, eg Beatson, 'Public Law Influences in Contract Law' in Beatson and Friedmann (eds) *Good Faith and Fault in Contract Law* (1995) 263; and 'Finessing Substantive 'Public Law' Principles into 'Private Law' Relations' *Acta Juridica* (1997) 1.

6   These designations imply that a particular party is already a 'contractor' and that it is dealing on the 'public' or the 'private' side of the divide (as the case may be). However, such characterisations might lie at the heart of the dispute; and each description is contestable. It must not be assumed, therefore, that when these designations are used, they are anything more than provisional in nature.

Where the private contractor claims that contract governs

8.38   Where a private party contends that contract law governs a particular relationship with a public party, this presupposes that there is a contract between the parties. However, as we saw in an earlier section[1], when we discussed the decisions in *Pfizer Corpn v Ministry of Health*[2], and *Norweb plc v Dixon*[3], the courts in those cases were persuaded neither that (in *Pfizer*) the supply of drugs under NHS prescription was contractual nor that (in *Dixon*) the routine supply of electricity to a tariff customer was contractual[4]. To be sure, these were not cases where the statutory scheme explicitly proclaimed that statutory provision of goods or services was not contractual; nevertheless, the reasoning in both *Pfizer* and *Dixon* is that provision under the statutory regime involved certain characteristics that were incompatible with contract[5].

1   See paras 1.17–1.19.
2   [1965] AC 512.
3   [1995] 3 All ER 952.
4   Similarly, see *Willmore and Willmore (t/a Lissenden Poultry) v South Eastern Electricity Board* [1957] 2 Lloyd's Rep 375.
5   Cf, too, *Rederiaktiebolaget Amphitrite v R* [1921] 3KB 500, 503, where Rowlatt J said that the Government's assurance
     was merely an expression of intention to act in a particular way in a certain event ... [It] is not competent for the Government to fetter its future executive action, which must necessarily be determined by the needs of the community when the question arises. It cannot by contract hamper its freedom of action in matters which concern the welfare of the State.
     As Rudden, 'The Domain of Contract' in Harris and Tallon (eds) *Contract Law Today* (1989) 81 at 97, has pointed out, it is unclear whether this means that 'such a contract can never even be formed or that apparently contractual promises may be broken with impunity'.

8.39   *Pfizer* and *Dixon* suggest that the interface between contract law and public law might be regulated by an inconsistency principle that is analogous to that regulating the interface between contract and negligence—although it should be observed, at once, that public law dominates this particular interface with contract. According to this principle, where the relationship between the disputants originates in a background public law (typically, statutory) scheme, then access to contract will be permitted so long as this is consistent with the background regime. This means that, where the public law scheme expressly or by implication excludes or restricts contractual relief, it will be so excluded or restricted[1]. Moreover, if the analogy holds good, it also means that, where recourse to contract would circumvent a feature of the public law regime that the courts wish to defend, then the general regulative principle will disallow access to contract. How well does the inconsistency principle fit with the key modern cases?

1   Legislation may explicitly regulate the possibility of contractual relief. See, eg National Health Service and Community Care Act 1990, s4(3), which provides that NHS contracts 'shall not be regarded for any purpose as giving rise to contractual rights and liabilities'.

8.40   In the modern case law, one of the central concerns is that private law procedures, and hence contract law, should not be available where this would constitute an abuse of process. The key reference point here is the principle of 'procedural exclusivity' as articulated by Lord Diplock in *O'Reilly v Mackman*[1]. According to his Lordship:

> [I]t would in my view as a general rule be contrary to public policy, and as such an abuse of the process of the court, to permit a person seeking to establish that a decision of a public authority infringed rights to which he was entitled to protection under public law to proceed by way of an ordinary action and by this means to evade the provisions of Ord 53 for the protection of such authorities.[2]

Whilst it is clear that, where a purely public law right is claimed, then public law procedures (such as judicial review) must be used, Lord Diplock recognised that there will be disputes involving a mix of public law and private law ingredients. Here, his Lordship accepted that there should be exceptions to the general rule, with the law to be decided on a case-by-case basis[3]. Reflecting on the implications of such a case-by-case jurisdiction, Lord Slynn recently took stock of the position in the following terms:

> The recognition by Lord Diplock that exceptions exist to the general rule may introduce some uncertainty, but it is a small price to pay to avoid the over-rigid demarcation between procedures reminiscent of earlier disputes as to the forms of action, and of disputes as to the

competence of jurisdictions apparently encountered in civil law countries where a distinction between public and private law has been recognised. It is of particular importance, as I see it, to retain some flexibility, as the precise limits of what is called 'public law' and what is called 'private law' are by no means worked out. The experience of other countries seems to show that the working out of this distinction is not always an easy matter. In the absence of a single procedure allowing all remedies—quashing, injunctive and declaratory relief, damages—some flexibility as to the use of the different procedures is necessary. *It has to be borne in mind that the overriding question is whether the proceedings constitute an abuse of the process of the court.*[4]

Given that judicial review procedures in public law are notoriously restrictive (including a short limitation period) and given that damages are not available, there are obvious incentives for claimants to seek access to more favourable private law (including contractual) remedial regimes—and, conversely, good reasons for public bodies to insist that public law procedures alone are applicable[5]. Following the current gloss on *O'Reilly v Mackman*, therefore, if the claim is not plainly caught by the general rule, the overriding question is whether allowing access in such circumstances constitutes an abuse of process. To illustrate the courts' thinking on these matters, we can consider two of the leading modern cases, *Roy v Kensington and Chelsea and Westminster Family Practitioner Committee*[6], and *Mercury Communications Ltd v Director General of Telecommunications*[7].

1   [1983] 2AC 237. For difficulties presented by this principle, see, eg Alder, 'Hunting the Chimera—the End of *O'Reilly v Mackman*' (1993) 13 LS 183; and Tanney 'Procedural Exclusivity in Administrative Law' [1994] PL 51.

2   [1983] 2AC 237 at 285.

3   [1983] 2AC 237 at 285.

4   *Mercury Communications Ltd v Director General of Telecommunications* [1996] 1 All ER 575, 581 (emphasis added). See, too, Lord Woolf MR's 'pragmatic' approach in *Dennis Rye Pension Fund Trustees v Sheffield City Council* [1997] 4 All ER 747, esp at 754–756 and in *Andreou v Institute of Chartered Accountants in England and Wales* [1998] 1 All ER 14, esp at 20–21. For comment, see Bamforth 'The Public Law-Private Law Divide' (1998) 148 NLJ 136.

5   Cf *Law v National Greyhound Racing Club* [1983] 3 All ER 300, where the NGRC moved to strike out the plaintiff trainer's originating summons, in which the latter claimed that his licence had been improperly suspended, on the ground that he must proceed by way of judicial review. Sympathising with the NGRC's concern about the increased incidence of doping, Slade LJ added (at 307):

> Furthermore, it is easy to understand why the NGRC would prefer that any person who seeks to challenge the exercise of its disciplinary functions should be compelled to do so, if at all, by way of an application for judicial review. In this manner the NGRC would enjoy the benefit of what Lord Diplock in *O'Reilly v Mackman* ... described as 'the safeguards imposed in the public interest against groundless, unmeritorious or tardy attacks on the validity

of decisions made by public authorities in the field of public law.'
Notwithstanding recent procedural changes, these safeguards are still
substantial.

The Court of Appeal held, nevertheless, that the relationship between the
parties was contractual and they declined to strike out the plaintiff's claim.

6   [1992] 1AC 624. Applied in *Hutchings v Islington London Borough Council*
[1998] 3 All ER 445, where the appellant's (private law) claim was thought to
be analogous with that in *Roy*, (private law) enforcement of which involved no
abuse of process (see esp at 450–451).

7   [1996] 1 All ER 575.

8.41 In the first of these cases, Dr Roy was a general medical
practitioner, who was on the list for the particular area covered by the
Kensington and Chelsea and Westminster Family Practitioner
Committee. The relationship between Dr Roy and the Committee
arose in, and was elaborated by, the National Health Service
legislation. Under the statutory scheme, the Committee was required
to cause full-rate payments to be made to Dr Roy provided that certain
conditions were met, including the Committee being satisfied that Dr
Roy was devoting a substantial amount of time to his NHS general
practice. A dispute arose between the parties when the Committee,
not being satisfied that a substantial amount of time was being so
devoted, reduced Dr Roy's payments by 20%. Dr Roy, contesting this
point and claiming that he had a contract with the Committee,
commenced his action by writ claiming, inter alia, payment of the
sums allegedly due under the terms and conditions of the statutory
scheme. The Committee's first line of defence was that it was an abuse
of process for Dr Roy to proceed as though the dispute concerned
private law (specifically contractual) rights and obligations; rather, it
was argued that this was a public law matter to be dealt with in
accordance with the statutory scheme and by way of judicial review.

At first instance[1], Judge White ruled that, although there were
'contractual echoes in the relationship'[2], there was no contract; the
Committee was exercising a public law function; and, it followed that
judicial review must be used. On appeal, the Court of Appeal applied
R v East Berkshire Health Authority, ex p Walsh[3]—in which the Court
had previously held that a dispute between the Health Authority and
one if its senior nursing officers, following the dismissal of the latter,
was simply a matter of private rights under the relevant contract of
employment—to hold that the relationship was contractual. Dr Roy
succeeded, too, before the House of Lords. However, the House rather
evaded the question of whether there was a contract by finding that,
provided Dr Roy was asserting private law rights of some kind, then
irrespective of whether such rights were contractual, there was no abuse
of process in invoking private law procedures.

Giving the principal speech, Lord Lowry equivocated on whether there was a contract. He was not persuaded that *ex p Walsh*, on which the Court of Appeal had relied, could be taken as decisive; there was at least one precedent, *Wadi v Cornwall and Isles of Scilly Family Practioner Committee*[4], giving a contrary indication on the point. On the other hand, Lord Lowry accepted that the 'contractual echoes' in the relationship, giving rise to rights and obligations, pointed strongly to Dr Roy having private law rights. His Lordship continued:

> I would here observe that the mere fact that the Act [ie the National Health Service Act 1977] and the Regulations constitute a statutory scheme which lays down a doctor's 'terms of service' (an expression which has contractual overtones) and creates the relationship between him and the committee, is not fatal to the idea of a contract, but that relationship did not *need* to be contractual. Moreover, the discretion which the scheme confers on the committee is not typically characteristic of a contractual relationship, and the same can be said of the appellate and supervisory role given to the Secretary of State.[5]

Given Lord Lowry's evident reluctance to commit himself on the question whether the relationship between Dr Roy and the Committee was contractual, it is hard to know quite what to make of *Roy*. At one level, the House has no difficulty in accepting that private law rights and obligations can nestle in the shadow of a public law background and that, where the public law background is incidental, then disputes concerning such private law rights and obligations can be properly resolved by ordinary private law processes. Moreover, in Dr Roy's case, there was no pressing reason to channel the dispute into a public law track—not least because issues of fact were in dispute (with regard to the amount of time devoted to NHS practice), and so ordinary private law trial processes might well have some advantage over a judicial review hearing. All things considered, therefore, Dr Roy's recourse to private law was not inconsistent with the integrity of the public law regime. At another level, however, the House quite clearly has reservations about whether the relationship between Dr Roy and the Committee can be characterised as contractual. The reservation, though, is not that if the relationship is so characterised then judicial review can be by-passed (because, as we have just said, the House has no concerns here about circumvention). Quite simply, the reservation is whether the essential ingredients for a contract are present.

1   [1989] 1 Med LR 10.
2   [1989] 1 Med LR 10 at 12.
3   [1985] QB 152; and see para 8.44.
5   [1992] 1AC 624, 649.

8.42   Similarly, on the facts of *Mercury Communications Ltd v Director General of Telecommunications*[1], the House of Lords thought that recourse to private law mechanisms involved no abuse of process. In *Mercury*, the dispute centred on a contract between Mercury and British Telecommunications, clause 29 of which made provision for the parties to negotiate in good faith about modifications to the contract. In the event that the parties could not reach agreement, they could ask the Director General of Telecommunications to make a determination. However, clause 29 stipulated that any determination so made by the Director General should be limited to certain matters set out in the licence conditions issued to British Telecommunications and to Mercury, and should be based on the principles set out in those conditions. The question was whether Mercury could use private law procedures to challenge a determination made by the Director General pursuant to a clause 29 reference, such use being opposed by both the Director General and British Telecommunications.

If we focus on the contract between Mercury and British Telecommunications, the dispute can be viewed quite plausibly as within private law. However, it can equally be viewed as a public law dispute if we focus on the licences issued to the parties. Thus, the critical question is whether access to private law procedures would involve an abuse of process. Lord Slynn, speaking for a unanimous House of Lords, saw no material objection to Mercury taking a private law path:

> [I]t cannot be said here ... that the procedures under Ord 53 are so peculiarly suited to this dispute (as they would be in a claim to set aside subordinate legislation or to prohibit a government department from acting) that it would be a misuse of the court's process to allow the originating summons to continue. On the contrary it seems to me that the procedure by way of originating summons in the Commercial Court is at least as well, and may be better, suited to the determination of these issues as the procedure by way of judicial review. In dealing with the originating summons the trial judge can have regard to, even if he is not strictly bound by, the procedural protection which would be available to a public authority under the provisions of Ord 53.[2]

Thus, putting this in terms of the inconsistency principle, there was no doubt that Mercury and British Telecommunications were in a contractual relationship; and, although the dispute had a public law element (ie the interpretation of telecommunications licence conditions), there was no inconsistency between the background statutory regime and the claimant using private law procedures.

1   [1996] 1 All ER 575.
2   [1996] 1 All ER 575 at 582.

Where the public contractor claims that contract governs

8.43 In view of the protections given to public contractors by judicial review procedures, as well as the way in which public governance considerations can trump standard private law arguments[1], it might seem strange that such contractors might have occasion to invoke private law arguments. However, in practice, public contractors have wished so to argue in a variety of contexts, including the termination of licences, the dismissal of public servants, decisions taken qua landlords, and decisions relating to procurement[2]. To illustrate the possible attraction of private law to public contractors, we can consider one of the more recent cases, *R v Legal Aid Board, ex p Donn and Co (a firm)*[3].

1 See *The Amphitrite* principle (para 8.38 note 5 [1921] 3 KB 500); and for the limited application of estoppel, see *Western Fish Products Ltd v Penwith District Council* [1981] 2 All ER 204. Generally, on the rule preventing fettering of (public) discretion by contract, see Arrowsmith 'The Impact of Public Law on the Private Law of Contract' in Halson (ed) *Exploring the Boundaries of Contract* (1996) 3 at 17.
2 See eg Arrowsmith 'Judicial Review and the Contractual Power of Public Authorities' (1990) 106 LQR 277.
3 [1996] 3 All ER 1.

8.44 The dispute in *Donn* originated in a tender submitted by a firm of solicitors for a legal aid contract under which the firm would represent plaintiffs in a multi-party action to be brought against the Ministry of Defence for compensation arising from Gulf War syndrome. The tender was unsuccessful, the contract being awarded to the only other party who tendered. The unsuccesful bidders applied for judicial review, alleging that the selection process was flawed in that the committee did not have a complete copy of the firm's tender document (the error occurring within the Legal Aid Board) and that it had been misled about a possible conflict of interest involving a member of the firm's team (who was a serving officer in the Territorial Army). One of the questions raised by the firm's application was whether the committee's decision-making process was amenable to judicial review. Or, was it simply contractual?

On behalf of the Legal Aid Board, reliance was placed on the earlier decision in *R v Lord Chancellor, ex p Hibbit and Saunders (a firm)*[1]. There, it was ruled that the applicant firm, which for many years had held the contract for shorthand report writing in a certain Crown Court area, was unable to use judicial review to challenge the Lord Chancellor's Department decision to award the contract to another firm[2]. Building on this ruling, the argument in *Donn* was that, even though 'the proper conduct of multi-party litigation is of public significance, ... it is no more so in this context than the importance of accurate court reporting ...'[3]. It was also argued that the statutory underpinning of the legal aid scheme was such that the tendering process must be regarded as essentially a contractual (private law) [sic] matter. Thus:

> The Legal Aid Board is a creature of statute. Had Parliament intended that it should conduct its tendering process in accordance with defined procedures, it would have said so. The failure to say so is said to be very significant in demonstrating that this was an exclusively commercial transaction only amenable—if at all—to private law remedies.[4]

In other words, the contention was that it would be inconsistent with the legislation to draw on public law [sic] relief because, by implication, the statutory scheme excluded such redress.

Against these arguments, the firm focused on the selection process itself, rather than any resulting contractual relationship, arguing that it was more akin to a governmental than a commercial function. In support of this approach, the firm emphasised that the Legal Aid Board allocated large sums of public money, and that it was plainly a matter of public importance that the solicitors chosen to represent legally-aided persons should be those who were best fitted to carry out the work.

Although Ognall J had difficulty in divorcing the selection process from the resulting contract, and preferred instead 'to treat both the nature and purpose of the selection process and its consequences as one indivisible whole'[5], he found in favour of the firm. Thus:

> The answer must, it seems to me, fall to be decided as one of overall impression, and one of degree. There can be no universal test. But bearing in mind all the factors drawn to my attention, I prefer the applicants' submissions. I believe that the function exercised by this committee ... , the purpose for which they were empowered to act and the consequences of their decision-making process, all demand the conclusion that it would be wrong to characterise this matter as one of private law. Even if there were to be arguably some private law remedy, or whether there is none, I am satisfied that, quite independently, the public dimensions of this matter are of a quality which makes it justiciable in public law[6].

Accordingly, where a situation falls within the domain of public law—and this, of course, is itself a vexed question[7]—judicial review will be available; and it will be no less available even if there is a concurrent remedy in contract law. Or, to put this in terms of the general regulative principle of inconsistency, public contractors will not be permitted to evade their responsibilities by having recourse to private law when this would be inconsistent with standards of public accountability, transparency, due process and the like[8].

1   [1993] COD 326, (1993) Times, 12 March, DC.
2   In *Hibbit and Saunders*, Rose LJ reasoned that the engagement of shorthand writers was no different from the engagement of civil servants, police surgeons, senior nursing officers, consultant surgeons, or prison officers. See, respectively, *R v Lord Chancellor's Department, ex p Nangle* [1992] 1 All ER 897; *R v Derbyshire County Council, ex p Noble* [1990] ICR 808; *R v East Berkshire Health Authority, ex p Walsh* [1985] QB 152; *R v Trent Regional Health Authority, ex p Jones* (1986) Times, 19 June; and *McLaren v Home Office* [1990] ICR 824. However, as Ognall J pointed out in *Donn*, when dealing with *McLaren v Home Office*, the question here was whether a Crown employee could raise a matter concerning his contract of service by private law processes (at 10).

Cf, too, Rose J.'s decision in *R v Football Association Ltd, ex p Football League Ltd* [1993] 2 All ER 833, holding that the Football Association is not a body susceptible to judicial review. Here, RoseJ said:

> [T]o apply to the governing body of football, on the basis that it is a public body, principles honed for the control of the abuse of power by government and its creatures would involve what, in today's fashionable parlance, would be called a quantum leap. It would also ... be a misapplication of increasingly scarce judicial resources. It will become impossible to provide a swift remedy, which is one of the conspicuous hallmarks of judicial review (at 849).

3   [1996] 3 All ER 1, 9.
4   [1996] 3 All ER 1 at 10.
5   [1996] 3 All ER 1 at 11.
6   [1996] 3 All ER 1 at 11.
7   See eg *R v Disciplinary Committee of the Jockey Club, ex p Aga Khan* [1993] 2 All ER 853, where the Court of Appeal held that the relationship between the Jockey Club and race-horse owners was contractual; that the relationship between the parties rested on the agreement to be bound by the Club's Rules of Racing; and that 'while the Jockey Club's powers may be described as, in many ways, public they are in no sense governmental' (per Sir Thomas Bingham MR at 867). Similarly, see *Law v National Greyhound Racing Club Ltd* [1983] 3 All ER 300. However, in *ex p Aga Khan*, the Court of Appeal was mindful of the modern tendency to extend the bounds of judicial review, reflected in particular in *R v Panel on Take-overs and Mergers, ex p Datafin plc* [1987] QB 815; but cf note 2.
8   Cf Fredman and Morris, 'The Costs of Exclusivity: Public and Private Re-examined' [1994] PL 69, and Arrowsmith, 'Judicial Review and the Contractual Power of Public Authorities' (1996) 106 LQR 277. The latter argues that 'the way forward now is for the courts to adopt the same approach to the judicial review of contractual powers as they do to the review of other activities of government' (at p 291). For, Arrowsmith contends, 'a public authority surely has no prima facie claim to the freedom of action enjoyed by private individuals in the exercise of contractual rights: it is the public nature of the body which should give rise to an obligation to treat citizens fairly and reasonably' (at 288).

Synthesis

8.45   If we think of public law as part of a background regime of rights and obligations, then the availability of contract law and, more generally, of private law procedures will depend upon their consistency with the background regime. Within that background regime, it is clear that, where the situation involves pure public law rights (however such a sphere of such rights is to be conceived), then private law processes are not applicable. However, where the situation involves a mix of public and contractual elements[1], the recent case law suggests: (i) that, provided the public elements warrant judicial review, then public law relief will be available (particularly to prevent an abuse of rights) even though contractual relief might also be available; and (ii) that contractual relief (and/or private law processes) will be available provided that this does not involve an abuse of process (as judged by the values represented by the background regime)[2].

1   Cf the remarks of Lloyd LJ in *R v Panel on Take-Overs and Mergers, ex p Datafin plc* [1987] QB 815 at 847.
2   Satisfying the proviso relating to abuse of process, of course, is a necessary but not a sufficient condition of contractual relief. There will be no such relief unless the independent ingredients for contractual relief are present: see eg *Roy v Kensington and Chelsea and Westminster Family Practitioner Committee* [1992] 1AC 624 (discussed in para 1.182 above) and *Andreou v Institute of Chartered Accountants in England and Wales* [1998] 1 All ER 14.

CHAPTER 9

The Rationality of Contract Law

The idea of rationality in the law

9.1 It is widely accepted that law aspires to be a rational enterprise[1]; it endeavours to progress by judgment rather than luck; irrationality is a cause for concern. Far from being exempt from this aspiration, the law of contract, as we noted earlier[2], takes an ordered approach, questing after ever greater rationality in the regulation of the economic life of the community.

What, though, does a commitment to rationality signify? According to Robert Nozick, '[to] term something rational is to make an *evaluation*: its reasons are *good* ones (of a certain sort), and it meets the standards (of a certain sort) that it *should* meet'[3]. When we evaluate the law for its rationality, it is suggested that we presuppose that it should meet three desiderata, these representing the standards that we judge that it should meet and the reasons that we count as good ones. First, to be rational, the law should be free from doctrinal contradiction; secondly, it should be effective in guiding action, and in achieving its intended purposes; and, thirdly, it should be legitimate (its reasons, in other words, should be good ones). We can call these desiderata, respectively, the requirements of formal, instrumental (generic and specific) and substantive rationality.

1 See eg Alexy *A Theory of Legal Argumentation* (1989); Brownsword 'Towards a Rational Law of Contract' in Wilhelmsson (ed) *Perspectives of Critical Contract Law* (1993) p 241.
2 See para 1.34.
3 Nozick *The Nature of Rationality* (1993) p 98.

Formal rationality

9.2   Formal rationality expresses the requirement that legal doctrine should not be contradictory. At one level, this is fairly straightforward: non-contradiction requires, for example, that the law should not say *both* (and at the same time) that postal acceptances are binding on posting and that postal acceptances are binding only upon receipt by the offeror. Equally, it is clear that the principle of non-contradiction does not require that there should be no exceptions to a general rule: thus, we do not violate the principle if the general postal rule (exceptionally) does not apply where it would produce absurd or unjust results[1]. It is also clear, at any rate in principle, that doctrines that complement one another involve no contradiction. For instance, where there is no completed contract and, thus, no contractual remedy, the fact that the plaintiff has a remedy in restitution (for benefit conferred on the defendant)[2] or in negligence (for status quo damages) does not involve doctrinal contradiction: rather, contract law is silent as to the possibility of non-contractual forms of relief and different strands of the law of obligations are simply complementing one another. Similarly, to take an example recently given by Lord Nicholls in *Malik v Bank of Credit and Commerce International SA (in liquidation)*[3]:

> [T]he fact that [a] breach of contract injures the plaintiff's reputation in circumstances where no claim for defamation would lie is not, by itself, a reason for excluding from the damages recoverable for breach of contract compensation for financial loss which on ordinary principles would be recoverable. An award of damages for breach of contract has a different objective: compensation for financial loss suffered by a breach of contract, not compensation for injury to reputation.

On the other hand, if the law of contract allows recovery of expectation damages for negligent misrepresentations, while reliance damages only are recoverable in a tort action for negligent misstatement, this looks more like a contradiction than a case of complementarity[4]; as, perhaps, do the different limitation periods in contract and tort where the law has recognised concurrent liability. Similarly, if contract law treats an agreement to negotiate in good faith as too uncertain to be enforceable, but recognises that an agreement to use best endeavours is sufficiently certain, it is arguable that there is a contradiction here because the underlying concepts (if not their respective linguistic formulations) are materially the same[5].

1   See *Holwell Securities Ltd v Hughes* [1974] 1 WLR 155.
2   See eg *British Steel Corpn v Cleveland Bridge and Engineering Co Ltd* [1984] 1 All ER 504.

3   [1997] 3 All ER 1, 10.
4   Cf Burrows 'Contract, Tort and Restitution—A Satisfactory Division or Not?' (1983) 99 LQR 217, 250–251.
5   See *Walford v Miles* [1992] AC 128. And see Neill 'A Key to Lock-Out Agreements?' (1992) 108 LQR 405.

9.3   In principle, we should also recognise the distinction between 'contradiction' and 'tension' in the doctrinal materials. Formal rationality militates against contradiction, but it does not preclude indeterminate tensions between particular doctrinal principles[1]. Suppose, for example, that one principle (P1) provides that in construing contractual terms the intention of the parties is relevant; while another principle (P2) provides that contracting parties are presumed not normally to agree to exclusions of liability for negligence. These principles may pull against one another, in one case P1 prevailing (in the sense that it is held that the parties' intention was to exclude liability for negligence), while in another case P2 prevails (in the sense that it is held that the parties did not intend to exclude liability for negligence), but this gives rise to no contradiction as such. However, if P1 provided that, for the purposes of construing the terms of a contract, the intention of the parties was paramount, while P2 provided that, for such purposes, the intention of the parties was never decisive (or that liability for negligence could not be excluded even where the parties so intended), this would involve a contradiction[2].

1   Cf Dworkin *Taking Rights Seriously* (1978) esp ch 2.
2   See further, Beyleveld and Brownsword, 'Privity, Transitivity, and Rationality' (1991) 54 MLR 48.

9.4   Potentially, doctrinal contradiction can arise in any one of several ways. First, doctrinal positions taken outside contract law in other areas of the law of obligations might contradict the position taken in contract. As we suggested in the previous section, it was a concern about precisely such a possible contradiction between contract law and the law of negligence that shaped the Privy Council's approach in the *Tai Hing Cotton Mill* case[1]. Secondly, contradictions might arise within the doctrines of contract law itself—as might seem to be the case, for example, in relation to the common law and equitable doctrines of mistake (on which see below); or the doctrines of consideration and promissory estoppel as they apply to contractual variations[2]; or the doctrine of consideration and the privity principle should the latter be relaxed[3]; or competing tests for terms to be implied in fact prior to *Liverpool City Council v Irwin*[4]; or between competing tests for discharge by breach prior to the reconciliation of the traditional classification test with the *Hong Kong Fir Shipping*[5] test in *Bunge Corpn v Tradax*[6]. Thirdly, contradictions might be found between particular cases within the same branch of contract law—for example, and famously so, between the coronation cases (on the question of frustration[7]) and the mistake of identity cases[8]. No matter how contradiction arises, lawyers see it as a blot on the rationality of law; and contradiction is particularly worrying perhaps where it involves general doctrines within contract law, for this cannot be dismissed as an interface question at the margins of contract law nor as the work of an occasional aberrant decision.

1   *Tai Hing Cotton Mill Ltd v Liu Chong Hing Bank Ltd* [1986] AC 80; see paras 8.8–8.15 above. And, to similar effect, see Deane J, in *Hawkins v Clayton* (1988) 164 CLR 539 at 584:

> The law of contract and the law of tort are, in a modern context, properly to be seen as but two of a number of imprecise divisions, for the purpose of classification, of a general body of rules constituting one coherent system of law. Where rules classified in different divisions would otherwise conflict or compete, an essential function of the whole system is to avoid, resolve or rationalize such conflict or competition, not to induce or preserve it.

2   See Adams and Brownsword *Key Issues in Contract* (1995) ch 4.
3   See the Law Commission *Privity of Contract: Contracts for the Benefit of Third Parties* (Law Com No 242) (1996) Part VI.
4   [1977] AC 239.
5   *Hong Kong Fir Shipping Co Ltd v Kawasaki Kisen Kaisha Ltd* [1962] 2QB 26.
6   [1981] 2 All ER 513.
7   See *Krell v Henry* [1903] 2KB 740; and *Herne Bay Steamboat Co v Hutton* [1903] 2KB 683; and see Adams and Brownsword *Key Issues in Contract* (1995) pp 333–335.
8   See *Phillips v Brooks* [1919] 2KB 243; *Ingram v Little* [1961] 1QB 31; and *Lewis v Averay* [1972] 1 QB 198.

9.5   On the face of it, one of the most obvious, and long-standing, contradictions in contract law concerns the different tests operated by the common law and equitable doctrines of common mistake in relation to so-called mistakes as to quality. For, whilst both doctrines hold that the validity of the contract will not be affected unless the mistake is 'fundamental', they have significantly different interpretations of what constitutes a fundamental mistake. In *Bell v Lever Bros Ltd*[1], the leading case on the common law doctrine, Lord Atkin held that:

> a mistake will not affect assent unless it is the mistake of both parties, and is as to the existence of some quality which makes the thing without the quality essentially different from the thing as it was believed to be.[2]

Of course, the concept of 'essential difference' is open to interpretation and, in principle, it might be applied quite restrictively or quite liberally. However, Lord Atkin went on to imply a highly restrictive reading, suggesting inter alia that there would be no fundamental mistake if the parties mistakenly believed that a picture was the work of an old master (when it was a copy), nor if the parties mistakenly assumed that a house was a habitable dwelling (when in fact it was uninhabitable)[3]. Moreover, the majority ruling in *Bell v Lever Brothers*, that there was no operative mistake at common law, only serves to underline the restrictiveness of the general test. Subsequently to *Bell v Lever Brothers*, however, the courts have been prepared to apply the equitable doctrine of common mistake to give relief in circumstances where the mistake seemingly would not have satisfied the stringent common law test[4]. Are we to conclude, then, that this is a contradictory (and hence irrational) state of affairs[5]?

1 [1932] AC 161.
2 [1932] AC 161 at 218.
3 [1932] AC 161 at 224.
4 See eg *Solle v Butcher* [1950] 1KB 671; *Grist v Bailey* [1967] Ch 532; *Magee v Pennine Insurance Co Ltd* [1969] 2QB 507; and *Laurence v Lexcourt Holdings Ltd* [1978] 1 WLR 1128.
5 Cf Atiyah and Bennion 'Mistakes in the Construction of Contracts' (1961) 24 MLR 421, 439–442 (for the view that mistake should be dealt with as a matter of construction of the risk allocation in the contract); Grunfeld 'A Study in the Relationship between Common Law and Equity in Contractual Mistake' (1952) 15 MLR 297; Andrew Phang, 'Common Mistake in English Law: The Proposed Merger of Common Law and Equity' (1989) 9 LS 291 (for the proposed merger of the common law and equitable doctrines).

9.6 In *Associated Japanese Bank v CrŽdit du Nord SA*, Steyn J (as he then was) set about putting the doctrines into a coherent order. The dispute in *Associated Japanese Bank* concerned a guarantee given by Cr•dit du Nord to Associated Japanese Bank which related to a sale and lease-back agreement between the bank and one Bennett. The sale and lease-back agreement purported to be for four machines. However, there were no machines, Bennett having committed a fraud on the bank and the guarantor. When the bank sought to enforce the guarantee, Cr•dit du Nord raised a number of defences, the first of which was that the guarantee was subject to a condition precedent that the machines actually existed. Steyn J held that there was such a condition precedent (express and/or implied), from which it followed that the bank's claim against the guarantor must fail. However, Steyn J went on to consider Cr•dit du Nord's second line of defence, namely that they were relieved from liability under the guarantee by either the common law or the equitable doctrine of mistake.

Steyn J started by remarking that two recurrent themes in the law of contract are 'respect for the sanctity of contract and the need to give effect to the reasonable expectations of honest men'[2]. Generally these principles pull in the same direction; but, occasionally they set up a tension—for example, in cases of common mistake. Now, as we have suggested, a tension between principles does not amount to a contradiction. However, to the extent that the more stringent common law doctrine of common mistake seems to prioritise the principle of sanctity of contract, and the more flexible equitable doctrine of common mistake seems to privilege respect for reasonable expectations, do we have a doctrinal contradiction? Steyn J thought not:

> No one could fairly suggest that in this difficult area of the law there is only one correct approach or solution. But a narrow doctrine of common law mistake (as enunciated in *Bell v Lever Bros Ltd*), supplemented by the more flexible doctrine of mistake in equity (as developed in *Solle v Butcher* and later cases) seems to me to be an entirely sensible and satisfactory state of the law É .[3]

The sense in which the equitable doctrine supplements the common law doctrine is as follows:

> Where common law mistake has been pleaded, the court must first consider this plea. If the contract is held to be void, no question of mistake in equity arises. But, if the contract is held to be valid, a plea of mistake in equity may still have to be considered.[4]

On the particular facts of *Associated Japanese Bank*, Steyn J indicated that he would have held that the guarantee agreement was void under the common law doctrine (in other words, that the non-existence of the machines did make the agreement essentially different) and that, if the common law doctrine had not so applied, he would have set aside the agreement under the equitable doctrine. In this way, although the guarantor was given two lines of defence in respect of the same mistake, the common law and equitable doctrines did not come into conflict. For, if the common law doctrine applied, the equitable doctrine was no longer relevant; and, if the common law doctrine did not apply (so that the contract was not *void*), it was still open to argue that the contract was *voidable* under the equitable doctrine[5].

1   [1988] 3 All ER 902, Treitel 'Mistake in Contract' (1988) 104 LQR 501; Cartwright 'Mistake in Contract' [1988] LMCLQ 300.
2   [1988] 3 All ER 902 at 903.
3   [1988] 3 All ER 902 at 912.
4   [1988] 3 All ER 902 at 912.
5   Cf Lord Scarman's concerns in the *Pao On* case about setting up an anomaly in the law if conduct falling short of duress were to render a contract void when proven duress rendered a contract merely voidable: see para 3.10.

9.7   Can it be this simple though? As Steyn J remarks in *Associated Japanese Bank*, the essential difference test of the common law doctrine is strikingly similar to the radical difference test that is now the accepted standard for frustration of a contract[1]—and, indeed, given the obvious parallels between questions of common mistake and frustration, this seems entirely appropriate. However, if the common law doctrine of common mistake is supplemented by an equitable doctrine of mistake that comes into play once the mistake fails the former (more stringent) test, and which is particularly designed to give relief against the party who benefits from the mistake unconscionably holding the other party to the contract, then why is the common law doctrine of frustration not supplemented by an equitable doctrine in a similar way? If we accept that the *Associated Japanese Bank* case resolves the apparent contradiction between the mistake doctrines, must we now accept that this sets up a contradiction with the adjacent area of the law on frustration of contracts? In fact, to be on the safe side, does the reasoning in the *Associated Japanese Bank* case push us towards acceptance of a general relieving principle of unconscionable behaviour? The problem with contract law is that its components are so closely connected with one another that we can never be entirely confident that doctrine is free of contradiction[2].

1   [1988] 3 All ER 902 at 910 and 912–913.
2   Cf Collins *The Law of Contract* (1997) at pp 118–119 for reflections on the relationship between common mistake and the objective theory of consent.

Instrumental rationality

9.8   Instrumental rationality can be of either a generic or a specific kind. The generic requirement is that legal doctrine should be capable of guiding action. Irrespective of whether contract law is duty-imposing or power-conferring, it purports to guide the conduct of would-be contractors. If the law is to have a purchase on conduct, it must conform to a number of instrumental requirements. Of course, this does not guarantee that the law will have a purchase on conduct, whether as a controlling or as a facilitative mechanism. However, generic instrumental rationality is a necessary, if not always a sufficient, condition of action-guidance. Specific instrumental rationality concerns the appropriateness of particular legal interventions in given situations. If we assume that particular interventions in contract (in the field of transactions) are backed by particular facilitative and protective purposes, then specific instrumental rationality focuses upon the efficacy of the steps taken to secure those purposes. If the intervention is intended to be facilitative, it should facilitate; if it is intended to be protective, it should protect. For example, if the intervention aims at eliminating certain forms of unfair dealing by conferring upon judges a general reviewing jurisdiction (ie a discretion to strike out unfair terms), specific instrumental rationality concerns the suitability of this particular technique. There is, of course, a degree of overlap between formal rationality and instrumental rationality (because contradictory law cannot serve as a guide to action), and generic and specific instrumental rationality must work in tandem. However, we can say more about this shortly when we consider in turn the two facets of instrumental rationality.

9.9   According to Lon Fuller[1], once it is accepted that the legal enterprise aspires to be an action-guiding enterprise, then it follows that certain minimal principles of rationality are presupposed, the so-called 'inner morality of law'. Legal rules should be general, promulgated, prospective, clear, non-contradictory, and relatively constant; they should not require the impossible; and, crucially, there should be a congruence between the law as officially declared and the law as administered.

The Fullerian principles can be regarded as 'procedural' matters in the sense that they generally have no substantive impingement. This is most obviously so, perhaps, with the requirement of promulgation, for this permits legal rules to have any content provided that they are published. Of course, promulgation might invoke certain resistances which would not be provoked by secret rules. Nevertheless, promulgation imposes no direct substantive constraint. The same is true for the requirements of clarity, congruence, constancy and non-contradiction (although, in these cases, reference to the content of other legal materials may be necessary in order to establish that a particular provision satisfies the requirements). The remaining Fullerian ideals (generality, prospectivity, and possibility of compliance) do have some substantive impingement, but they stop short of subjecting law to the governance of a master 'external' (as Fuller would put it) moral standard. For present purposes, it is unnecessary to consider whether the Fullerian procedural principles are correctly characterised as 'moral' principles[2]; here, their significance is that they provide some important leads in relation to the notion of generic instrumental rationality.

1   Fuller *The Morality of Law* (1969).
2   But see Brownsword 'A Synthesis of Rights and Community: In a Different Register?' in Watts Miller (ed) *Socialism and the Law* (ARSP Beiheft 49) (1992) 131.

9.10   We have already treated the principle of non-contradiction as a matter of formal rationality. However, as we have indicated, non-contradiction is significant too in the dimension of instrumental rationality. In this context, it can be conveniently set alongside the requirements of clarity, constancy, and promulgation.

For many judges and commentators, the cardinal sin is for the law of contract to fall into a state where contracting parties and their advisers are left uncertain as to their legal position. In particular, for commercial contractors, legal calculability is of the essence. Recall, for example, Lord Wilberforce's observations in *Photo Production v Securicor*[1]:

> After this Act [viz, the Unfair Contract Terms Act 1977], in commercial matters generally, when the parties are not of unequal bargaining power, and when risks are normally borne by insurance, not only is the case for judicial intervention undemonstrated, but there is everything to be said, and this seems to have been Parliament's intention, for leaving the parties free to apportion the risks as they think fit and for respecting their decisions.
>
> At the stage of negotiation as to the consequences of a breach, there is everything to be said for allowing the parties to estimate their respective claims according to the contractual provisions they have themselves made, rather than for facing them with a legal complex so uncertain as the doctrine of fundamental breach must be. ...
>
> At the judicial stage there is still more to be said for leaving cases to be decided straightforwardly on what the parties have bargained for rather than on analysis, which becomes progressively more refined, of decisions in other cases leading to inevitable appeals.

This serves to highlight an important point. Whilst the distinction between contradiction and tension is important in the context of formal rationality, it is of no great moment in the context of instrumental rationality. The fact of the matter is that if the legal position is unclear, it matters little why the problem exists. Whether the source of the difficulty is that the law vests judges with an unpredictable discretion (as Lord Wilberforce feared might become the case with UCTA), or that there are contradictions or tensions in the materials, either way, instrumental rationality is jeopardised. And, of course, precisely the same considerations apply to the requirements of constancy and promulgation. If legal doctrine is restless, and constantly changing, contractors cannot be confident that they can rely on extant principles remaining settled. If the law is not promulgated, the position is even worse: contractors have no doctrinal basis for reliance and they must operate more in hope than (doctrinally grounded) expectation.

1   [1980] AC 827, 843.

9.11 The demand for certainty in the law can be taken to generate two related claims: first, that the law should be transparent in its operations; and secondly that, where discretions are employed in doctrine, they should be structured in a way that makes it possible for reasoned argument to take place as well as to minimise the uncertainty attaching to the application of such discretions[1].

With regard to the first point, judges have not always agreed that transparency is a good thing[2]. Lord Hoffmann, however, has criticised evasive reliance on concepts such as the reasonable man, arguing that 'it does the legal profession no good to keep its reasoning in mystery', that 'it makes the results of cases very difficult to explain', and that 'judges should always give the real reasons for their decisions'[3]. So, rationality requires that the reasons given should be clear, and that the reasons given should be the real reasons. The requirement that the reasons given should be real is one that we will take up shortly under the heading of congruence in the administration of the law.

With regard to the second point, the use of statutory discretions—such as the provisions for just retention and just payment found in the Law Reform (Frustrated Contracts) Act 1943, ss 1(2) and 1(3), and the reasonableness requirement in the Unfair Contract Terms Act 1977—gives the courts some flexibility, but the modern predilection for discretion poses obvious questions about calculability[4]. In the case of the UCTA reasonableness requirement, which (as Lord Wilberforce underlined) could operate as a loose cannon in the law, the Sch 2 guidelines structure the discretion as it arises under UCTA 1977, ss 6 and 7, and judicial practice is to treat the guidelines as being of general application[5]. Similarly, the Unfair Terms in Consumer Contracts Regulations 1994, Sch 2 gives the concept of good faith a public shape and structure, thereby easing concerns about the judges administering an unpredictable jurisdiction of palm tree justice. More generally, as we have emphasised on several occasions, the protection of the contractors' reasonable expectations (which, necessarily, involves judicial discretion in the weak sense of requiring judgment) is no threat to rationality in the law so long as the exercise does not collapse into judicial licence. It is true that expectations are, so to speak, layered, drawing in part on background rules, but also on the understandings (often unspoken) found in particular contractual settings and generated by particular dealings, and, to be sure, this means that the protection of reasonable expectation is not a mechanical exercise[6]. In principle, though, the attempt to give effect to reasonable expectations is entirely consistent with the quest for certainty in the law. These are matters to which we will return in the final part of this section.

1   Cf Reynolds 'Drawing the Strings Together' in Birks (ed) *The Frontiers of Liability: Volume 2* (1994) 156, 157 (for a suggestion and a comment on the use of structured discretion in the context of marrying equitable techniques with common law rules).
2   See eg Paterson *The Law Lords* (1982) pp 140–143.
3   Lord Hoffmann 'Anthropomorphic Justice: The Reasonable Man and his Friends' (1995) 29 The Law Teacher 127, 134.

4 Cf Treitel, *Doctrine and Discretion in the Law of Contract* (1981).
5 See eg *Stag Line Ltd v Tyne Shiprepair Group Ltd, The Zinnia* [1984] 2 Lloyd's Rep 211; *Rees-Hough Ltd v Redland Reinforced Plastics Ltd* (1985) 2 Con LR 109; and *Phillips Products Ltd v THyland and Hamstead Plant Hire Co Ltd* [1987] 2 All ER 620.
6 Cf chapter 9.

9.12 Even if the law is clear, non-contradictory, and promulgated, there must be a question mark against its generic instrumental rationality if, nevertheless, it violates the principle of 'ought implies can' by prescribing the impossible. Since much of liability in contract is strict, does this entail instrumental irrationality? After all, where strict liability applies, the defendant will be liable for breach even though all reasonable steps—maybe even all possible steps—to perform have been taken. Two short points can be made about this. First, where the law of contract sets up a permissive framework in which contractors can freely agree to accept strict liability risks, there is nothing instrumentally irrational about the law if the parties make use of that facilitative framework. Secondly, however, if strict liability applies, not because the parties have freely agreed to it, but because the law so prescribes independent of agreement, then the position is more complex. Briefly, where the law has protective concerns (eg for consumer purchasers of goods or services) a strict liability regime may be instrumentally rational. Whilst it may not be possible for the party subject to strict liability (eg the seller or supplier) to perform, it is perfectly possible for this party to compensate the other party for a strict liability breach[1]. Granted, this may not, in the final analysis, serve the specific protective end: costs may be transferred to consumer purchasers, sellers and suppliers may avoid high-risk enterprises, and so on. Nevertheless, strict liability, even imposed strict liability, cannot be written off without a good deal more as instrumentally irrational[2].

1 For a convincing articulation of this point, see *Beshada v Johns-Manville Products Corpn* 90NJ 191, 447A 2d 539, 546 (1982) (per Pashman J).
2 For the question of substantive rationality, see Beyleveld and Brownsword, 'Impossibility, Irrationality, and Strict Product Liability' in Howells and Phillips (eds) *Product Liability* (1991) 75.

9.13 For Fuller, the requirement of congruence (coupled with that of generality) articulates the essential ideal represented by the Rule of Law. In contract, a lack of congruence has characterised much of appeal court adjudication this century as the classical paradigm has been challenged by the new interventionism. So, for instance, until the enactment of the Unfair Contract Terms Act in 1977, the disjunction between declared doctrine and the real reasons for decisions was strikingly apparent in relation to the regulation of standard form contracts and exemption clauses. While the judges insisted that they were doing no more than effectuating the parties' intentions, they manipulated the rules on formation and the canons of construction in order to protect weaker bargaining parties, especially so that a fairer deal could be struck for consumers. Officially, freedom of contract ruled, but, in practice, the judicial script was written in terms of fairness and reasonableness[1]. This phenomenon, however, was not restricted to the regulation of exemption clauses; it has been implicated, too, in much adjudication concerning, for instance, the privity doctrine[2] and the right to withdraw for breach of contract[3].

1   Cf Reiter 'The Control of Contract Power' (1981) 1 OJLS 347, esp at 360–361. See chapter 4.
2   See BCLS: CL (1999) chapter 6.
3   See BCLS: CL (1999) chapter 7.

9.14   Generic instrumental rationality, as it has been emphasised, must be complemented by specific instrumental rationality. Legal interventions will be viable only if they are compatible with the features of the particular field within which they are to operate[1], that is, if they can overcome any relevant resistances—individual or sub-systemic[2]—within the field. Thus, rational lawmakers must consider which of the many legal techniques within the regulatory repertoire (or, which combination of techniques) is likely to prove most effective in a particular case. Each technique will have its own debits and credits: on the one side, its limitations, costs, and resistance, on the other side, its positive prospects. Unless such calculations are made, the particular intervention may simply make no impact, or, worse, produce unintended—and undesirable—side-effects[3].

Clearly, it is important that lawmakers are aware of the so-called problem of the 'gap'—the disjunction between the law-in-the-books and the law-in-action. One aspect of the gap concerns the lack of conformity between the intended purpose of the declared rule and the conduct or response of *non-officials*. On the one hand, if the law is meant to facilitate, it may not actually be used in practice—although such a failure of use may not always give rise to great cause for concern. On the other hand, if the law is intended to be protective, a failure to function as such may be serious. It is one thing for commercial contractors to make little use of the law of contract in their dealings[4]; it is quite another thing for tenants to fail to make use of fair rent provisions and rent tribunals[5], or for poorer consumers to remain unclear about the cost of credit despite legislation designed to improve their knowledge and understanding of such matters[6]. Not only must lawmakers be aware of this problem, they must act on an understanding of why the gap exists—an understanding of why the law fails to regulate as intended.

The other aspect of the gap concerns the conduct of *legal officials* rather than non-officials. In relation to judges, it is not simply that there is sometimes a lack of congruence between the law as declared and the law as administered; for the way in which the gap develops depends in no small part on the particular judicial ideologies in play. Legislative reform in the area of contract law, for example, has to reckon with the different approaches that judges display towards the interpretation of statutes, as well as with the particular ideologies that judges have with regard to consumer protection, the facilitation of commerce, and the like[7].

It should not be thought, however, that rational lawmaking is simply a challenge for the draftsman. We have to come to terms with the fact that judges do not have uniform ideologies, that the impact of regulation is not always easy to predict, and that no amount of attention to drafting can be guaranteed to produce the desired response.

1   See Jenkins *Social Order and the Limits of Law* (1980).
2   Cf Teubner 'After Legal Instrumentalism? Strategic Models of Post-Regulatory Law' in Teubner (ed) *Dilemmas of Law in the Welfare State* (1986) p 299; and Collins *The Law of Contract* 3rd edn (1997) p 2.
3   Cf eg Teubner 'Legal Irritants: Good Faith in British Law or How Unifying Law Ends Up in New Divergences' (1998) 61 MLR 11.
4   See Macaulay 'Non-Contractual Relations in Business' (1963) 28 American Sociological Review 55; and Beale and Dugdale, 'Contracts Between Businessmen: Planning and the Use of Contractual Remedies' (1975) 2 British Journal of Law and Society 45.
5   See Partington 'Landlord and Tenant: The British Experience' in Kamenka and Erh-Soon Tay (eds) *Law and Social Control* (1980) p 166.
6   See eg Howells 'Contract Law: The Challenge for the Critical Consumer Lawyer' in Wilhelmsson (ed) *Perspectives of Critical Contract Law* (1993) p 327.
7   See chapter 6. Generally, see Adams and Brownsword *Understanding Contract Law* (2nd edn; Fontana, 1994; Sweet and Maxwell, 1996); see, too, 'Law Reform, Law-Jobs, and Law Commission No 160' (1988) 51 MLR 481.

Substantive rationality

9.15   The requirement of substantive rationality should not be equated with that of substantive fairness as the latter appears in the contrast with procedural fairness[1]. Substantive rationality has an altogether broader sweep, covering all aspects of contract doctrine, and requiring that all rules of contract law, whether concerned with matters of formation, content, performance, or remedies, should be based on good reasons. In the first instance, this means that the empirical reasons upon which particular doctrines are premised (for example, that family agreements should be presumed to be non-contractual otherwise the courts would be overwhelmed by domestic litigation[2]) should be plausible. Beyond this, however, substantive rationality demands that, even if the empirical part of the justification is sound (that the floodgates really would be opened, or whatever), the principle or policy reason upon which the particular doctrine ultimately rests must itself be defensible as legitimate.

To demand that final reasons should be legitimate, however, invites two obvious questions. First, are there not many rules of contract law that are morally neutral, that are akin to rules of the road, and in respect of which it makes no sense to demand that contract doctrine must make the right choice? Secondly, even allowing that some aspects of contract law are not morally neutral, what sense can we give to the idea of making the right choice when many questions of morality not only are hotly disputed, but also are thought to be beyond rational resolution? The first of these questions can be dealt with quite shortly; but the second is much more complex.

1   Generally on which, see eg *Hart v O'Connor* [1985] AC 1000 (Lord Brightman), and Atiyah *Essays on Contract* (1988) ch 11.
2   Cf *Balfour v Balfour* [1919] 2KB 571, esp at 579 (for Atkin LJ's appeal to the floodgates argument).

9.16   Are there not many rules of contract law that are akin to rules of the road? Granted, we need to have rules determining whether offers and acceptances are binding on despatch or receipt, whether formalities are required for certain categories of transaction, and so on. However, does it make sense to suppose that the particular doctrinal choice that we make in relation to such apparently neutral questions is capable of being substantively 'right' or 'wrong'? Does not substantive rationality make some allowance for neutral choices?

In principle, an adequate theory of substantive rationality will recognise that a particular doctrinal choice is rationally prohibited, rationally required, or rationally permissible (meaning that it is neither prohibited nor required). Accordingly, all that we need if we are to respond to the first question is a category of rational permissibility. Given this category, some doctrinal choices will be correctly regarded as optional.

9.17   The second question is altogether more complex, asking whether rationality dictates there are any substantively right answers at all. Indeed, this sceptical question presupposes that the height of modern rationality is represented by the appreciation that we can have a rational debate about the right answer relative to a given criterion of rightness, but that in the final analysis no such criterion can itself be shown to be rationally required. On this view, rationality runs out once a hitherto accepted criterion of rightness is challenged.

To bring this question more clearly into focus, we can distinguish between *positive* criteria of substantive rationality and *critical* criteria. Whereas positive criteria enjoy some level of acceptance or recognition (whether as the community's standards of fairness, or as the agreed standards within a particular context or practice), critical criteria are argued in opposition to (or, at any rate, independent of) positive recognition and acceptance. What the sceptic contends is that we can never give substantive rationality a firmer footing than actual acceptance, recognition, or commitment. To be sure, we can exchange our personal convictions, sometimes with great passion, but this is all that our critical criteria can amount to. On the sceptical view, substantive rational debate cannot get underway until the participants agree upon their criterion of substantive legitmacy.

Whether or not the sceptical view can be shown to be incorrect is a matter for high philosophical debate[1]. For the practical purpose of legal argument in contract cases, there are several candidates that might serve as the criterion of substantive rationality, and we can conclude this chapter by outlining the principal options.

1   For a bridge into those debates, see Adams and Brownsword *Key Issues in Contract* (1995) ch 10.

9.18   One option is to put our trust in the convictions of the judiciary. In support of this idea, it can be said that judicial training instils a sense of fairness, that judges are to some extent insulated against the pressures of day-to-day politics, and that the tendency of much of the modern law is to leave questions of contractual fairness to the discretionary judgments of the courts. However, there are several fairly obvious objections to this proposal.

First, even if the culture of law and legal practice ensures that there is a high level of homogeneity within the judiciary, it is apparent in contract law, as in other areas of law, that there is by no means a single view on the issues arising for decision. Far from it, judges often disagreee with one another, different judges prioritising different values. It follows that, even if we thought it appropriate to take 'the convictions of the judiciary' as the criterion of substantive rationality, we would have as many different criteria as there are different convictions.

Secondly, as Patrick Atiyah has observed[1], the modern tendency is for Parliament, rather than the Courts, to take responsibility for laying down the general doctrines of the law of contract. Indeed, the discretionary judgments that the Courts are asked to make are often *ex casu* decisions set in the context of an authorising statutory framework. In this light, to take judicial convictions as the criterion for the legitimacy of legislative enactments seems not only undemocratic but distinctly anachronistic.

Thirdly, the second objection could be reformulated to take account of the globalisation of contract law[2]. So revised, it would be objected that it would seem at odds with the tide of modern developments, particularly with the movements to harmonise European contract law, to accept the views of the English judges as the criterion of substantive rationality. This is not to say that the convictions of the judiciary do not merit respect; but this is some way from treating their views as conclusive.

1   Atiyah *From Principles to Pragmatism* (1978).
2   See chapter 7.

9.19   It is sometimes said that the virtue of a strict system of precedent is not so much that it promotes consistency and calculability in the law but that it confines judicial idiosyncrasy. Accordingly, a second option for the criterion of substantive rationality is that we should be guided by the standards of fairness already recognised, whether explicitly or immanently, in positive contract doctrine. For several reasons, however, this is an option that has limited appeal.

First, it must be recalled that the discourse of substantive rationality is directed at evaluating the defensibility (in the sense of the legitimacy) of doctrine. If there has to be some distance between the criterion of legitimacy and positive doctrine, then the fact that a particular rule or principle is employed at a particular time cannot be the reason for treating it as legitimate. Doctrine, in other words, cannot validate itself as legitimate. Yet, if this is so, the idea that we should use existing doctrine as the standard against which to measure the legitimacy of new and evolving doctrine hardly makes sense. To be sure, considerations of formal rationality push for a smooth fit between new doctrine and what remains of prior doctrine, but the avoidance of contradiction is no warrant of substantive legitimacy.

Secondly, even if we were to concede that it might be proper to use existing doctrine as our guide to legitimacy, we have reason to doubt how far current doctrine would assist in this respect. James Gordley, for instance, has contended:

> Many jurists are now pessimistic about the very possibility of discovering general principles or doctrines that can explain the rules of positive [contract] law or the results most people regard as fair. Their pessimism is understandable. The attempt to build coherent doctrine seems to have ended in failure.[1]

Moreover, as it was argued earlier in this chapter[2], contract doctrine bears the imprint of a number of ideologies, such that there is little prospect of finding governing criteria of legitimacy in the law-for-the-time-being.

Thirdly, it might also be objected to the use of existing doctrine as the standard of legitimacy that this would stultify any proposal for revision or reform (unless this could be shown to be a way of bringing the law more into line with its deeper principles). No doubt, we could modify this option to allow for reforming 'improvements' to existing doctrine; but such a modification already presupposes a criterion of legitimacy beyond existing doctrine (a criterion enabling us to recognise an 'improvement' when we see one) and it thus invites doubts about the wisdom of taking positive doctrine as the standard of legitimacy in the first place.

1   Gordley, *The Philosophical Origins of Modern Contract Doctrine* (1991) at pp 230–231. But cf Smith 'In Defence of Substantive Fairness' (1996) 112 LQR 138, where it is argued that a 'contract at an abnormal price is similar to an unannounced change in tax policy' (at p 151), thereby impeding autonomous planning and self-direction, and thus violating a meaningful principle of substantive fairness.
2   See especially chapter 6.

9.20   A third option is to invoke the standards of fairness recognised by the community. On this view, the legitimate function of contract doctrine is to protect the expectations of transactors relative to the standards of fairness recognised by their community. This is an idea that has been touched upon several times earlier in this chapter, particularly as a way of finding a more acceptable alternative to both a narrow text-bound reading of contractual obligations and judicial licence to rewrite contracts as seems fair and reasonable relative only to the judge's own convictions. Two aspects of this proposal, however, invite further clarification. First, what do we mean by a 'standard of fairness'? And, secondly, which 'community' is the reference point?[1]

With regard to the first question, it is important to recognise that there must be some formal (definitional) restrictions on what counts as a standard of fairness. Of course, it is a matter for philosophical debate precisely what those restrictions are[2]. However, it is clear that mere positive or negative evaluations will not do. Such evaluations can only be counted as standards of fairness if they are held sincerely and independently, if they do not rely on plainly erroneous factual premises[3], if they are free of manifestly arbitrary distinctions, if they display the elements of impartiality (or universalisability) and categoricality that we take to be (formally) distinctive of a moral standpoint, and so on. Far from being a licence to pick and choose to suit one's own preferences, this formal appreciation of what counts as a standard of fairness calls for a careful examination and filtering of what passes for common standards of fairness[4].

The second question is no more straightforward. So far as domestic contract law is concerned, we might argue for a restricted local version of community (being little more than that represented by the English legal system), or we might argue for a broader regional version (placing English law in the wider context of European law), or we might go even wider (trying to place English contract law in the context of internationally recognised standards of fairness). As we suggested earlier[5], the publication of principles of contract law for these wider constituencies puts pressure on English contract law; but it also gives the lie to the objection that it is simply a matter of speculation what packages of contract doctrine would be acceptable to these communities. It does not follow that English contract law will succumb to the pressure to take a broader view of the community in which it is located; but an evolution in this direction is surely more likely than not.

1   We might also ask: what do we mean by a 'community'? Cf para 5.22, esp note 1.
2   See, eg Dworkin *Taking Rights Seriously* (rev edn) (1978) at pp 248–253 for his helpful distinction between a moral position in an 'anthropological' and in a 'discriminatory' sense. Unlike the former, the latter is a position free of 'prejudices, rationalisations, matters of personal aversion or taste, arbitrary stands, and the like' (at p 248).
3   Cf para 9.15, where it has already been said that the plausibility of empirical premises (offered as part of the reason for a particular doctrine) is the first element of substantive rationality.
4   Such a constrained (filtered) approach, rather than a particular substantive position, might also be equated with the views of 'right thinking' members of one's community. Cf Steyn 'Contract Law: Fulfilling the Reasonable Expectations of Honest Men' (1997) 113 LQR 433.
5   See chapter 7.

9.21   Finally, if the standards of fairness of, say, Europe are taken as the criterion against which the substantive rationality of contract doctrine is to be assessed, what does this mean in practice? It is suggested that, so far as consumer contracting is concerned, we should be guided by the European view of a fair balance between, on the one hand, the interests of consumers of goods and services and, on the other hand, the interests of suppliers and producers. Insofar as the regulatory framework for consumer contracting is set by EU Directives, identifying and implementing the European view is relatively straightforward. So far as commercial contracting is concerned, however, the position is more complex. At one level, there might be problems about identifying a common European standard of fairness on a particular doctrinal question. At another level, community-wide European standards of fairness will almost certainly require that contractors' reasonable expectations, based on background standards of fairness, on the standards accepted in a particular sector of business, and on the signals sent out by one's fellow contractor, are to be protected. The difficulties associated with implementing this kind of contractual regime, it is suggested, are likely to present the courts with a challenge that will run on well into the next century.

Index